Praise for
THE FRESHMAN SURVIVAL GUIDE

"THE FRESHMAN SURVIVAL GUIDE is the most comprehensive guide for college students. The information in this book is invaluable for students as they find themselves starting the scary and exciting journey of higher education."

> —Fr. Martin Moran, executive director, Catholic Campus Ministry Association

"Helpful and readable...It takes students quite seriously...It speaks their language candidly, frankly and honestly...I suspect a lot of us will say, 'I wish I had said that.'"

> —Charles Currie, SJ, president, Association of Jesuit Colleges and Universities

"THE FRESHMAN SURVIVAL GUIDE helps illustrate how to engage and understand religious diversity to build the all-important bridges of cooperation rather than barriers."

> —Dr. Eboo Patel, executive director, Interfaith Youth Core

**Nora Bradbury-Haehl
and Bill McGarvey**

THE
FRESHMAN
SURVIVAL
GUIDE

REVISED AND UPDATED

Soulful Advice for Studying, Socializing, and Everything in Between

**CENTER
STREET**

New York Boston Nashville

Copyright © 2011, 2016 by Nora Bradbury-Haehl and Bill McGarvey

Cover design by Christopher Tobias
Background image © Martin Holm/istockphoto
Photograph of Cup © ryasick/istockphoto
Photograph of Stains © Dovile Butvilaite/istock
Cover copyright © 2016 by Hachette Book Group, Inc.

Center Street
Hachette Book Group
1290 Avenue of the Americas
New York, NY 10104
centerstreet.com
twitter.com/centerstreet

Originally published in 2011 by Center Street.
First Revised and Updated Edition: April 2016

Center Street is a division of Hachette Book Group, Inc.
The Center Street name and logo are trademarks of Hachette Book Group, Inc.

The publisher is not responsible for websites (or their content) that are not owned by the publisher.

The Hachette Speakers Bureau provides a wide range of authors for speaking events. To find out more, go to www.HachetteSpeakersBureau.com or call (866) 376-6591.

The Library of Congress has cataloged the original edition as follows:

The freshman survival guide : Soulful advice for studying, socializing, and everything in between / Nora Bradbury-Haehl and Bill McGarvey.
    p. cm.
    ISBN 978-0-446-56011-5
    1. College student orientation—United States.   2. College freshmen—United States—Conduct of life.   I. Bradbury-Haehl, Nora.   II. McGarvey, Bill.   III. Title.
    LB2343.32.F74 2010
    3781'98—c22

                                                              201001381

ISBNs: 978-1-4555-3900-0 (revised trade paperback), 978-1-4555-6703-4 (ebook)

Printed in the United States of America

LSC-C

10 9 8 7 6

Contents

Introduction

"There are options." The words were neatly printed in the empty space under question number four on our student survey. The surveys had arrived at our offices in New York City from the campus of the University of Iowa in Iowa City. It was just a single piece of paper in a thick stack of replies we had received, but amid all the dashed-off handwritten responses we tried to decipher that day, those words stuck out. A twenty-two-year-old University of Iowa senior was responding to our question: "What was the best advice you got as a freshman?"

That was well before *The Freshman Survival Guide* was first published. Looking back now with a few more years of perspective and over sixty thousand copies of the book in use by students across North America, it is even clearer how true that student's insight was. So much of the input we've received from students and administrators over the years has been helpful, but *There are options* was different. It jumped out at us like a clear, simple response to the much bigger questions we'd been asking ourselves about this book before the first edition was published: What is it really about? What do college students actually need to know? What wisdom can we possibly offer to students who have been bombarded with advice from all angles?

When we embarked on writing this fully updated edition of the book, we realized that Iowa student's statement was more relevant now than ever. The number of options and complexity that students face seems to grow exponentially every year.

Fortunately, this undergrad had unwittingly offered us a Zen koan–like bit of wisdom that got to the heart of what we wanted to offer college students. If this book does anything at all, we hope it gives you the sense that you have options during your college career. Not just academic, social, or lifestyle options but options in every sense. You will be faced with more choices in the next few years than you've ever imagined. Those choices will be accompanied by seemingly endless questions, ranging from small issues like how to get along with a difficult roommate to the big existential questions college is famous for inspiring: Who am I? Why am I here? What do I believe? What should I do with my life? Asking questions is an essential part of what college is all about; *The Freshman Survival Guide* brings together the advice and experiences of college students, professors, administrators, counseling staffs, campus ministers, and other professionals to help you deal with the big questions, the small questions, and all the countless questions in between.

There are many guides for getting into college, choosing a college, paying for college, and getting good grades in college, but this is the *first* to offer a holistic look into the lives of college students and life on campus.

What does *that* mean? Our version of *holistic* simply means that we're approaching your life as a student on every level by combining up-to-date practical advice on academics and student life with guidance on coping with the intangible emotional, spiritual, and values issues that college students encounter every day but that are rarely talked about.

There's no doubt that your experience in college will force you to grow intellectually, but it would be a mistake to think that is the only area in which you'll develop over these years. Your mind is accompanied on this journey by your body and your spirit—none of these three are simply along for the ride; they're all active participants that need to be integrated and in balance.

The world is an increasingly complex place with lots of competing ideas and approaches that can be difficult to make sense of. Sometimes you may be tempted to resist that complexity so you can settle for simple answers instead, but that really isn't much of an option. Your time at college is supposed to be a period of questions and exploration. That's the only way any real learning takes place. "The test of a first-rate intelligence," F. Scott Fitzgerald famously wrote in his book *The Crack-Up* decades ago, "is the ability to hold two opposed ideas in the mind at the same time, and still retain the ability to function." We have no doubt that you will come across a lot more than two opposing ideas during your college career; our goal isn't simply to help you function, but to help you actually flourish during these years.

The Freshman Survival Guide treats the issues of mind, body, and spirit as overlapping and recognizes them as intimately connected instead of distinct.

All too often, advice about college life presumes that students are just a collection of brains, hormones, and appetites entering some sort of ivy-clad educational pressure cooker that will help their brains grow bigger, hopefully without the side effects of letting their hormones and appetites get too out of control at the same time. The fact is a lot of the stories you've heard about college are true. There will be tons of challenging information offered to you over the next few years to enhance your knowledge and intellect; there will also be plenty of opportunities to indulge your appetite and let your hormones run wild (we're guessing those are the opportunities you've heard most of the stories about). Within these pages you'll get the most honest, current information possible on the reality of college life today.

Whether it's academics, dating, sex, drinking, drugs, roommate problems, dorm life, sexual identity, safety, mental health, nutrition, or any number of other issues you're liable to come across in college, you will find the information and advice you need inside these pages.

And if for some reason it's not here, you'll be able to find it at our website: http://TheFreshmanSurvivalGuide.com. We've added additional information online as well as numerous interactive features. Since the first edition of this book was published, one of the most helpful online features we've had has been our Interactive RA (iRA), where resident assistants and residence life professionals from colleges around the country are available to answer your questions online or through their work on our blog. The iRAs have been a tremendous asset to us from the beginning, as they are on the frontlines dealing with students and their struggles every day. We've included their reflections and insights in numerous chapters throughout this second edition. They are some of the most helpful pieces in this expanded version. The iRA is done in partnership with http://Resident Assistant.com, the nation's leading online resource for residence life—a free service of Campus Advantage, the largest private student housing firm in North America.

Along with this dose of reality, we will also offer you *options*. Without your parents watching over you, you'll be in a position to make a lot of decisions that will have an enormous impact on your college career.

- Can you stay out all night drinking and sleep in without getting in trouble?
- Can you skip your classes without somebody reporting you to your mother?
- Can you spend all of your time on Facebook or in training to become the greatest League of Legends player your dorm has ever seen?

The answer, of course, to all of the above is yes, and we have little doubt you will come across people who seem determined to do all of those things and more during college.

This book offers you the tools and accumulated wisdom of hundreds of students, administrators, professors, counselors, and campus ministers to help you take advantage of the options in front of you and make good decisions in the years ahead. We've surveyed hundreds of students and recent grads from small private colleges and huge public universities in every region of the United States to give you as complete a picture as possible of what life on campus is truly like. We've also interviewed professors, resident assistants working in college dorms, administrators, and health professionals to get a sense of what you should expect when you arrive.

We've spoken to campus ministers from the Catholic, Jewish, Hindu, Muslim, Protestant, Jain, and Buddhist faith traditions to get their sense of what's going on in the spiritual lives of students. They have a unique perspective on campus life and the sometimes hotly debated intersection of faith and reason. Their insights into the spiritual, religious, and intellectual lives of college students are revealing, to say the least, and are among the book's most provocative and compelling passages.

Ultimately, however, *The Freshman Survival Guide* has been generated *for* students *by* students. The upperclassmen and recent graduates who helped make this book possible were once in the same position you're in now. The first wave of students who used this book as freshmen have now actually graduated, and some of them have added their own wisdom to this second edition. Not that long ago, they were incoming freshmen with the same sense of anticipation, anxiety, exhilaration, and fear you're now experiencing. They've made the transition to college and have lived to tell the tale. We hope that once you've survived, you'll come back and tell the freshmen that come after you yours.

We're always looking for feedback and insights that could help new batches of incoming college students. If you would like to see other issues addressed or learn about things that might be helpful to you, please be sure to e-mail us at feedback@thefresh mansurvivalguide.com.

User Guide

A "How to" (and "Who Is") for Using *The Freshman Survival Guide*

 The Freshman Survival Guide's greatest value is its versatility and depth as a tool and a resource for the transition to college. Though it is addressed to students, the reality is that parents, mentors, educators, counselors, ministers, and friends are putting it to use as a textbook, as an orientation manual, as a discussion starter, as a workshop springboard, as a curriculum component, as a graduation gift, or simply as an opportunity for honest conversation with students embarking on their collegiate careers.

When the first edition of *The Freshman Survival Guide* was published, we were confident that—after years of research—the information, insights, advice, and real-world, on-campus experience found in these pages would prove to be helpful to students heading off to college. With tens of thousands of copies sold, that initial confidence has been validated many times over.

What we hadn't anticipated, however, were the audiences beyond the students themselves who also found the book helpful. In fact, there's a small army of people helping students make the transition to college—parents, high school guidance counselors, teachers, freshman orientation and first-year experience staffs, residence life staffs and RAs, college administrators, campus ministers, on-campus counseling providers, and so on—all of whom have a deep interest in the tools and information that *The Freshman Survival Guide* offers.

We've visited numerous high school and college campuses around the country and worked with the full range of those helpers to adapt our book's resources to each specific community's needs. There's a tremendous amount of information in the chapters that follow, but not all of it is relevant to everyone. We suggest you browse around and read the chapters that are the most interesting and pertinent to you, and keep the book handy for when questions come up in the future (as they inevitably will).

Below you'll find some suggestions for how *The Freshman Survival Guide* can act as a toolbox that you and your community can use for programming, classroom discussion, or when specific issues arise.

 Online Survival Guide: *Visit http://TheFreshmanSurvival Guide.com and click on "User Guide" in the drop-down menu under "About" for even more tips as well as a free, downloadable Condensed Survival Guide and a "Survival Guide Shortcuts" PDF.*

We love to hear from our readers directly to get feedback or consult on what strategies may benefit you or your organization. We've helped develop customized programming free of charge for a number of high schools and colleges that have bought the book in bulk for their students. We encourage you to contact us via e-mail at info@thefreshmansurvivalguide.com to discuss how we might help.

How to Use *The Freshman Survival Guide* for ...

High School Juniors and Seniors

A great deal of energy and attention is given to applications, scholarships, and how to choose the right college, but a crucial question is sometimes left out in the admissions scramble: *How will you manage once you're actually in college?*

Reading through *The Freshman Survival Guide* now will help you consider some of the issues beyond simply getting in, such as: How will you maintain the friendships you have now? (See chapter 2.) What kinds of friends will you look for once you start college? (See chapter 2.) What are your biggest worries? Are you a procrastinator? (See chapter 14.) Where do you struggle academically (chapter 13), socially (chapter 6), or emotionally (chapter 10), and what can you do now to prepare to deal with the problems that might arise?

Some suggestions:

- Make this book your own. Highlight important information and take notes. Keep a journal of questions it raises for you and things you want to remember.
- Bring your questions to a trusted mentor, teacher, minister, or even a friend who is already in college, or e-mail the Interactive RA (ra@thefreshmansurvivalguide.com) on our website.
- Find a few friends or a teacher/mentor who will commit to reading this book with you and form a discussion group to talk about each chapter.
- Talk to your parents about the issues *The Freshman Survival Guide* raises. You deserve the support and guidance of the people who have gotten you this far in life.

College Freshmen

There is a big difference between reading a book about college life months before you arrive and actually setting foot on campus. Here are some shortcuts for using this book once you've hit the ground.

- Struggling academically? See chapters 13–16.
- Homesick? See chapter 5.
- Struggling spiritually? See chapters 11 and 19.
- Bored or lonely? See chapter 18.
- Not feeling healthy? See chapters 24–27.
- Take a look at the Interactive RA (iRA) section of our website. Our veteran team of resident assistants—Danielle Shipp (MD), Michelle Lowry (LA), and coordinator Natalie Vielkind (NY)—is ready to help with any questions. E-mail them at ra@thefreshmansurvivalguide.com. The iRA blog is also updated regularly with timely content addressing real issues facing first-year students in dormitories across the country.

Commuters

Just because you're not living on campus doesn't mean you should sell yourself, or your college, short. Check out chapter 21 and follow these tips to fight that "I'm just a commuter" mentality:

- Get involved in campus activities; it's a great way to meet new people and feel more connected to what's happening on campus. (See chapter 18.)
- Use your school's resources: Study groups, the library, writing and math labs, and professors' office hours are there for your use. (See chapters 13, 15, and 16.)

- Set up your schedule so you'll have some time on campus a few days a week. If you're also working, it can be tempting to pack your classes in the morning so your afternoons and evenings can be spent off campus. If at all possible, though, consider leaving some gaps in your schedule so you'll have time built in to hit the offices (financial aid, academic advisement, the registrar), go see your professors, visit the library, or attend student activities.

Parents, Siblings, Aunts, Uncles, and Other Relatives

The first concern for many parents sending kids off to college is survival in the literal sense of the word. Too often our campuses have been places where a poor decision or simple bad luck can have tragic consequences. We encourage parents to read this book and use it as an opportunity for family discussions about the things that matter. Fortunately, most challenges in college don't have life-and-death consequences, so make sure you also emphasize the small, everyday habits that build success and happiness.

Chapter 29 deals with emergencies and how to handle them. Chapter 4 could be a good starting point for talking about the first few weeks of on-campus living. Chapter 22 deals with all the different places on campus to find help.

Remember:

1. Listen as much as you talk.
2. You've already done most of the work.

You've been teaching life lessons since this kid appeared on the scene. Find out how much he or she has picked up. Consider setting aside time each month during senior year to talk through the worries and concerns you both have about college.

High School Educators, Teachers, College Counselors, Guidance and Mental Health Professionals, Principals, Librarians, Ministers, and Others

The Freshman Survival Guide has been used as a text for half-year courses for high school seniors and as the springboard for panel discussions, off-to-college nights, and leadership programs. It has been used with parent groups and in student-parent discussions, and as gifts for members of the senior class and senior award winners. It can be a great tool for preparing first-generation or at-risk students for the issues they will face. One way it may be helpful to divide the material for use in workshops and minicourses is as follows:

- Balance: dealing with time management, procrastination, mind-body-spirit health, choosing activities and extracurriculars (chapters 10, 13, 14, 18, and 25–27)
- Relationships: parents, dating and sex, homesickness, friendship, maintaining old friendships and finding new ones that will help you grow (chapters 2, 3, 5–8, and 22)
- Identity: setting goals, decision making, habits (chapters 9, 11, 17, and 19)
- Academics: learning how to be a college student, creating a study budget, dealing with profs (chapters 12–16)
- Risk: positive risk taking (stepping outside your comfort zone) and negative risk taking (drugs, alcohol, sex, criminal behavior) (chapters 4, 6, 11, 23, 24, and 29)

College/University Educators, Residence Life Staff, RAs, Freshman/First-Year Orientation Staffs, Counseling Center Staff, Campus Ministers, and Others

We've worked with administrators, professors, professional staff (counseling, orientation, and residence life), and campus ministers at institutions ranging from large state universities to small private colleges and everything in between.

Just a few of the ways *The Freshman Survival Guide* has been implemented at colleges and universities so far include:

- It was mailed out to an entire class of 1,500 incoming freshmen as summer reading.
- It was used as a textbook for a semester-long, small-group, first-year experience class (for credit).
- Residence hall staffs have used it as a discussion text for mandatory floor meetings.
- Campus ministries have purchased it for their university congregations and hosted workshops.
- The challenges that affect incoming college students are as varied as their individual personalities, but some perennial issues include:
  - Roommate drama (chapters 2–4)
  - Struggles making adjustments to college academics and time management (chapters 12–16)
  - Drinking and drugs (chapter 24)
  - Sex and dating (chapters 7, 8)
  - Mental and emotional health (chapters 9, 10, and 22)
  - Emergencies (chapters 22, 23, and 29)
- Visit http://TheFreshmanSurvivalGuide.com and click on "User Guide" in the drop-down menu under "About" for additional tips as well as examples of how other colleges have implemented the book.

THE FRESHMAN SURVIVAL GUIDE

CHAPTER 1

That Was High School...
This Is COLLEGE

Survival Strategy #1: The months leading up to your first day of college can often be a blur. At its best, all of this kinetic energy can generate a momentum that can help launch you into a successful college career. At its worst, it can obscure issues that could easily derail your college years before they start. It's important to use this time to ask yourself some important questions and take an honest look at what high school habits you'll need to change to succeed.

Do you bear scars? Anyone dealing with the pressure and anxiety of senior year in high school—either directly as a student or vicariously as a parent, a grandparent, a sibling, a teacher, or simply as the local letter carrier—knows that the last year of high school is a battleground on a number of levels.

For many it's a whirlwind ride of excitement and anxiety as you, and everyone else who is concerned with your health and well-being, obsess over which schools you should apply to. Which ones you will get into? Which one should you ultimately attend? How will you pay for it? and so on.

Whether a student has questions about his or her future

schooling and career or he or she is simply pushing boundaries at home, senior year is a time of transition for many family relationships. In the words of a colleague who works with high school students, "Senior year exists so that parents aren't sad when their kids leave for college." She was only partially joking.

The reality is that for many second-semester high school seniors, once the confusion about where they're going to attend in the fall is sorted out, the transition is already underway. The last few months before graduating is the perfect time for you—and those close to you—to start preparing for the next step.

Four Questions Before College

Once the anxiety surrounding the annual Springtime Rites of Acceptance/Rejection has subsided, it's a good opportunity to ask a different set of questions. These four questions speak to the core meaning of a student's education and development far more than where he/she was accepted. While they can be answered by you alone, ideally it will have more impact if it is done as an exercise between you and your parent, mentor, or teacher, with both sides answering the questions separately and sharing their responses—the two of you can even try trading written responses and reading each other's answers before attempting a conversation. Honest responses, shared respectfully, will go a long way toward a better experience for all concerned.

Question 1: What Do You Hope Happens to You/for You in College?

Both student and mentor should go beyond the obvious (i.e., a good education, new friends, and so on) and focus on how both parties would like the student to grow over the next four years. What qualities as a person do both of you hope the college experience will develop in the student? Perhaps a broader experience of people, cultures, or beliefs? Greater self-understanding? A job? This should spark an interesting conversation about values and goals.

Question 2: What Are You Most Afraid Of?

It's helpful for the student to name their fear in order to better understand their vulnerabilities. It can also be a good reality check: Is this a reasonable fear or just one of those floating anxieties that needs to be addressed with a little logic and life experience? For the parent/mentor this is a helpful way to communicate real-world concerns and their own deepest fears. One father recently reached out to discuss the answer he gave to his son's question, "Why don't you trust me?" "It's not that I don't trust you," he said. "I'm afraid that I haven't properly prepared you to face the world, and the consequences of that can be the worst of all. I could lose you."

Question 3: What Are Your Biggest Weaknesses and Strengths?

A student often already knows his or her own Achilles' heel, and this needn't be the time to visit old failures except to talk about the important lessons learned from falling down and getting back up again. Take some time to talk about the gifts and skills, the successes and strengths, that will help them meet the challenges in front of them.

Question 4: Who Will You Call with Problems or Big Life Questions?

Over the next four years students will inevitably encounter challenges; some might seem overwhelming. Keep in mind that nobody at college knows what is normal for you. Don't go it alone. Who do you call when you're in trouble or you have big life questions? Students should write down the name of the person(s) they will contact. Parents: If you are doing this exercise with your child, don't be offended if you aren't on their list. Write down names of people you hope your child will contact. Agree that whomever they decide to reach out to should also be in touch with you in case of an emergency.

Don't wait until the drop-off day at school to begin these conversations. So much has led up to this point, and so much more is at stake than what school they were accepted to. These may very well be difficult conversations to have, but, trust us, the cost of *not* having the conversation is potentially much higher.

Colleges are usually a lot bigger than most high schools, which can be intimidating but also can really give you the chance to be yourself, branch out, and get involved. The new environment gives you a chance to discover things about yourself you never knew. So step out of your comfort zone. Allow yourself to feel uncomfortable sometimes. Some of the greatest friends and hobbies come from the most unexpected situations. Make a plan and seek advising when necessary. But in the process, be sure to have fun and create memories that last a lifetime. The college experience comes up quickly and ends even quicker.

—Kate, Temple University

6 Bad Habits in High School (and What They'll Look Like in College)

Regardless of whether you are at the top of your class, the bottom, or somewhere in between, everyone is challenged by some bad habit or another when it comes to school. If you're a high school junior or senior, you may already be painfully aware of the bad habits that get you into trouble and make your life more difficult than it needs to be. The real danger with high school bad habits, though, is that they often cause big problems when you bring them with you to college. The good news: Habits can be broken, and new habits—good ones—aren't that hard to form.

We've compiled a list of six high school bad habits below, along with some advice for how to form better habits instead.

1. Charm School

- **High School:** In high school you may be one of those lucky few that can slide through your classes on charm and BS. You float along rarely doing the homework, relying on your stellar performance in class participation, your great retention abilities, and that knack you have for getting the right answer on the test.

- **College:** In college, class participation really does count, so your charisma and gregarious personality are definitely going to work in your favor. Being able to test well is also a real skill, as is retaining what the professor teaches in class. Those aspects of this bad habit are actually beneficial. The problem, though, is that college-level learning relies on reading and homework. You've got to do it. In college, there is a lot more information to absorb in a much shorter period. Blowing off homework can quickly result in falling too far behind to catch up.

- **Making the Change:** Even if you have a bad case of senioritis, try to establish a homework habit now so that freshman year will be less of an adjustment. Schedule study time and get those assignments in when they're due.

2. Who Needs Sleep?

- **High School:** Do you pride yourself on your capacity to operate on little to no sleep? Congratulations. You're a

superior human being. Put that trophy on the shelf before
you head off to college, though. It may be true that some
people can function on less sleep than others, but this one's
definitely a bad habit you should break now.

- **College:** Staying up too late in high school isn't usually a
big deal. You might get a little run-down or fall asleep in
the back of your bio lab. But at college, getting run-down
and sick, missing a week of classes, or drooling on the desk
in the lecture hall can be disastrous. They've even found
that shorting yourself on sleep can cause weight gain.

- **Making the Change:** Practice giving yourself a bedtime
and sticking to it. Break the habit of late-night screen
time, whether computer, phone, or TV. Being short on
sleep makes you moody, shortens your attention span, and
messes with your ability to get stuff done. Speaking of
which...

3. I'll Do It... Later

- **High School:** Procrastinating in high school means the
occasional late night to catch up on your work and sometimes a bad grade or two. You work best under pressure
anyway, right?

- **College:** Actually, no. In college, pushing off work until
later can mean a week (or more) without sleep when your
deadlines come crashing down on you—blowing a crucial
project or required course, or even bombing a semester.

- **Making the Change:** Studies have shown that your ability to make yourself do things you don't want to do (called
self-regulation by the procrastination scientists) goes up
dramatically when you're getting enough sleep. Another

way to break the "I'll do it later" habit is by forcing yourself to spend five minutes *now* on a task or an assignment you dislike or can't seem to get started on. You can trick your brain into doing just a little and then next time your resistance to the task will actually be lowered.

4. The Joiner

- **High School:** You're well-rounded and busy with a capital *B*—three sports, theater, band, student government, clubs, service commitments, and so on.

- **College:** That same long list of activities that got you into college can be your undoing if you're not careful, especially first semester in freshman year. The bad habit of overcommitment in high school turns into being overwhelmed in college.

- **Making the Change:** Take some time now to think about all the activities you've been involved in during high school. Which ones did you love? Which ones seemed to energize you? Which ones did you stay in out of a sense of obligation or because you were trying to build your résumé? If you could pare down your list of activities right now, what would you give up? Take some time to consider those questions, and remember that you may want to try something new at college, too. If your default setting is "Yes!" to anyone who demands your time, you'll need to start being picky about what you're willing to commit to. Activities need to justify their place in your schedule. Try saying no to the next thing someone wants you to do that isn't something you love. The benefit of a little more time is your reward.

5. The Human Garbage Can

- **High School:** If your bad habit is bad food, beware. It's even easier to eat junk at college.

- **College:** College weight-gain culprits are the vending machine at the end of the hall, snacks instead of meals, and the high-carb and high-calorie options offered in the dining hall. Just because you *can* have FroYo at every meal doesn't mean you *should*.

- **Making the Change:** The good news is that it's actually the freshman five, not fifteen like everyone says. Most freshmen don't gain that much weight. Take time now to develop some healthy eating habits and find snacks that are cheap, easy, and healthy. Ask your folks to teach you a few basic cooking skills. Master more than ramen, and your waistline will thank you.

6. What, Me Worry?

- **High School:** If you respond to stress with unhealthy habits—binge drinking, eating your feelings, harming yourself, or behaving impulsively—it's time to develop some new coping mechanisms.

- **College:** College is stressful. It just is. There's a lot of change to deal with along with increased academic and social pressure. At the same time, you're dealing with the absence of your most vital relationships.

- **Making the Change:** You've got to find things that help you blow off steam without causing you more problems. Exercise, counseling, mindfulness practices like prayer and meditation, and hobbies that calm you down or help you focus can all help. If you're coming from a difficult situation at home, know that that won't just disappear on its own. One campus minister we know has this adage: "If you're running away from trouble at home you're going to run into trouble at college." Take the time to deal with your issues now. If you're already in counseling, your current therapist or doctor can guide you to help on or near your campus.

Why Can't I Quit You?

Habits—good or bad—are habits because they're familiar. We often start a habit without realizing it and then keep a habit—good or bad—because it's what we're used to. Our brain, to get a little technical, likes its old familiar neural pathways and wants to return to them; but forming a new habit creates a new channel for your thoughts to travel. It takes intention to end a bad habit, but it's easier to break a bad habit by replacing it with a good one. So if you want to break your habit of late-night mindless TV, it will be easier if you replace it with a good habit like reading or mild exercise. Your bad high school habits don't have to become your bad college habits. Start working on changes now, and the transition from life in high school to life on campus will be significantly smoother.

 Online Survival Guide: *Unsure of what to bring, buy, and so on for your freshman year? Check out our iRA online posting "Do I Really Need 20 Pillows?" (http:// TheFreshmanSurvivalGuide.com/interactiverablog /do-i-really-need-20-pillows/).*

Leaving for College–The Interactive RA

Leaving for college may not seem like such a big deal when it is still months, weeks, or even days away. The reality of the impending change won't hit most college kids until it is the day that you actually start packing. As you begin to pack away your clothes, pillows and blankets, games, and other personal items that made your room *yours*, you may start to feel sad and nervous about the situation. And that is just your bedroom. You still have all of the people in your life to say good-bye to. How do you do it? How do you cope with all of those emotions you are probably feeling?

1. **Have One Last Outing with Your Friends:** Do yourself a favor and don't wait to do all your packing the day before you leave. That way you can spend your last day in your hometown with your friends doing whatever it is you all love doing. Most important, don't focus on it being your last day, otherwise that is all you and your friends will find yourselves focusing on, and it won't feel as genuine as it usually does hanging out with them.

2. **Guys, It Is Okay to Cry:** Okay, so I was a tough eighteen-year-old guy leaving for college at one time, too, so I get it. You have this masculine principle that "Guys Don't Cry" to uphold. Well, from one guy to another, what if I told you that it is okay to cry? I'm not afraid to admit that the day my best friend and I had to say good-bye, he and I both cried. It is natural to be going through dozens of emotions, and you would be amazed how crying actually helps to convey these pent-up feelings. Because before you know it, you and your friends will have cried yourselves into smiling and joking about the situation, and it makes it that much easier to deal with the circumstances. Guaranteed.

3. **Don't Say Good-bye:** This is something I found myself

doing after my freshman year of college when it was time for me to go home for the summer. Instead of saying good-bye to all my friends, I simply said, "I'll see you later" or "I'll see you soon." Sometimes "good-bye" just sounds too gloomy and melancholic, but saying "I'll see you later" is somewhat of a casual promise that you will see each other again soon.

—Josh Martin, iRA
Director of Residence Life, Culinary
Institute of America at Greystone

SEEK → FIND

 The transition from high school to college may be one of the biggest transitions you ever make. Some people assume that the transition from college to the "real world" is necessarily bigger, but college life is very real, especially if you take it seriously. For the first time, you are the agent of your own destiny in a way that you've never been before. The decisions you make about the courses you take, the clubs you join and, ultimately, who you choose to be—are yours.

Take time to think carefully about the decisions you make. Gather as much data as you can: Pay attention to your interests, what captures your imagination; listen to your instincts, and also ask the thoughts and opinions of a mentor or someone you trust. Then make—and own—your decisions. You'll probably get some decisions right and probably get some decisions wrong—but you'll learn from both—and along the way become the person you choose to be!

—Conor O'Kane
director of campus ministry, Fordham University

THE TAKEAWAY

Once you've been able to settle some of the drama around where you're going in the fall, you'll have a few months before you hit campus, but the truth is your transition to college life has already begun. Taking stock of what you truly want out of your experience and what you need to work on will serve you well and give you a solid foundation to build on.

CHAPTER 2

Be Generous with Your Friendship but Stingy with Your Trust

 Survival Strategy #2: Making good friends in college is important, but it takes time. Be patient, be smart, and stay connected to your support network—the friends and family who helped get you this far.

The friends you have back home didn't get to be your friends overnight. It took months—or more likely, years—to establish those relationships. If you're like 97 percent of freshmen entering a four-year college, you're either eighteen or nineteen years old.[1] The fact is you already have years of experience under your belt building the kinds of relationships you'll need in the next few months and years. You've been through tough times with your old friends and have learned their strengths and weaknesses. You trust them because they've proven themselves trustworthy. They know and keep your secrets, and you know and keep theirs.

At college, new people can feel like your old friends. You're eating together, studying together, crashing in each other's rooms, and sometimes spending more time with them than you ever could with your friends from back home. The relationships *feel* familiar, comfortable.

But be aware that there can also be a kind of artificial intimacy early on in freshman year. These new friends need to earn your trust. Don't just give it to them. The people you meet in your first few weeks of school may be great, some of them may turn out to be the best friends of your life, and some of them may turn out to be criminals (seriously). Every freshman class has its gems and its jerks; which are which will become clear over the next few months. Remain open to new friendships, but wait until you get to know people a little before you loan them your car, give them all your passwords, or share your deepest secrets with them.

The first couple of weeks on campus Danielle and Laurie had really connected; they had a lot in common, shared a major, came from similar backgrounds, and just enjoyed each other's company. When Danielle wanted to borrow her sweater, Laurie was really pleased. She felt as if she was back home with her old friends. Lately, though, Laurie began having second thoughts about the friendship. It seemed Danielle was always in crisis and half of Laurie's wardrobe was now missing from all the "borrowing." When Laurie wanted to go out, Danielle wanted her to stay in and talk about her latest problem.

The last straw was the night Laurie had a paper to finish but spent the night with Danielle crying on her shoulder instead. Laurie was feeling isolated and overwhelmed. It wasn't terribly surprising; Laurie had always been the one her friends turned to in high school. She was a good listener and a patient friend, but she also had a tendency to be the one people took advantage of.

Laurie thought about places on campus where Danielle could get support and suggested them to her: their RA, the counseling center, even other friends in their dorm who might be willing to invite Danielle out and help her make some new connections. For her part, Laurie began to seek out some friends that could offer *her* support instead.

As you make friends, don't let the relationships become limited or isolating. Remain open to new friendships, and as a matter of habit check the pulses of the ones you're in. After your first week, reassess your new friendships. Do it again after your first month. If the friends you connected with initially don't seem to be a good fit, keep looking. Think of your entire first semester, not just the first two weeks, as a chance to keep meeting new people. It can get tiring, especially if you're not an outgoing person, but the benefit of finding the right friends for yourself is really worth the effort.

There's a tendency to settle in with the first group of people you meet. It feels safer, somehow, when everything else is suddenly different, to have at least that part of life handled. But the people you choose to be friends with can make a huge difference in nearly every aspect of college life: study habits, interactions with other groups of people, how you spend your free time. Choose carefully and remember you can make a new choice anytime.

Have you ever heard the saying "Tell me who your friends are and I'll tell you who you are"? If all your buddies are always on you to come out with them when you've got work to do, it's going to take superhuman strength to keep saying no. If you're struggling to work more and party less, look for friends who are doing okay academically and imitate their habits. Conversely, if you feel as if you're spending all your time in the library, find some friends who are involved in campus activities and get out there a little yourself. Need help sorting through all that? Check out "The 6 Kinds of Toxic Friendships" later in this chapter.

SEEK → FIND

 Look for companions who are positive, who have healthy lifestyles, who are exploring wellness or healthy alternatives in how they approach various things, whether it's their physical bodies or their religious seeking or their relationships. Seek people who have a positive approach as opposed to a negative, self-centered, extremely individualistic one. When you surround yourself with companions who have something deeper, something healthier, then you yourself are protected from the negative influences that are out there and so endemic.

—Ven. Bonnie Hazel Shoultz, Buddhist chaplain,
Syracuse University

Don't just hang out with the people on your floor, or in your major. Not only is that boring after a while, it will drive you crazy because with groups of friends comes drama! Instead, join a few great clubs, talk to people in your classes, and meet your friends' friends. Just be a friendly person, and in time you'll get close to some people from all over campus. I met my closest college friend because we had been making small talk on a bus home. I asked her to dinner that night. Be yourself. People like that.

—Becky, Providence College

In with the New (and Keep Up with the Old)

One of the biggest challenges is worrying about all kinds of new issues at the same time you're building a new support network—the friends and mentors who will help you navigate this unfamiliar situation. Make sure you take time to tend your relationships, the old ones and the new ones.

You may get along great with your parents, or maybe not. Either way, parents can be one of your most important supports right now; in many ways they know you better than anyone else. "You have to make your own decisions about when to talk to your parents and how much to tell them about your life," says Dr. Richard Kadison, chief of Harvard University Mental Health Services. "But when making that decision, remember that being an independent adult doesn't mean going it alone. Part of being mature is learning when to share problems and concerns and when to ask for help. Even if your parents can't understand exactly what you're going through, their love goes a long way—what they don't get, they'll usually try to understand and work with you to get through it."

Take time with new friends to really get to know each other and keep in touch with friends from back home. When the chips are down and you need some encouragement to keep moving forward, you'll be glad you invested in your relationships. Whether or not you've been great about keeping in touch, an old friend or mentor is usually thrilled to hear from you, even if it's just so you can whine for a little while.

Don't let guilt or worries about deadlines keep you from tending these life-sustaining relationships. When stress or loneliness starts to get the best of you, fight back by reaching out. You won't always need this kind of support, but especially during the first few weeks of college, you're entitled to it.

I called my parents. I would fight with them a lot during my senior year [in high school]; I didn't have a good relationship with them. I wanted to leave! But once I came to college, it was different. I would call my parents, and the next thing I knew, our relationship had changed. It was more mature, trusting, and more of a friendship. Granted, they still are my parents and the "authoritarian" figures, but being able to communicate with them on another level and having a different level of trust improved my relationship with them. I came to realize that they will always be there for me!

—Junior, University of California, Los Angeles

I got involved in a lot of clubs and things and made some great friends just by being myself. This kept me too busy to really think about how homesick I might have been. Also, I called my family on the phone every day for the first few weeks. There is nothing wrong with that.

—Sophomore, Stonehill College

Be careful who you make friends with. Have a thick skin, because those friends might not last for four years, but there will be some special ones that do.

—Senior, Dominican University

The 5 Best Ways to Meet New People in College (According to Students)

1. **Get involved.** We've all heard it a million times, but it's true. You're not going to meet people by sitting in your room watching TV—you have to get out there. Try going to smaller events that allow for more one-on-one interactions.
2. **Live in a dorm.** There are all sorts of great reasons to live off campus, depending on the university, but when you first get there you'll find no better way to meet people than to live in the dorms.

3. **Keep an open door.** Keeping your dorm room door open when you're there increases your opportunities to connect with other people on your floor. "On my hallway people were always in and out of each other's rooms getting to know everyone."

4. **Take classes with strangers.** Definitely. "Don't take classes with friends; take one with completely new people. Trust me, it's better. Why? Because if you hang out with someone random from your one random class in the dining hall, then you'll meet their friends and your social network just increased threefold."

5. **Eat in the dining hall.** A ton of people are always there, and you can almost always find someone sitting alone. It's easy to find people to eat with, and there is always something to talk about (the food and how good or, more accurate, how bad it is). Also, if you can't find someone new, there is almost always someone you know to sit with.

A Table That Fits

- Chat with people in the dining-hall line who seem interesting and ask to sit with them when you all get your food. That way you're all at the same part of the meal. There is nothing worse than sitting down when everyone else is about to get up.

- Ask someone you recognize—from class, orientation, extracurricular activities, and so on—and would like to get to know better if you can join him or her, even if you don't know anyone else at the table.

- Stick to the big tables. Much of the time people who sit at the small tables do so for a reason. Go to the big tables and try to sit with a diverse group of people who look like they're all having a good time.

The 6 Kinds of Toxic Friendships

Just as there are really great people on every campus, there are also creeps. The selfish, the dishonest, the bullies, the social climbers—they got into college, too, and they'll be living in your dorm and sitting next to you in class. Here are six types to watch out for:

1. **The Constant Crisis:** Friendship is give-and-take. If you find you're always listening to other people's troubles but they never listen to yours, or your friends are in a constant state of crisis, do your best to connect them with help while you're connecting with some new friends.

2. **The Joker:** Teasing in a friendship is okay, but if you find you're always on the wrong end of the joke or your friends can dish it out but can't take it, ditch those friendships and find people who are nice to you.

3. **The Furious Friend:** Don't remain in friendships with people who throw things or throw punches. Violent people often escalate their level of violence when they're under stress, and college is a stressful environment; it will only get worse as the semester wears on.

4. **The Liability (aka: You're *Not* Their Mother!):** If you always find yourself searching the room for these friends when it's time to go home or cleaning up after them in the wee hours of the morning (if you haven't had any experience with this yet, trust me, it's not a pretty sight), move on to slightly more responsible friends. A lot of people are going to screw up or go too far, but if it's a habit, stop hanging out with these people and let somebody else be their mother.

5. **The "No" Friend:** Are you always having to do what they want to do, go where they've decided to go, hang out with the people they choose to? Or maybe these friends just never

want to do anything. Either way, there are enough people on campus who *do* have the capacity for compromise that you don't have to hang with people who are pushy or inflexible.

6. **The Arm-Twister:** Not the friends who get you to try a new sport, but the friends who press you, sometimes by nagging, other times by mocking, to do things that are against your values or leave you feeling guilty afterward.

 Online Survival Guide: Share your own stories (or types) of toxic friendships by going to http://TheFreshmanSurvival Guide.com/chapters/ and clicking on "Chapter 2."

Some of these relationships are just annoying and others can really be poisonous. You'll have a lot on your plate as a new college student, so if you find yourself in a friendship that takes away more emotional energy than it gives you, don't be afraid to let that friendship fade and replace it with more life-giving ones. Check in with your old friends and talk it through, or if you're really struggling to get free of a toxic friendship—and if the "3 Ways to Disengage" (see below) don't work for you—check out chapter 22 for finding help on campus.

3 Ways to Disengage

1. **Get busy.** Join a new activity. This will give you the opportunity to make new friends and get away from the ones you may be having problems with. People can't get mad at you, or at least they can't reasonably be angry, if you have a practice, meeting, or rehearsal. And if they do get mad, point out that they should try joining something.

2. **Branch out together.** In most cases toxic relationships are isolating, so instead of finding yourself in a situation

where you're stuck again with needy friends, invite others along. This takes the pressure off and allows you, and possibly the toxic friends, to meet new people. If they don't want to join in with others, then go ahead and have fun yourself. You are not responsible for making others happy.

3. **Let your feelings be known.** Reveal what you feel to the one you want to disengage from, not to others. Don't talk about people behind their backs—that's the easiest way to hurt feelings and to be a pretty bad friend. But if the friends you're trying to distance yourself from confront you, tell them the truth—in the way you'd want to be told. Try using statements like "I came to college to expand my horizons and networks, and right now it seems like this is the best way for me to achieve that."

Online Survival Guide: *How do you disengage? Go to http://TheFreshmanSurvivalGuide.com/chapters/ and click on "Chapter 2."*

THE TAKEAWAY

Friendship is one of the most important aspects of college life and one of the most challenging. Stick up for yourself and find people to hang with who will also stick up for you. A recent college graduate really summed it up well: "Your friends have an enormous influence on the person you are and the person you'll become. Choose them carefully, and choose friends that are like the person you hope to be."

CHAPTER 3

Living with a Weirdo and Other Roommate Issues

 Survival Strategy #3: You may not get along with your roommate, you may become best friends, or—most likely—you'll fall somewhere in between. The most important elements of the roommate relationship are communication and compromise. Forging a respectful roommate relationship will make a big difference in your satisfaction with life on campus.

You get your roommate assignment and go into shock. You can't pronounce her name and she's from a country you haven't heard of. Or maybe you friend him on Facebook and find out he's a country music fan who listens to Rush Limbaugh—and you protest to stop climate change and love hip-hop. You might be a little disappointed—or terrified—but don't decide ahead of time that this match can't possibly work. Even if you're nervous, try to enter into your roommate relationship with an open mind and let go of your prejudices. Your roommate may be perfectly normal or might actually be pretty weird. Either way, you may be pleasantly surprised to find a person you didn't expect.

Even if you and your roommate click immediately, expect the relationship to be at least a little bit of work. You both need and want different things within the same small (*very* small) space, and you're bound to run into a few conflicts—it's just the nature of living with another person. Learning to communicate when things are uncomfortable is an important life skill.

There's a good chance you've probably already learned some of the basic skills you'll need in order to have a good roommate experience. Recent research on college roommates at the University of Michigan Institute for Social Research supports the notion that having genuine compassion and concern for others is an essential element in building good roommate relationships. The institute studied more than three hundred college freshmen who were assigned to share rooms with strangers at the start of the first semester. The goal was to see how students' approaches to relationships affected their relationships with roommates and their own emotional health. During the first week, 32 percent of students reported always or almost always feeling lonely; by the tenth week of the study, however, only about 17 percent reported those same feelings.[1] The good news here is that even roommates who started out as strangers can pretty quickly begin offering each other support.

Students who were concerned with their own popularity were less likely to report that their relationships with their roommates were getting better. "Basically, people who give support in response to another person's needs and out of concern for another person's welfare are most successful at building close relationships that they find supportive," said Amy Canevello, one of the researchers. "We get support, in other words, by being supportive."[2]

If your good communication skills and concern for the well-being of others don't seem to be helping and you're still having roommate issues, don't worry—there are people around to help. Resident assistants and directors (RAs and RDs) are there for the times when things aren't working out in your living situation, so don't be afraid to speak up. Your room is a home away from home—it should feel that way. Here are more tips that will empower you to create a great roommate relationship.

Don't Be a Doormat

Be honest right from the start with your roommate about what you like and don't like. If her perfume gives you migraines, say so. If you don't like him borrowing your shampoo, speak up. Establish a habit of directness about little things so that when the big things come up later, you've already had some practice. You don't have to be a nitpicker—and there will be plenty of things that don't really matter, so you don't have to address them—but if you find yourself irritated with something your roommate is doing, you owe it to him or her to say so and to say so directly. There's nothing worse than finding out your roommate has been complaining to everyone else on the floor about your irritating habits without the courtesy of keeping you up to date. Establishing a pattern of addressing problems as they arise will encourage your roommate to be honest, too.

> *You don't have to be tight with your roommate. Think of it like teammates on a sports team: You don't always like them, you just have to respect them. Communication is the key. If there are any issues, you need to talk about them before they get out of hand. Don't let too many white elephants pile up in your living space.*
>
> **—Robert, sophomore, Philadelphia University**

Sit down within the first week you move in and draw up a contract of responsibilities and expectations that you and your roommate agree to abide by. If it seems a little geeky to one or both of you, go ahead and acknowledge it: "I know this seems a little geeky but it'll give us the chance to discuss what we like and don't like." Setting the expectations in writing at the beginning will give you something more concrete to rely on if there are conflicts in the future.

The most valuable thing I've learned from living with all sorts of people throughout my college career has been to be vocal. Leaving nothing uncommunicated, in my opinion, is the best way to set the stage, whether you're living with your best friend or a random roommate. Even if you know your roommate wouldn't mind you borrowing something or having one of their drinks, just making the effort to ask and make your actions known makes all the difference. Even if you're sure you know the answer, ask.

—Jenna, Boston College

Don't Be a Princess/Prince

That's when you expect everyone to adjust to your way of doing things. You don't start your first class on Monday until ten, so you leave the lights blazing and music blaring until late Sunday night, but then when morning comes, you expect your roommate to tiptoe around in the dark getting ready for his early class. Or maybe you just expect that everyone will love your adorable boyfriend as much as you do in spite of the fact that he helps himself to anything in the fridge, no matter who it belongs to, and is napping on your roommate's bed when she gets back from her afternoon class. Be considerate and expect consideration.

RA Wisdom

- Get to know each other, but go slow. Don't bare your souls to each other the first night.
- Make other friends your roommate doesn't know. This can prevent and relieve "roommate fatigue," where there's nothing really wrong, but you're just a little sick of each other because you hang out together *all* the time.
- The ideal situation is probably when your best friend is *not* your roommate. Sometimes living with your best friend makes it hard to bring up annoying little issues, the things a friend should overlook but that can drive a roommate crazy (like when he shaves over your desk every morning and leaves a disgusting dusting of facial hair there—true story).
- Most students don't go to their RAs enough. University of Scranton RA Bryan Heinline says people are often reluctant to admit they're having trouble with roommates (and lots of other things RAs can help with). So keep in mind that there's a reason your college put a person up the hall from you whose job it is to keep an eye out for you. It's almost as if they *know* you might need help.

The first shock of dorm life can be lack of personal space; often a student's living space is one-half the size of his or her living space at home. After a week or two, the camplike feel of the living situation can grow stale. "At home my room is my place to get away from my family, to play my music, to play video games with my friends, and to be as loud as we want," says one student. "In the dorms—nothing against my roommates—it just isn't my space." Actually, that is the key: It really isn't just your space, and if you haven't shared your bedroom with anyone before, you may be in for a shock.

Online Survival Guide: *Ask our online resident assistants about college life by visiting "Interactive RA" at http://TheFreshmanSurvivalGuide.com and clicking on "Ask."*

Keeping the Peace

Two issues tend to make things fall apart between roommates: noise and visitors. Address these problems before they become unbearable and trigger World War III. Sometimes the other person is unaware, and sometimes he or she is just inconsiderate.

Here's a quick list of strategies for communicating positively and keeping things friendly:

- Don't accuse. Use "I" statements. Don't say, *"You* are so inconsiderate." This accusation may well be true, but instead say, "When you leave your wet towel on my bed, *I* feel like you don't care." This lets your roommate know about the problem behavior but gives him or her room to change it. Accusations lead to arguments. "I" statements can lead to solutions.

- Catch your roommate doing something good and say thanks. "Hey, you cleaned! I'm so busy this week I really appreciate that. Thanks." It reinforces the behavior you want to increase without being negative. Warning: This must be done without a scrap of sarcasm, or it completely ruins the effort.

- Offer a little support. If things are getting tense (but you're still speaking to each other), ask how your roommate is doing. Sometimes stress shows up as inconsiderate behavior. If he just found out he's failing chemistry and he is a chem major, you might need to show a little kindness instead of laying down the law until the crisis passes.

Creating Roomie Love—The Interactive RA

Dorm life can be the best experience of your college career or it can be a nightmare. Most of you have heard roommate horror stories, but here are a few tips to create long-lasting roomie love.

Tip 1: Communication—Like any good relationship, communication is key; the same with having a roommate. If you can, talk to your roommate before you are thrown into the same room together and start class. After class starts chaos occurs, and you may never get the chance to talk to your roommate unless you are waking her/him when you get back from a late night at the library. Here is a list of what you should discuss before you move in:

How clean a person are you?—Talk about when and how often you are going to clean your room. Are you going to clean together or just your space?

Morning bird vs. night owl—This is an epic battle that only the strong will win. Make room rules about when lights go out, when they can be turned on, when you can play music. Basically be courteous to your roommate. If he or she is sleeping, be as quiet as possible.

Food/clothes use—Food can be a touchy subject. Discuss if you are going to be sharing or not sharing food. Talk about whether you are going to share clothes. Are you going to have an "ask before you use" policy? How are you going to ask permission? In person? Text? Before? After the fact?

Boyfriend/girlfriend/guest—Tell you roommate if you have a GF/BF, or if you are supersocial. Set times and days when guests can come over. Tell your roommate when you would like some alone time with your guest, and please never ever have alone time with your GF/BF when your roommate is in the room. Three's a crowd. Remember that your room is also your room-mate's room and they have a right to be there. So if your roommate has a problem with your guests, meet your guests elsewhere to hang out.

If you talk about these things before moving in, you can both have a set of expectations for living together.

Tip 2: The honeymoon period will end—The first few weeks of class is a great time. You might love your roommate and that you're living together. But by the time the first exam rolls around, you may be ready to tear each other's hair out. The hair-tearing-out time is a good time to sit down and make a roommate contract. You can do this on your own or with your RA if you need a mediator. Put in the roommate contract all the answers to my communication tips.

Tip 3: Gossip—Never talk about your roommate behind his or her back. Do not complain to other people on your floor or your friends (especially if you share friends). Your roommate will hear about it because people love gossip. If you have to complain to someone, talk to your very, very close friends, parents, siblings, or your RA. Your RA is living on the floor with you for a reason. Use them for advice on how to deal with or talk to your roommate.

Tip 4: Clean—Please clean your room! Do your laundry, take your trash out, and using a well-placed air freshener is an excellent idea. Your roommate will thank you. Your floor mates will thank you. Your RA will thank you. Smells travel through walls and closed doors. It is a mysterious phenomenon.

Living with someone, especially a stranger, can be very stress-ful. Talk to each other, and don't let problems build up. Leaving a note for your roommate can be a good or a very bad idea. If the note is about when you're coming back to the room or when dinner is, that's okay. But if the note is about an issue you have with your roommate, please talk to your roommate in person, not through a piece of paper. You are adults now—discuss your feelings.

Living with someone can also be really fun, and I have seen tons of freshman roommate go on to be best friends and even live together their sophomore year.

—Kailynn Cerny, iRA
West Virginia University

College Essentials

Your college's website may have a packing list that's specific to the region and includes your school's rules regarding what appliances are permitted. Talk to your roommate(s) about who will bring which appliances, such as a minifridge, microwave, or TV. You'll definitely need:

- Clothes: everyday casuals, workout clothes, swimsuit, coat, one or two dressy outfits (not twelve...)
- Lots of socks and underwear
- Weather gear appropriate to the region: umbrella, rain/snow boots, hat, gloves
- Backpack
- Shower stuff: toiletries, bathrobe, towels and washcloths, flip-flops
- Bedding: sheets (check mattress sizes), extra blankets, your favorite pillow
- Laundry supplies: detergent and fabric softener or dryer sheets, drying rack, hangers, mini-iron and board, hamper or laundry bag
- First-aid kit, including antacids, cold/allergy medicine, ibuprofen

- Mini tool kit and sewing kit
- Duct tape, masking tape, stapler, printer paper, notebooks, pens
- Extension cords, power strips, desk light or book light, flashlight
- Headphones (noise-canceling are best)
- Cleaning supplies: bucket, all-purpose cleaner/wipes, dishpan, dish soap, sponges, garbage bags
- Dishes: plate, cup, silverware, water bottle, a giant mug, can opener, ziplock bags
- Laptop, thumb drive
- Pictures of family, friends, pets

Optional: mattress padding, dry-erase board, football/ Frisbee, prepared foods/snacks

Don't bring: expensive items you don't need, family heirlooms or jewelry, candles or appliances that violate your school's rules

 Online Survival Guide: Download a PDF of our list of college essentials—and add any of your own essentials that aren't already listed by visiting http://TheFreshman SurvivalGuide.com/chapters/ and clicking on "Chapter 3."

It can seem complicated to share so much time, space, and stuff with one person, but it comes down to one thing: respect. You have the right (and the responsibility) to have (and to be) a respectful roommate. Respect isn't just about being nice, either; it includes the way your roommate treats your belongings, sleep, study habits, health, safety, and general sanity.

Freshman year, Erin ended up with a roommate, "Nancy," who was really negative. Nancy's constant complaining was driving everyone else in the suite to spend all their free time anyplace but in their room. Nancy gossiped about whoever wasn't there at the time, was always in crisis, and occasionally was openly hostile—calling people names and blaming them for her unhappiness. Erin had tried cheerful compassion, sincere empathy, and specific requests. Nothing worked. Finally, Erin and another saner roommate gently suggested that perhaps Nancy would be happier in a different situation. She responded by trying to oust Erin from their current setup instead. Finally, Erin and the "good" roommate went to the residence life office for help. Even though the office staff couldn't offer a switch right away, they were able to give Erin and her friend some strategies to keep the peace in the short term. Much to everyone's relief, the unhappy roommate—who really just wasn't ready for life on campus—moved home shortly thereafter and commuted.

SEEK → FIND

Our ability to tolerate others is based on our capacity to empathize with them, understand who they are and what is important to them. That said, there is a threshold where what works for one person's living situation doesn't necessarily work for another's.

—Rabbi Yonah Schiller, executive director of Hillel at Tulane University

If you are not happy with your first roommate, I would strongly recommend getting a new one. My first roommate was a nightmare. She was rude, judgmental, and refused to say hello to me. I was miserable and alone. Finally, I decided to move out. It was the best decision I have ever made, and my new roommate and I are great friends. If you and your roommate aren't friends but you can get along, I wouldn't move. In my case, however, it was necessary. Any situation where he/she doesn't respect you or treat you like another human being is something you need to get out of as soon as you can. It's worth it!

—Freshman, University of Iowa

The Roommate Dirty Dozen: To Deal or Ditch?

Every roommate experience is unique—for both of you (let's face it, we've all got our own weird habits). Here are twelve of the most common types of college roommates. With each description are some suggestions about when you should stay and *deal* with the situation or when it's time to *ditch* the roommate. (No need to thank us, it's our job.)

1. **The Slob.** Very few people are flawlessly neat, but the Slob takes messiness to new levels. An unmade bed is one thing, but dirty laundry everywhere? Unwashed dishes that smell? His or her stuff invading your space? *Deal for a bit but ditch before the mice and cockroaches move in.*

2. **The Neat Freak.** A certain amount of neatness in the room is definitely a matter of respect for each other's space. A roommate constantly harping on you to be neat, though, is no good. Check your own habits—*is* your mess out of control? Give it some thought, but trust your judgment. Your roommate may be a Neat Freak, and while

that's great for his or her stuff, it shouldn't add to your stress. *Deal if you can.*

3. **The Witch.** This can be a guy or a girl, but you'll know you're living with one whenever that person's mood becomes *the* mood. You're having a great day and the Witch comes back to the room fuming and complaining, and all of a sudden the bubble has burst and everything looks bleak. It happens to everyone once in a while, but if it's an everyday occurrence, find some positive friends who can improve your outlook. Don't let this crabby roommate push your buttons. *Deal if you can, ditch if you must.*

4. **The Mooch.** "Sure, you can borrow my scarf." "I'll spot you the cash this time." "Yeah, take my last granola bar." STOP! Sharing is great, but when you're only ever asked to give, give, give, it's time to reconsider. Is there any balance? Maybe you share stuff but your roommate offers you support and edits your papers. If it's a two-way street, the scatterbrained-but-sweet Mooch can actually be nice to have around. But the suck-you-dry Mooch needs a firmer approach. *Deal if you can set clear boundaries. Ditch before you get really resentful or go broke.*

5. **The Druggie.** The Druggie can come in many forms and is usually, to some extent, a combination of many of the roommates in the dirty dozen. Maybe he smokes a lot of pot and is totally unmotivated by anything besides Doritos. Or maybe she likes taking hallucinogens, and she starts seeing things after drinking two bottles of Robitussin for fun. Or maybe he's into uppers like cocaine or even prescription drugs like Adderall; he's certainly motivated but is really annoying because he won't ever shut up and stays up for days at a time. No matter what, you

need to think of the way your roommate's illegal behavior is affecting you. No one wants to rat out a roommate, but definitely consider whether you could be more of a help in the long run if you tell someone about your roomie's problems. And remember, it's your room, too. You have every right to say you're not comfortable with drugs being kept in your room, because if campus security finds something, it could quickly become your problem, too. *Ditch.*

6. **The Masturbator.** This roommate comes in two varieties. Type 1: If you often come back to find your roommate frantically trying to exit out of something on the computer or covering himself with sheets, just remember—knock and pause before entering! Type 2 is more of a problem: Every night when the lights go down and you're trying to sleep, you realize from the rustling of sheets in the next bed that your roommate's taking a little pleasure trip, leaving you feeling awkward and more than a little grossed out. This one will actually require an awful conversation. *Deal if possible. Ditch Type 2 if he doesn't smarten up after your uncomfortable talk.*

7. **The No-Study.** This roommate can be very annoying. While you're constantly studying and working your hardest, he or she is taking long naps and playing video games. Not only can this distract you and encourage you to slack off, it can hurt your sense of pride as well. If in spite of all his or her slacking off, your roommate continues to pull in As while you're busting your butt for Bs, you may feel the urge to drop your study habits altogether. Don't. *Deal.*

8. **The Party Animal.** The Party Animal is the best roommate during orientation week and the worst roommate

during finals week. Picture it: After living in the library for the last two days, you return, exhausted, to find your roommate has become the host of the never-ending study-break party. You have to either kick out the hordes of people drinking their way through finals, or try to sleep while people blast dubstep underneath your loft bed. It's times like these when you need to draw the line. The best way to deal with the Party Animal is to set ground rules early and hard. Agree that if anything is going to be hosted in your room it will be a group decision, and agree on quiet hours and set days when showing up wasted is okay. If the Party Animal seems to think rules are made to be broken, that's the time to confront or bring in your RA for help. *Deal until it's clear the Animal can't be tamed.*

9. **The Angry Guy.** He plays his music loud. He yells a lot. He punches things. And that's all when he's sober. When he drinks, he yells louder and starts punching people. *Get out.* If you're stuck, give him room, be as positive as you can, and keep your RA posted. But if at all possible, *ditch.*

10. **The Absentee Roommate.** You haven't seen him in a week and you're starting to think maybe he dropped out, but all his stuff's still there. She goes home every weekend or she's always at her boyfriend's. This roommate's not so much a problem, just a disappointment if you were hoping for something more from the relationship. Check up on the Absentee occasionally to make sure he or she is okay, and look for companionship elsewhere. *Deal.*

11. **The Needy One.** There's a new crisis every day or perhaps just an ongoing concern. Lots of tears and sullenness. Be a sympathetic ear but don't do it alone. Make sure that the Needy One has lots of people he or she can

rely on so you're not handling the endless problems on your own. Keep your RA in the loop in case things get serious. *Deal compassionately as best you can; ditch if you're getting dragged into the hole, too.*

12. **The Sexiler.** You're locked out (in college parlance, *sexiled*) half the nights from Thursday to Sunday because your roommate has hooked up—again. If you need to come to a mutual agreement about who gets the room to him- or herself, fine. If not, put your foot down and let your roommate know his or her sex life needs to relocate. *Deal as best you can, but if the roomie won't listen to reason, ditch.*

 Online Survival Guide: *Share your own roommate Deal or Ditch stories by going to http://TheFreshmanSurvival Guide.com/chapters/ and clicking on "Chapter 3."*

The Freshman Survival Guide's Roommate Bill of Rights

Our Bill of Rights is adapted from those posted by residence life offices across the country. Check your college's residence life website to see your school's official policy.

- The right to sleep and study free from undue interference (noise, music, television, gaming, guests) in your room.
- The right to expect that a roommate will respect your personal belongings.
- The right to a clean living environment.
- The right to free access to your room and facilities without pressure from a roommate.
- The right to privacy.

- The right to be free from the fear of intimidation or physical and/or emotional harm.
- The right to expect cooperation in the use of "shared" appliances and a commitment to honor agreed-upon payment procedures.
- The right to be free from peer pressure or ridicule if your lifestyle choices differ from those of your roommate.
- The right to redress of grievances. Residence hall staff members are available for assistance in settling conflicts.

Online Survival Guide: Go to http://TheFreshmanSurvival Guide.com/chapters/ and click on "Chapter 3" for a downloadable PDF of our roommate Bill of Rights.

Dealing with Differences (Religion, Race, Sexuality, Etc.)

So your roommate has a different religious tradition, country of origin, race, sexual orientation—nearly any difference can be managed, even though it might seem insurmountable at the start. Learning to deal with differences maturely and respectfully, without prejudice or jokes, without demeaning the other person or yourself, is a vital life skill that will hold you in good stead in the rest of your college career and in work and relationships beyond college.

Understand that your attitudes, beliefs, or background may be challenging to your roommate. He or she may have a hard time adjusting to some of those differences, but your patience, understanding, and honesty can go a long way toward teaching tolerance to someone who hasn't had much experience dealing with diversity. Don't feel obligated to share your entire personal history, especially early on. (For more on dealing with differences, see chapter 6.)

Michelle Goodwin, associate director of the University Catholic Center in Austin, Texas, has seen a lot of students go through the first-semester discomfort of learning to live with a stranger. "This is the time in life to learn who you can live with and who you can't," she says. You don't always know before college what will bother you once you're in the situation. "Even if you filled out the likes/dislikes form the dorms sent you, it may take one semester to understand more clearly what you can and cannot tolerate." Goodwin recommends:

- Give your roommate a chance. Your roommate may look different, have different tastes in music and interests, and be the best person in the world—but you will never find out if you don't give him or her a chance.
- Set and keep boundaries.
- Be considerate of time, noise, space, and friends.
- Your roommate may not want to be your best friend. You can live with someone and not be close to him or her.
- If conflicts arise, try to work them out with your roommate first and then go to your RA for help.
- You may need to change roommates. It really isn't the end of the world.

THE TAKEAWAY

Roommate issues can be some of the biggest challenges in adapting to college life. Remember, you have rights. Be considerate and try to communicate. But know when to deal and when to ditch.

CHAPTER 4

For the First Few Weeks, Live Like a Monk

Survival Strategy #4: Monks take vows of chastity, poverty, and obedience. A little restraint can go a long way toward helping you keep yourself together when you're new on campus.

There's plenty of fun to be had at college and lots of time to have it. The first few weekends can be a bit of a free-for-all and are often when you're at your most vulnerable. Give yourself time to get acclimated to your new surroundings before you start taking chances that could have negative (and lasting) consequences. Those chances will probably look a lot less attractive once you're feeling more comfortable. Michelle Goodwin, associate director of the University Catholic Center in Austin, Texas, describes it this way: "There are so many ways to be lost on a campus: physically, spiritually, socially, or intellectually. College is all about creating an internal gyroscope that keeps balance. At first you are completely out of balance, but then you find your center."

Live like a monk? You can probably do without the vow of silence, but the other three vows are a good rule of thumb as you begin your college career.

Chastity

College may be the place where you meet the love of your life, but you probably won't know that the first week of school, especially on Friday night after a couple of drinks. It's too soon to tell who's who. Give yourself some time to settle in before adding a boyfriend or girlfriend to the mix or hooking up with someone who may turn out to be bad news (see the list of creepy people to avoid dating in chapter 7). It may be hard, especially with so many new people to meet, to avoid connecting with a guy or girl you find particularly attractive or fun. But the same rule applies here as with new friends and roommates: It's nearly impossible to tell who's safe or sane early on, or to know enough about a person to decide whether he or she is someone you want to get involved with or not. A month from now you'll have a better sense of who the players are and what they're about.

 Online Survival Guide: What's your dating IQ? Test it at http://TheFreshmanSurvivalGuide.com/chapters/ and click on "Chapter 7."

Not only will early-semester chastity help your sanity, it will also improve your dating life in the long run. I knew a lot of girls and guys who were making out with tons of different people the first few weeks of freshman year. They would get drunk and make out with whoever happened to be around. In most cases it didn't go beyond that, but the fact that these people were making out with different people at least every weekend got them the reputation of being people who were just looking for a good time and not a relationship. They had a hard time finding people who took them seriously after that.

—Brittany, graduate, Case Western Reserve University

SEEK → FIND

From the Jewish perspective, when woman and man first came together [the Torah] says that "Adam knew Eve." We have understood this to mean that they had relations and produced offspring. Yet upon closer examination, in Hebrew, "to know" can be understood with more consequence. A sexual relationship is another way for two people to really "know" one another. The idea that during the common hookup there's real communication and something is being shared is not something many students think about. In fact, I think the most damaging sexual relationships are the ones that lack communication and [true] "knowing." When people feel sexually used, most likely one person was communicating all over the other person while the recipient never got a word in edgewise.

—Rabbi Yonah Schiller,
executive director of Hillel at Tulane University

It seems to me that people jump into a lot of relationships freshman year because they think college is all about experimenting or something. A lot of people are glad they did this, but I am glad I didn't. It became obvious after freshman year that the guy who had wanted to date me—who I had agonized over starting a relationship with but hesitated because it didn't feel quite right—was completely wrong for me.

—**Amelia, Gonzaga University**

Poverty

Don't blow all your money your first weekend at school. In a few weeks you'll be amazed at what you can live without. If you have the luxury of calling home for cash, your parents will be a lot happier if you don't do it the second week of school...And not blowing all your money right away is even more important if you worked all summer for money that has to last the semester.

Are you a comfort shopper? You know, *I'm feeling anxious, angry, unhappy, stressed out. Hey! Let's go shopping!* If you're a person who tends to deal with strong emotions with retail therapy, be especially careful. There will be lots of strong emotions in your first semester, probably more than your budget can handle. You will see big spenders flashing their cash the first few weeks of school, but resist the urge to follow suit. Be a miser for a month and see where that gets you. There will be college sweatshirts at the bookstore for the next four years; you can pick one up anytime. And does it make sense to buy pizza when your food at the dining hall is already paid for? Okay, sometimes it does, but not every night.

Online Survival Guide: Are you using shopping as a way to deal with stress? Go to http://TheFreshmanSurvival Guide.com/chapters/ and click on "Chapter 4" for our "Are You a Stress Shopper?" quiz.

---

7 Saving Strategies

1. **Look on campus first.** If you're looking for an evening's entertainment, most campuses have multiple free events each week—concerts, talks, art shows—and they're often accompanied by free food. On-campus social events will almost always be less expensive than going out to a club.
2. **Wait a day.** Fight impulse purchases by practicing the "wait a day" rule. If you see something you like, don't buy it immediately. Give yourself at least twenty-four

hours to consider whether your budget can handle it and if it's something you actually need.

3. **Buy books cheaper.** As long as you're careful to get the right edition (some profs will care, others won't—make sure you check with them first), you can save a lot of money getting your books online or at a local used bookstore. Another way to save is by waiting to see if your professor actually uses the book in class before you buy it.

4. **Check your balance.** There's no better way to keep an eye on your money than keeping an eye on your money. Keep a shortcut to your financial institution's website on your computer desktop, or get your bank's app on your phone. When you check your e-mail in the morning, also check your account balance. There's nothing worse than hitting the ATM to find out you're down to nothing or you've overdrawn your account.

5. **Don't drink (or at least drink less).** Alcohol, even the cheap stuff, will eat into your budget. There are lots of good reasons to not drink or drink less. Your wallet is one of them.

6. **Use your meal plan.** Restaurant food is the most expensive food. Even if you only get coffee a few times a week or hit the vending machine in the afternoon for a Coke, you can easily rack up from $20 to $150 a month or more, depending on how much of a caffeine addict you are and how fancy you like your Starbucks. If the meal plan is paid for, use it and save your money.

7. **Check out the library.** Stacy, a recent University of Akron grad, shared this tip: "Most college libraries have a lot of books, magazines, and movies for entertainment purposes. Don't be afraid to check out the library for fun. You are paying for it."

Online Survival Guide: *For more resources on how to manage your money, go to http://TheFreshmanSurvival Guide.com/chapters/ and click on "Chapter 4."*

I failed to keep track of the money I was spending. It's so important to know how much money you have in case of emergency, and I wasn't paying attention. Thank goodness I didn't go too overboard—I would be completely broke right now. Money is so important in college, especially when you will have student loans to pay off. You may have the money to do something now, but you should keep in mind where it will need to go in the next five years.

—Freshman, University of Iowa

One of the things that helped me survive the tough first few months of freshman year was the ability to go off campus for a meal or some other activity. When I was feeling very homesick, enjoying a good meal or going to see a movie off campus picked up my spirits. The important message here is not learning not to spend but learning to spend wisely.

—Sophomore, Middlebury College

Obedience

Go to class! This seems obvious—it *is* why you're in college—but you wouldn't believe how many freshmen skip their way out of school. Do a little math and figure out how much it costs for you to have your butt in that chair per hour. You'll be less willing to blow a class off. Most professors will allow one or two absences, but save them for the end of the semester when you've got mono and three papers due in the same week.

Fr. Rick Malloy says, "It will help tremendously if the student has gone to every class. Missing class is a loud message to the professor: 'I want an F for this course!' On the other hand, if you are in class every day, how can a professor admit he or she was unable to teach you anything?"

It sounds pretty easy. Just show up and the rest will fall into place, right? Well, not exactly. "We are *not* high school teachers in any way, shape, or form," explains one professor. "Fortunately or unfortunately, most professors do not think it is their job to make the classroom entertaining. Few will reward you for just showing up to class and sitting there lifeless, but almost all will deduct points if you skip." Going to class is no guarantee you'll pass—but *not* going assures that you won't.

If you've always been able to skate along without really working too hard, that may just catch up with you now. Develop a plan of attack, and set aside time to study and do homework. Spend your time carefully, and don't let your study time fill up with other things. You're the one who chooses how to spend those unoccupied hours now, so choose carefully.

Online Survival Guide: *Download your own PDF copy of the "Study Budget" by going to http://TheFreshman SurvivalGuide.com/chapters/ and clicking on "Chapter 4."*

Manage your time well. Make sure that school always comes first, because this time you are paying for it. It doesn't mean that you can't be social and do things with friends, but make sure that you always, always go to class!

—Sophomore, University of Montana

The best advice I got was to get to know people. It's no fun to be stuck in class surrounded by a bunch of people you know nothing about. By actually talking to a few people, I got to share some common interests, and sooner or later we began forming study groups, making class a whole lot less stressful.

—Abay, New York University

Be a little overcautious early on. So many people crash and burn in their first few weeks because they try to keep a superhero's schedule—class all day and party all night—and are unpleasantly surprised when they accidentally sleep through a whole morning's worth of classes or get hit with a nasty cold because they're exhausted and run-down. Your body does have limits. With so many options, it can be hard to slow down and take good care of yourself. Try keeping a schedule similar to the one you had back home, or at least count how many hours of sleep you're getting and shoot for eight most of the time, knowing that there'll be nights where you want to, or have to, shortchange yourself.

The biggest thing about freshman year was getting used to the fact that at college I didn't have my usual responsibilities—chores, family stuff—the ones I had as a "kid." Now I had to get myself to classes, get work done (no more reminders from teachers), and step up to the bat and take care of business, on my own.

—Ania, senior, Cornell University

THE TAKEAWAY

Three of the biggest issues you'll face in college are sex, money, and making choices. So remember, early on live like a monk: Practice poverty, chastity, obedience. And until you've gotten to know a few people and have figured out, at least a little bit, who you want to be in this new place, consider treating the big three with caution.

CHAPTER 5

I Miss My Old Life!

Survival Strategy #5: Homesickness is a fact of college life, but it doesn't have to defeat you. Develop habits and relationships that will help you ward off the longing for home.

One of the most common struggles, especially in the first few weeks of college, is homesickness. Even if it wasn't your favorite place, home was familiar, and as human beings we are all creatures of habit. Familiarity makes us feel safe, and the opposite is also true, which is why missing home can turn into such a big deal.

Another reason homesickness can hit with such ferocity, especially in the first few weeks, is that everything else has changed at the same time; you're missing home while you're meeting a whole new set of academic and social demands. Are you pining for your own room, your dog, the sights and sounds of the house you grew up in? You're not alone. According to the UCLA Higher Education Research Institute, 66 percent of college freshmen suffer homesickness.[1]

You have a right to be sad. It may seem strange; you've

finally gotten the independence that you waited for all through high school. You can stay out all night, you can leave your socks on the floor, and nobody is nagging you to do chores. But there will be days where what you've lost seems like a lot more than what you've gained. The company of your family—even if they were irritating as anything—and the sense that somebody was always looking out for you are not small things, and it's okay to miss them.

Busy Is Good

Getting involved in at least one activity or club right off the bat can provide a good distraction and something to focus on besides schoolwork. It will also give you some immediate social connections with people who have a common interest with you. Keeping busy with new friends and campus activities, exploring your new surroundings both on campus and around town, and finding physical outlets—a morning run or a walk after dinner—all these things can help fight the feeling of homesickness.

Centers for spiritual and religious life on campus can be a real refuge in your first weeks on campus, and now is a great time to connect with the helpful and friendly people available to you. Religious services are a great anchor to your week. "It helped me tremendously in the first few weeks in terms of staying connected to home," says one Middlebury student, "because I knew that the same Mass I was hearing was being said at home. These campus spirituality centers can also just be a good place to go hang out and talk with someone who is understanding."

The only time I ever thought of leaving college was when I was homesick. I felt a small feeling of loneliness, and I wanted to go back to who I was in high school. I wanted to go home the moment my parents drove away. But I stayed, because I found friends who invited me to things and who wanted me to stay. I made friends with sophomores who had a year under their belts, and they helped keep me grounded.

—Victoria, senior, Marian University

Fight Homesickness Without Going Home

It can be really tough to resist, but one of the worst ways to fight homesickness is by heading home for the weekend. Tough it out for a few weekends and make the effort to get out and do something. You'll miss out on a lot of college life if you hit the road every Friday and spend all your weekends back home. Plus, when you get back on campus Sunday night you can end up feeling even more isolated.

If you really can't make it without a little homemade TLC, try a nice long phone call or video chat first, or see if you can con your folks into coming to visit you, preferably with some home-cooked food and a little extra pocket money!

I would try to make a point to call home at least once a week. Just talking to my mom or hearing a familiar voice really helped freshman year.

—Mack, graduate, Allegheny College

It may not feel like it at the beginning, but first semester will go by fast. Things can seem slow at the start; it's as if you're in a weird time warp, because everything is so new and you're without your old routines. But count the number of days until Thanksgiving break, then the even-shorter span until winter break. Don't let the whole semester loom large. Fight homesickness by breaking up the semester into smaller chunks, and look only as far ahead as the next long weekend, parent visit, or break.

At the same time, don't wish away your days at school. It's only four years, which may seem like an eternity right now, but it will go by more and more quickly all the time. Don't waste the time by drowning in homesickness.

I saw so many people get homesick and go home every weekend, and they ended up alienating themselves from their peers and having a harder time adjusting. Everybody's going to get homesick at some point, but really try to push yourself to stay on campus for the first few weekends. Socialize as much as possible. Going back home may make you feel more comfortable, but it will only make going back to school on Monday that much more difficult.

—Jennifer, senior, Fordham University

Online Survival Guide: *For more college students' stories of homesickness, go to http://TheFreshmanSurvivalGuide .com/chapters/ and click on "Chapter 5."*

SEEK → FIND

I think students feel stressed out and depressed when they do not feel welcome. We have a group of seniors that partner up with the freshmen for a number of months and help them get acclimated. Seniors become part of the solution. That helps reduce the amount of stress and anxiety about not feeling at home.

—Imam Yahya Hendi, Muslim chaplain,
Georgetown University

Don't Isolate Yourself

With the explosion of communication technology, students staying in their rooms on their computers all day has become a growing problem on campuses (see chapter 17 on computer hazards). One of the benefits of going away to college is that you can expand your horizons and challenge yourself. It can be really tempting, especially if you're feeling nervous or lonely, to call or text parents or old friends throughout the day. Fight the urge.

The more you hang on to home, the less you'll be able to connect on campus. If you've got "helicopter parents" who keep hovering over you to make sure everything's okay, let them know when *you'll* call *them* next (then call when you say you will). If your mom and your best friend keep calling or texting you all day or start getting nervous if you don't reply immediately, reassure them that you'll check in later, but you really need to focus on the people and activities around you.

Mike said the first couple of weeks on campus weren't too bad. He met a lot of people at orientation, though nobody he'd really clicked with. He'd gone to a bunch of parties with his suitemates, but it wasn't really his scene. He also started to suffer from a bad case of homesickness that was becoming a major distraction. He was embarrassed; he felt as if he ought to be able to conquer college on his own, and he *really* didn't want to tell his parents how he was feeling.

Mike decided to call his aunt. She'd always been somebody he could count on. In just a few minutes she'd gotten him to admit that he was struggling, and they strategized a little about making new friends. Just having someone who knew him and could sympathize helped him over the homesickness hurdle and got him through that first month.

If you're constantly on your phone calling or texting friends at home, people will notice, and trust me, it gets annoying and can really hinder the beginnings of friendships. So instead, put the phone away, turn it off even, and make plans to talk to your friends later in the evening or online. I allowed myself one visit home before fall break, but only one. So many students go home the first weekend and as often as they can, but this can be a mistake. You get to finally have fun with your friends on the weekends—it's hard to make friendships like that if you aren't around for it.

—Junior, Juniata College

Online Survival Guide: *Ask our online resident assistants about college life by visiting "Interactive RA" at http:// TheFreshmanSurvivalGuide.com and clicking on "Ask."*

Of course, not everyone gets homesick, but try to be understanding of those who are having trouble with transitioning and offer your support.

Sometimes it works in reverse and your parents are the ones missing you. If they're calling a lot or inviting you to come home too often, try to keep in mind that your being away might be a difficult transition for them. If they are interrupting study time with calls, call them back later. But don't lose touch. When something goes wrong you'll want them to know what's going on and who is in your life.

Reminisce (but Not Too Much)

Look through your pictures and think about all the people who are rooting for you! Just don't spend so much time with memories that you start to wallow in self-pity. As long as those thoughts remain a source of strength, stay with them. You'll know it's time to put the pics away if every time you look at your high school buddies, you're choking back tears or plunging into that well of loneliness.

See if you can identify what it is that you miss the most—the chance to be alone, a full fridge, somebody to take care of you—and consider whether it's something you can duplicate on campus. If you miss solitude, find a quiet corner in the library or a little-traveled area of campus, and make it a priority to spend some time there. If you're missing your parents, don't be afraid to call them for a daily catch-up on the news from home. You won't always need to call so often, but starting out they'll understand. Not only that, chances are they're missing you just as much. If you miss the food from home, ask for a few easy recipes and get cooking. Make sure you pack a few familiar objects: a favorite mug, your football, the pillow that's got just the right level of squishiness, whatever will be a little piece of home on your toughest days.

When Is It More Than Homesickness?

If you start to feel as if you're actually in danger, if the despair reaches a point where you feel you may hurt yourself, immediately talk to your RA, your parents, or someone in the counseling center. (See chapter 22 for people who can help.)

8 Weapons in the Battle Against Homesickness

1. **Busyness.** This serves both to distract you from feeling sorry for yourself and to engage you in your new com-

munity. Clubs, activities, and community service can shift your focus in some really positive ways.

2. **New friends.** Taking time to build up these relationships will give you something to do and help you through the next few months.

3. **Old pictures.** Photos of friends and family can remind you of everyone who's pulling for you back home.

4. **Sleep.** Being well rested makes everything easier to deal with. If you find yourself weepy or moody, sleep should be your first defense.

5. **Your favorites.** That pillow, sweater, teddy bear, music, snack, mug—in the midst of chaos something familiar is a big comfort.

6. **The Internet.** One student taught her mom to use Facebook before she left for college so keeping in touch would be easier.

7. **Get stuff done.** Go to class and do your homework. It'll keep you busy *and* help you develop your new routine. The sense of accomplishment will improve your mood too!

8. **Immersion therapy.** This is a step beyond just doing the work. You'll likely be reading some of the most interesting stuff you've ever read and studying under some of the smartest people in their fields. Really getting inside the material you're studying can inspire you and open up your mind.

Online Survival Guide: How do you beat homesickness? Share your own stories by going to http://TheFreshman SurvivalGuide.com/chapters/ and clicking on "Chapter 5."

THE TAKEAWAY

Becoming an independent person won't happen overnight, but it will happen. Give yourself a break until you're over the worst of homesickness. Take good care of yourself, keep busy, and stay in touch with family and friends old and new.

CHAPTER 6

Dealing with Differences

Survival Strategy #6: Depending on where you go to college, you may find yourself rubbing elbows with a much more culturally, economically, sexually, and religiously diverse group of people than you ever have before (or will again). Dealing with differences in backgrounds and beliefs can be intimidating at first, but college campuses are ideal environments to explore both common ground and complex differences.

Expanding your horizons and coming to understand that the world is more diverse and complicated than you thought is a fundamental aspect of the college experience. Use this opportunity to explore some of the differences all around you. If your life experiences thus far have had you spending most of your time with people a lot like you, you may be a little nervous about interacting in a more diverse environment. But don't let that fear keep you from forging new and different relationships. With globalization and an unprecedented ability to connect and communicate instantaneously, the truth is, dealing with diversity isn't really a choice at all; it's a necessity. It may be easier to hang out exclusively with people who are just like you, but you'll be doing a disservice to yourself and your education

if you don't meet new people and seek out experiences beyond
your comfort zone.

Whether it's dealing with differences in terms of cultural,
family, and socioeconomic backgrounds or issues like sexual
orientation and religious beliefs, you may find yourself concerned about saying the wrong thing or looking stupid when
interacting with people from different backgrounds. Don't
worry; that's normal. Of course, it's generally a good idea to
enter any new environment with an open mind and a degree of
caution, but remember, *everybody* is new here: You're not the
only fish out of water.

In structured and unstructured settings during college you
will encounter other students whose lives and experiences seem
dramatically different from your own. There are usually plenty
of activities and events on campus designed to give you exposure
to different cultures in a learning atmosphere. Take advantage
of these. If a classmate asks you to sample some foods that are
native to his country, give it a try. If a friend invites you to join
her for a religious celebration from a faith tradition different from
your own, go. Rather than perceiving new experiences as a threat
to your own culture or beliefs, try to understand other people's
life experiences. It's essential to developing a fundamental sense
of empathy with other human beings. But start slow. Before you
try to talk about your core convictions, politics, or any other hot
topics, just get to know each other on a human level first.

Some Ground Rules for Finding Common Ground

- You're all new and you've all ended up at the same place.
  Early on, share stories of family, friends from back home,
  how you ended up at this college, and how you like it so far.

- Do a little homework. If you're getting to know an international student, find out about his or her country. If you have a new acquaintance with a different cultural or religious background, learn a little about it, not so you can be an expert but to reduce your chances of making wrong assumptions.
- Once you've established rapport, don't be afraid to move into more difficult territory. Ask if the person minds sharing information about differences. Invite him or her to make observations. A great transition from "safe" topics into more challenging areas can be a discussion about what's the same and what's different about college compared to home.
- Your questions may help others feel better about their own curiosity and free them up to ask you some challenging questions as well.
- For minority students it can be tiring to feel like representatives of their religion, race, or sexual orientation. So be sensitive to their need to just be one of the crowd at times—don't overquestion. If you find yourself in the minority on your campus, try to find a balance between getting out there and interacting and making sure you have support from those who share your values and beliefs.

Different and the Same: Culture and Race on Campus

The experience of an African-American student who grew up in a culturally diverse urban neighborhood will be different from that of a small-town white student with little exposure to people from different backgrounds. As varied in experience as you are, you're all at the same college, of the same generation, with at least the common goal of getting an education. The tension between finding what we have in common with others and discovering what makes each of us unique forms the challenge and the blessing of diversity.

Most of us have prejudices, either buried or on the surface, about people from different backgrounds. As much as possible, approach each person you meet with an open mind and leave your assumptions about who he or she may be behind. If you come from a family where racism or discrimination was acceptable or from a community where there was a lot of tension between different racial or ethnic groups, you may have some work to do.

Diversity Dos and Don'ts

Don't contradict: Even though you and the "different" student are in the same place doing the same things, each of you is viewing these experiences from a unique perspective. If a classmate shares an experience of racism or sexism, discrimination or difficulty, don't try to explain it away. Listen and seek to understand. Telling someone who feels discriminated against that his or her perceptions are wrong will only compound his or her sense of alienation.

Do reach out: It may sound too easy to make a difference, but smiling, making eye contact, and inviting other people to sit with you, especially at the beginning of the semester, can do a lot to break down barriers and give you the opportunity to connect.

 Online Survival Guide: Ask our online resident assistants about college life by visiting "Interactive RA" at http:// TheFreshmanSurvivalGuide.com and clicking on "Ask."

Haves and Have-Nots

Have you ever had to bow out of an event or activity because it was just too expensive? Or have you ever had a friend turn down an invitation to something only to find out later that the reason he said no was that he just couldn't swing it financially?

College may seem like the great equalizer, where everyone is around the same age, dresses similarly, and had similar experiences and opportunities growing up, but that isn't a smart assumption to make. One of the great changes that has taken place in the past few decades is that a college education has become accessible to a much broader group of students, not just upper- and upper-middle-income families. So an awareness of the economic differences, whichever end of the spectrum you're coming from, can be really helpful. Leave behind preconceived ideas about people who've grown up with less, or more, than you and head into the college experience with an open mind.

What may seem like a bargain price for a spring break trip to Cancún might be completely out of the question for your roommate, who works a job to help pay his tuition and has never been out of the state before. If you come from a relatively affluent background, you shouldn't assume that everyone else on your floor has traveled overseas or owns a summer home. If you were brought up in relatively humble economic circumstances, don't try to compete with better-off classmates in terms of your spending. Whatever you do, don't blow your savings trying to keep up or get a credit card and begin charging yourself deep into debt in an attempt not to be left out. Anyone who calls herself a friend should try to be aware that not everyone in her circle has unlimited amounts of disposable income and that creating prohibitively expensive trips or nights out might place an undue burden on—or necessarily exclude—some friends.

Whatever your economic circumstances might be, college is as good a time as any to begin learning a lesson so fundamental that it's practically clichéd: Basing your self-worth—or judging anyone else's for that matter—on levels of material wealth is a waste of time and energy. You will meet people of great affluence who might be among some of the most wonderful people you encounter and others who might be insufferable bores. The same is true for economically challenged people as well as the vast majority of us who fall somewhere in between those economic poles.

Kyra was excited to be accepted by her first-choice college and only a little intimidated by the school's academic reputation. She'd worked hard and gotten excellent grades all through high school, despite holding down a part-time job to save for college. What she hadn't bargained on were all the hidden costs. Her savings were being quickly depleted by purchases for things she didn't realize she'd need, such as chipping in with suitemates for takeout, getting around in the city, and unexpected but necessary supplies. It was clear that many of her classmates didn't have to worry about money, and she realized that trying to keep up with them was getting to be a problem. Finally, when her roommate, Beth, was pressuring her to join her suitemates on a weekend road trip she knew she couldn't afford, she gently explained that the only money she had for college was what she had earned and saved herself, as her parents were not in a position to help. It made Kyra a little angry to have to say it, but doing so did help in the long run. From that point on Beth was a lot more sensitive, and Kyra didn't feel as much pressure to keep up with other students.

Sexuality

In terms of sexuality, many college students are already pretty tolerant. Unlike many people in previous generations, you've grown up knowing and understanding what homosexuality is and may already have come to terms with a friend or yourself being gay, lesbian, bisexual, or transgender. We don't mean to imply that a person's sexuality isn't a big deal—it is—or that intolerance doesn't still exist—it does.

According to one Gallup poll, adults aged 18 to 29 (6.4 percent) are more than three times as likely as seniors aged 65 and older (1.9 percent) to identify as LGBTQ.[1] You're going to encounter people with different sexual orientations in college: straight, gay, bisexual, transgender, and people who are still questioning, and both men and women whose sexual behavior and attitudes may be very different from your own. All these people— you included—are deserving of respect. People's choices and values may not be the same as yours, but resist the temptation simply to judge everyone else. Seek information and understanding. If you're encountering attitudes, speech, or behavior from others that you find intimidating because of your sexuality, talk to your RA and search your campus website for resources and support.

Online Survival Guide: For additional online resources regarding sexual identity, visit http://TheFreshmanSurvival Guide.com/chapters/ and click on "Chapter 6."

Religion: I'm Right, You're Wrong

If you're one of the many students who has been raised in a religious household, your beliefs and practices are probably among your most deeply held values. But if your exposure to other faiths has been minimal, it may take some adjusting for you to get comfortable with the variety of beliefs (or nonbelievers) you come into contact with on campus. Most of us tend to assume that everyone sees the world from *our* point of view. Spending some of your time in college pulling yourself away from your own perspective and trying to listen to and understand other people's should not threaten your own faith. Instead, view it as an incredible opportunity to deepen and enrich your own sense of belief.

Rabbi Yonah Schiller sees it as part of his responsibility as a chaplain on a college campus to build tolerance: "Those are the kinds of conversations where a lot of work can be done." As the world becomes a smaller place, with people from every race and religion interacting in business and political affairs, knowing how to conduct yourself respectfully among those different from yourself is a vital life skill. You can still hold fast to your own tradition without being discriminatory or superior to someone who holds a different set of beliefs.

There are a lot of religious truths common to every tradition— it's interesting and valuable work to find that out for yourself, as well as finding out what's different. Take a world religions course. Go with a friend to a service in another tradition. Once you know someone is open to the discussion, don't be afraid to dig deep and talk through the differences. These can be life-changing and mind-opening conversations.

When it comes to religion, having a basic knowledge of your own tradition can sometimes make it a little easier to interact with a level of confidence. Still, in an interfaith environment you may be afraid of doing or saying the wrong thing. If you are a bit nervous, that's a good indicator that you are tuned in enough to know that you're treading on sensitive territory. Proceed with caution and good manners, and you should be fine.

Different, Not Divided

According to the chaplains and students we've spoken with, students realize how connected people are in the world. They already accept diversity as a given. What they really want to know is what makes their own faith tradition distinct.

SEEK → FIND

Every year, we have a meeting with leaders of all our religious groups. We've talked about how similar we are—our differences exist, but we have the same values. What the students said this year is, "We really want to talk about our differences: what makes a Jew a Jew, a Muslim a Muslim, and a Pentecostal a Pentecostal." They don't want to sit around and sing "Kumbaya" together. That's not helpful because we don't get to know each other. We need to build trust to get to the hard stuff.

—Rabbi Serena Fujita, Jewish chaplain,
Bucknell University

The most successful interfaith conversations are the ones that make someone more deeply rooted in his or her faith tradition and simultaneously develop understanding or knowledge about another faith tradition.

—Imam Abdullah T. Antepli, Muslim chaplain,
Duke University

Online Survival Guide: *Curious about others' beliefs? Find out more by visiting "Chapter 6" at http://TheFresh manSurvivalGuide.com/chapters/.*

Dealing with Pressure Groups and Pressure People

There are religious groups on every campus that use pressure tactics to recruit. Sometimes they're referred to as *cults* or *pressure groups*. When a student is not able to articulate what he believes in and why, these pressure groups spot a vulnerability and start disassembling that student's faith tradition, if he has one, then try to put their own beliefs in its place. That's always a risk for new students on campus. Beware of anyone who is too friendly too fast, or who seems to have scripted questions designed to make you doubt the faith you grew up with. Be very wary of any group that subtly tries to separate you from your family and friends, even for seemingly sincere "religious" reasons.

SEEK → FIND

In our Jain tradition we are an interfaith group. Fundamentally we respect all religions—not that we always do everything right. Learning about other religions makes you convinced that every religion has a lot of good things to come out of it—it is not made up only of the fundamental and violent minorities that we [sometimes] see. That [violence] is not the real religion; [zealots perform violent acts] in the name of religion. When you come into contact with a person who truly represents a tradition, you will see what the true good in that religion is.

—Fakirchand J. Dalal, president, Jain Society of
North America

Online Survival Guide: Find out how to spot a cult or pressure group by visiting "Chapter 6" at http://TheFresh manSurvivalGuide.com/chapters/.

THE TAKEAWAY

Diversity on campus can be a stumbling block for some and a stepping-stone for others. It will trip you up if you feel you must do battle at every turn, correct other people's wrong thinking, or defend your own beliefs to everyone who disagrees. If you use the opportunity to improve your understanding of others, the differences you encounter can enrich, inform, and challenge you in some really positive ways.

CHAPTER 7

Save the Date? Is Dating Dead on Campus?

Survival Strategy #7: You will probably never again be in such close proximity to as many datable people as you will in college. Don't squander the opportunity! Get your courage up and take some positive risks. It could end up paying off in some great ways.

College dating has changed. First of all there's not as much of it anymore. A third of college seniors have been on fewer than two dates in four years.[1] College students these days are prioritizing academics and career over relationships and have a more casual approach to connecting romantically. Mark Regnerus, associate professor of sociology at the University of Texas, conducted more than two hundred interviews for his book *Premarital Sex in America: How Young Americans Meet, Mate, and Think About Marrying*. Regnerus contends that because there are more women on campus these days (56 percent),[2] men don't have to work as hard. "Less seems to be required to be in the company of a woman," he says.

Boston College professor Kerry Cronin also sees a number of other factors at play. When Cronin first taught her junior/senior seminar on Relationships, Spirituality and Personal Development a number of years ago, she discovered that the hookup culture had largely replaced dating culture on campus, and that many of her students didn't know how to ask someone out. She calls dating a "lost social script," something that previous generations knew how to do and what to expect from it. Somewhere along the way it was lost, and we've settled for hooking up, which in the short term can be...er...satisfying, but in the long term no one is really happy with. So she decided to try to reintroduce dating and created a unique assignment for her students.

The assignment has rules:

1. You must ask someone out in person (or at least over the phone, but *not* by text).
2. It has to be someone you have a legitimate interest in.
3. It has to be a level one date: forty-five to ninety minutes, no alcohol, no physical contact beyond a friendly hug at the close.
4. Plan the date yourself and pay. If you ask, you pay.

It may seem silly to make dating an assignment, but if you've ever gotten a text asking if you wanted to hang out, you may have wondered what that meant. *Is that a date? Is he/she interested in me or just bored or lonely?* Or if you've had a series of slightly drunk hookups with someone who never talked to you when it was light out or when they were sober, then you may start to see the method to Cronin's madness. While the pressure is lower in a dimly lit, alcohol-soaked hookup environment, the chance to really get to know another person and figure out whether you'd like to spend more time with them is somewhat diminished.

The benefit of the date, besides the obvious opportunity to get to know somebody you're actually interested in, is it's also a chance to flex your courage and take a positive risk. According to Cronin, "Too many students let their vulnerability or fear of rejection rule their decisions." And another dating fail she sees all too often is students crushing on someone for a long time and never asking for what they really want. Lots of people give their hearts away without anyone ever knowing.

Professor Cronin's Top Ten Dating Tips for College Freshmen

1. If you want to date, don't hook up. People are paying attention, and if you're doing it, they'll assume that's what you want.
2. Ask someone who is a legitimate interest or at least a romantic question mark for you. Don't wait for your soulmate to fall out of the sky. Dating is something you get better at if you learn how to date well and break up well. First and second dates ought to be about finding out if the romantic interest is there and mutual. If it doesn't work out, be up front and dignified in taking a pass.
3. Get courageous. Step up and try to ask the person out in person. This is for men and women. The dating scene takes courage, and because the hookup script is so dominant (that is, loud) on most college campuses, it's just wrong to assume that men should be the only courageous ones.
4. When you ask, suggest a plan within the next two to three days. If you ask someone out for "next week," it just won't happen.
5. The first date should be sixty to ninety minutes long, max.
6. Weekdays are the best days for a first date. More casual, less pressure, less alcohol.

7. Be prepared to move on if the person you're interested in doesn't want to date. If she/he prefers the hookup scene, that probably won't change. Save your heart and move on.
8. Find two to three friends who support you in your desire to date. These might not even be your closest friends. Unfortunately, lots of good friends unconsciously sabotage us in our efforts to avoid or walk away from the hookup scene.
9. Don't just opt out. College is a great time to date. Dating is a great way to find out important things about yourself and others. Try.
10. Figure out how to break up well. If college students knew how to manage dignified and drama-free breakups, they would date more.

When it comes to dating in college, you have people who fall on opposite ends of a fairly polarized spectrum: on one side, the "I can't be tied down because college is supposed to be fun" crowd; and on the other, the "College is where you're supposed to meet the love of your life" camp. I knew people on both sides who were so set in their ways that they failed to live fully in the messy, beautiful, exhausting, exhilarating experience of our college years. The most important advice I can give about dating is to remember that who you'll be at twenty-two is a world away from who you are at eighteen. There are some couples who will meet freshman year and whose romance will strengthen over time, fostering personal growth for its partners; other people may date casually, or even seriously, and ultimately find that they outgrow these relationships and college isn't the place where they meet the One. Both of these scenarios are okay. Take it from a bride-to-be (who didn't meet her partner in college, for the record): Treat others as you would want to be treated, make sure that others are treating you the same, and your college dating experience will be a success—whatever that means in the context of your journey. Keep moving toward your personal and professional dreams, and eventually—maybe at twenty, maybe at thirty-five—you'll find a fellow traveler worth coming home to each day.

—**Emily, University of Central Florida**

6 Creepy People to Avoid on Friday Night

1. **The Guilt-Tripper.** He's bought you a drink, not that you asked him to; she's hung by your side all night, no matter how hard you tried to shake her off. Now the crowd is dwindling and he's implying that you owe him something, or she's saying that you have to walk her home. Under no circumstances should you be alone with either the male or female version of this creep. For the girl, you can offer to call security to make sure she gets home safely. The guy obviously didn't get the memo that buying something for someone doesn't entitle him to anything more than a thank-you. You can catch him up or just say good night and leave with a friend.

2. **The Groper.** Cute enough to get away with it, charming enough that you almost didn't notice when he pretended to be too drunk to realize his hand kept ending up in inappropriate places. Don't be afraid to tell this guy, "Hands off."

3. **The Lurker.** This is the guy or girl hanging in the corners, making eye contact for just slightly beyond the comfortable point, perhaps trying to be seductive...but

he or she kinda makes your skin crawl. The person might just be shy, but trust your gut.

4. **The Booty Caller.** If he or she is calling after 2 A.M., well...

5. **The Scary Girl.** She started out the night talking in her baby voice. Without slowing down on the shots, she began to alternate between squealing and screaming. When she switches to crying, get out—she'll soon be getting her stomach pumped, and it won't be pretty.

6. **The Super Creeper.** This is the kid who invites himself into your open room, sits down with you and your friends without being asked, never stops talking, and tries to put his arm around you all the time. Maybe he just has boundary issues, but more likely he's counting on that you're too nice to tell him to cool it.

When Tom met a girl he liked in his hall in his first week on campus, his parents were a little concerned, because he tended to get attached quickly. But he was pretty lonely and she was pretty cute, and being with someone made him feel a little less homesick. Things moved along fast. After hanging out at a couple of parties together, they became a couple and things got physical. Tom was really falling for her when suddenly she lost interest and moved on. She wasn't really interested in a serious relationship. By fall break he was in pretty bad shape. Tom ended up having to deal with a breakup—and bumping into this girl all the time because she still lived in his dorm—along with everything else he already had going on.

Always know you have a choice. And never do something to please someone else. If it doesn't make you happy then don't do it! You don't have to go to that party because everyone else is going and you don't have to date that guy just because all your friends are dating someone.

—Michaela, Monroe Community College, Rochester, NY

Don't date anyone first semester. Wait until second semester and you have established friendships. I see so many people who never bothered to make friends because they started dating the first week of their freshman year. When they break up with their BF/GF, they have no close friends. Wait.

—Gretchen, freshman, Rensselaer Polytechnic Institute

Chances are you're going to have to see these people for the next four years of your life, so if you don't think it's a good idea to hook up with them, it's probably not. And if the prospect of seeing them everywhere after you break up seems horrible, maybe don't start dating them.

—Rachel, State University of New York at Brockport

5 Dates on $5 or Less

Don't let college poverty stop you from asking someone out. Cash is not a necessary ingredient for dating. Sure, it makes things more convenient, but anybody can get a dozen roses or a pricey dinner. Think of your lack of funds as an opportunity to get creative. More personal = more romantic.

1. **Go together.** Whatever's happening on campus—a show, a party, an event—make a point to go together. Walk to the other person's dorm and pick him or her up, just as you would on a pricey off-campus date.

2. **Local sites.** Get off campus and into town. Visit something enlightening or cultural, or hit the waterfront—the river, canal, ocean, bay, or lake. If you're near water, there's inevitably a park for walking in.

3. **Major date.** Share a major with your crush? One of the cool things about college (and college dating) is that you'll find, sometimes for the first time in your life, others who are as interested in the same geeky stuff as you. Political science majors who are politics junkies, music majors who have a shared affinity for Wagner—do something related together that "normal people" wouldn't be interested in. English lit majors, visit a local Shakespeare festival. Computer science majors, hit a free tech show. Geology majors, find a cool local land formation to visit.

4. **Show off your skills.** Take him to the lab. Invite her to your recital.

5. **Eat dinner in.** Dinner can be as simple as a box of pasta, a jar of sauce, and a package of cupcakes from the vending machine. Follow it with game night: Teach him your favorite card game or break out the Scrabble (just don't get too competitive).

I think going to college with a boyfriend from back home can be really tough. I spent my entire freshman year going back and forth too many times just to see my boyfriend. I didn't make as many friends that year in college, and I didn't see my parents as much as I should have for the amount of time I went home. If you are dating someone from home, make sure you don't spend too much time going home. And the time that you do go home, spend time with your family, too. You don't know where you'll be after college even if you think you do. My plan probably changed at least every semester and then even after college. It's not wrong to date some-one from back home, but make sure it's not monopolizing your free time. Sometimes we want to put our BF/GF first, when we should really be putting ourselves first. If they stick with you when you do take the time to have your own social life at school, then that shows that they care about your new life at school, not just your life back home with them.

—Anonymous

When you go in to college expecting to find "the one," you are going to miss out on a lot. Just have fun. Don't try to force anything. The best relationships, whether one week or one lifetime, come when you least expect it. You don't have to meet the one, or even anyone, for that matter. This isn't the '50s. Just concentrate on you, and the rest will come! Another thing is to be safe! You are not above any statistic, and yes, it can happen to you, too. Make sure that you are sure in any decision you make, and be aware of what could happen. Make sure you know and trust the person you are with and that you are both on the same page at all times. Lastly, if you end a rela-tionship, you don't have to hate each other. It doesn't have to end in flames. You can still be friends when it ends. If it's not working, just let the other person know. The longer it drags on, the worse it will be. Don't stay with someone just because it is convenient or comfortable. You wouldn't want someone to do that to you, so don't do that to someone else! Have the decency to tell them when it isn't working.

—Lindsay, University of Buffalo

Never be afraid to stand up for yourself. It seems silly, but you know you better than anyone else. Don't be afraid to say no, because you may need to.

—Molly, Nazareth College

Online Survival Guide: *What's your dating IQ? Test it by going to http://TheFreshmanSurvivalGuide.com/chapters/ and clicking on "Chapter 7."*

Far, Far Away

Everybody knows that long-distance relationships are difficult: lonely nights when everyone else seems to be with somebody, trying to convey devotion and work out problems over IM, texts, and Facebook. Besides missing the physical closeness of your significant other, you risk missing out on a lot of college life if you're trying to keep up a connection with a faraway boyfriend or girlfriend. Does that mean you break up with your high school sweetheart? Not necessarily. The challenges don't always outweigh the benefits. Here are a few points to consider:

- **No worries.** Some students say having a boyfriend or girlfriend who wasn't on the same campus freed them up to devote their time to studying or participating in clubs and activities.
- **Stormy weather.** If your relationship has a lot of ups and downs, you may want to think twice about trying to maintain it over a distance. Conflicts that were challenging in person are even more difficult to deal with when you're far away. They can become a serious distraction for the new college student.
- **Here and now.** If you're more of a present-moment kind of a person, be honest with yourself and the person you've left behind. Save your boy- or girlfriend the heartbreak and yourself the guilt of broken promises.
- **The real thing.** If both of you are committed to maintaining the relationship and can manage the distance without

(too much) jealousy, drama, or depression, hang in there. Lots of couples have managed to stay together even when they've been far apart.

SEEK → FIND

> *Try. Challenge yourself to ask someone out in person in the next two weeks. Try. If you get a no, don't overanalyze; just move on and ask someone else. Find a friend who'll do this as well, and support each other in your plan to try dating. This is as much about courage as it is about romance. More people on campus than you think would like to go on a date. A lot of people participate in hookup culture, because they think that's the only option. Try.*

> —Kerry Cronin,
> Center for Student Formation, Boston College

Online Survival Guide: *For more simple recipes or to share your ideas for a date on $5 or less, visit http:// TheFreshmanSurvivalGuide.com/chapters/ and click on "Chapter 7."*

THE TAKEAWAY

Some of your best times on campus, and some of your worst, will surely fall under the category of dating and relationships. Be brave and honest about what you want, and you could end up with some experiences that really help you grow as a person.

CHAPTER 8

Sex and the University

 Survival Strategy #8: The subject of sex cuts to the core of who you are and what you're looking for in ways that few other issues can. Think ahead about the choices you're making and how those choices are shaping your identity.

The movies often depict college as a four-year sex fest with "getting some" being the primary goal of the majority of students. While there may not be statistical categories for "sex fest" or "getting some" just yet, the data clearly backs up the perception that students are sexually active on campus. According to the 2013 National College Health Assessment, 44.5 percent of college students nationwide had had sexual intercourse with one partner in the previous year. Almost 10 percent of college students had had sexual intercourse during the past twelve months with four or more partners.[1]

Of course, the numbers tell only a fraction of the story. Statistics don't have unrequited crushes. They don't get into relationships. They don't have one-night stands. They don't fall in or out of love, and they certainly don't get their hearts broken—people do. It's important to remember that behind the data offered here about sex and dating are the individual experiences of college students just like you. They had the same doubts about the differences between the high school and college dating scenes that you do. They had the same questions about what they're looking for.

They also had the same choices you now have. The ability to choose is so much of what college is about. Without your parents and family there to check on your every move, you'll need to begin making decisions about your values and behavior. Do your actions reflect the values you claim to hold? Is your behavior consistent with your sense of the person you want to be? How are you treating other people? How are you treating yourself?

Even if you typically err on the side of caution, it's hard to completely avoid errors in judgment, and there's a very good chance you could have your heart broken somewhere along the way. Armed with the information, advice, and experiences included in this chapter, you'll at least have some tools to help you choose wisely and pick yourself up if things go wrong.

The Lay of the Land

While it's true that a majority of college students are sexually active, students—and everybody else—tend to think there's a lot more sex happening on campus than there actually is. The hookup culture on campuses gets a lot of attention, but what the news and the statistics don't normally show is the broad variety of relationships on campus and the choices individual students are making. The idea that everybody, all the time, is having indiscriminate, spontaneous sex with multiple partners is simply not true. In her book *Hooking Up*, sociology professor Kathleen

Bogle points out, "The hookup culture is not as out of control as some observers (and college students) believe." More than one study shows that students dramatically overestimate how much sex their peers are having. One researcher found that nearly half (45 percent) of the students he interviewed reported that they'd never hooked up. But the students in that study thought hookups were the norm for their peers, with 90 percent believing that having had at least two hookups was "typical" for their peers.[2] Another study shows one in four college students is a virgin and only 20 percent of students reported having six or more partners after turning eighteen.[3]

Does it matter? Of course, you're going to make your own choices, but having a clear read on what is going on with other students on campus, knowing that other students are making many different choices about how far to go, how frequently, and with a limited number of partners, can be empowering. The range of what's normal when it comes to college students and sexual behavior is a lot wider than the culture would have you believe.

Maybe you dated a lot in high school or maybe not at all. Either way, one of the other great things about campus is also one of the danger zones: Nobody here knows you. It's easy to feel kind of anonymous, especially when you first get to college. Unlike high school, where you probably knew a lot of your classmates, and they expected you to behave as you always had and the way others in your group of friends did, nobody's really watching you—nobody has any particular expectations of how you're going to act. But to be clear, nobody here knows you *yet*. The choices you make every day—and night—are defining you.

The best advice I got before going to college was to make a decision about what I was willing to do sexually before I got into those situations. You can decide to sleep with people you love. You can decide to sleep with nobody. The truth is that as long as you make your choices carefully and consciously, then you won't have very many regrets. A huge number of my college friends really regret the things they did.

—Graduate, Cornell University

Dating in college is so much different than dating in high school. All of a sudden it seems like there are less rules and more confusion. My best advice is to be honest with your partner and true to yourself. It's easy to let yourself hold on to or get into a relationship because it feels like it gives you someone to turn to when you feel like you need love and attention. But make sure that you aren't just in the relationship for those reasons.

—Darby, sophomore, Northwestern University

Getting Good Information

If you went to a high school that didn't offer a class in reproductive health, or you didn't take the class, or just weren't paying attention, you can and should catch up. Northwestern University has launched an online course that anyone (including you) can take. Faculty at Northwestern were finding that many students did not have enough information to make competent decisions about their health and that a "lack of knowledge contributes to the epidemic of sexually transmitted diseases as well as unintended pregnancies among college students."[4] Professor and reproductive expert Teresa Woodruff, vice chair for research in obstetrics and gynecology at Northwestern University Feinberg School of Medicine, created the class, which can be found at https://www.coursera.org/learn/reproductive-health (or go to the Coursera website and search for "Introduction to Reproduction"). Your on-campus health center as well as your own doctors can point you in the direction of good and vital information.

Give Yourself Permission *Not* to Have Sex

You're on a campus full of people who are all searching right now. Soon people will start settling in and settling down. With everybody else (seemingly) so busy hooking up, you may start to feel as if you're the only one going home alone. But remember this: The people who have decided *not* to hook up are not usually making a big deal about it. Not hooking up is a legitimate choice, and a choice that a lot of students make for all types of reasons. Some have religious traditions and values that are important to them. Others have gotten burned and have decided to hold off for a while. Still others want to wait until they find the right person.

There's nothing prudish or backward about making choices about your own body and how intimate you want to get with another person. If you've decided to wait, don't let anyone pressure, guilt, shame, or wheedle you into going further than you've decided to go.

> *People tend to think that virginity is a onetime thing. Once you've lost it, it's all over. While that's true to some extent, it doesn't mean you can't decide* not *to have sex once you've already done it.*
>
> **—Sophie, Loyola University Chicago**

Defining Sexual Consent

On many college campuses there is what could politely be described as a lack of initiative regarding administrations' response to sexual violence. There are too many stories to count of date and acquaintance rape that have gone unpunished and campus climates that do little to prevent rape. However, on other campuses, a quiet (and sometimes not so quiet) revolution is taking place. More and more schools are starting to pay a different kind of attention to the importance of consent and are educating their students accordingly. The definition of consent has transitioned a great deal in the last few years from "no means no"—if one partner verbally declines, then the other partner must not pursue intercourse—to affirmative consent. Many campuses have raised the bar, often in response to new state laws that require a verbal yes to legally have sex with someone. Know your campus policy and know the laws of the state where you are going to college! An estimated 1,400 institutions of higher education now use some type of affirmative consent definition in their sexual assault policies. In New York State the law reads: "Affirmative consent is a knowing, voluntary and mutual decision among all participants to engage in sexual activity." It goes on to clarify: "Consent to any sexual act or prior consensual sexual activity between or with any party does not necessarily constitute consent to any other sexual act."[5]

In nearly every state a person who is too impaired by alcohol or drugs to give verbal affirmative consent is considered unable to legally give consent.

Tips for Making Choices You Can Live with in the Long Run

- **Sex is *not* a universal language.** Sometimes the actions that mean *I love you and want to be with you* to one person can mean *You've been great to hang out with tonight, and besides I was really horny* to another. To avoid being hurt and to avoid hurting someone else, don't make the mistake of thinking that sex or any kind of physical intimacy means the same thing to the other person that it does to you.

- **Go with a plan.** Decide before a date or party if and how much you're going to drink and how far you're going to go sexually. Don't be afraid to share those decisions with a friend who can hold you accountable.
- **Don't go to a party alone.** Ask the same friend who holds you accountable to keep an eye on you. You do the same for him or her.
- **Guys and girls are different—really.** According to Kathleen Bogle, *in general* girls are hoping that a hookup might lead to a relationship, and *in general* a guy is just looking to hook up. The adage "Guys give love to get sex and girls give sex to get love" turns out to be generally—and statistically—true. Many girls will play it cool but then end up getting hurt when a hookup doesn't turn into something more. Many guys will play it sweet and then are surprised when a girl seems to have expectations beyond their hookup.
- **You're new here.** Be careful at the beginning; be aware of your new environment, the people around you, and your own self-control.
- **Don't go there.** Don't try to fool yourself or the person you're with. There's a whole series of opportunities to say no—or at least "not now"—before the *big no* if you don't want to get too involved physically. Be sure to send clear signals.
- **Take responsibility.** The National Institute on Alcohol Abuse and Alcoholism's (NIAAA) Task Force on College Drinking reports that each year 400,000 students between

the ages of eighteen and twenty-four have unprotected sex, and more than 100,000 report having been too intoxicated to know if they consented to having sex. Don't let drinking or stress be an excuse for behaving irresponsibly, hurting someone, or making stupid decisions. Unplanned pregnancy and sexually transmitted infections/diseases are a big deal with big consequences.

I'm an RA (Resident Assistant) and a junior at a small private school. Last year, I had very sweet resident named James. Throughout the year, we became good friends and I got to know him very well. James is a small guy with a big heart. He loves to get to know new people and have fun. One night, I was on duty, which meant that I had to stay up late to make sure that the residence hall was safe and sound. At about 2 A.M., I walked by my resident's room to find him walking in with a very large, much older man that reeked of marijuana. Because I knew him so well, I immediately knocked on his door and pulled him aside to ask him if everything was okay. He said that it was fine, and that he met his new friend on Grindr and that they were just hanging out. I was afraid that James was in trouble and something might happen to him without his consent. I went through my student manual and called my director. We found a few loopholes, and I was able to use residence hall policies that required his guest to leave. After he'd left, James told me that he was so happy that I did that because he had begun getting very nervous that he was losing control of the situation. I trusted my instincts and saved my friend from a potential date rape. There are people in your residence halls that can help you, too! Don't ever be afraid to talk to the RA on duty about something that makes you feel uncomfortable. There are policies on campus for a reason—you deserve to be safe!

—A Concerned RA

SEEK → FIND—Sex and God

One of the messages that the culture gives about sex is that it's just one more commodity that you have to have as a successful human being. Students engage in sex for lots of reasons, obviously, but one of the results is that they commodify each other, and that's where the dissatisfaction comes in. Nobody wants to be used. This is another place where we can help students see the disconnect as to why they're feeling terrible about the experience: They're feeling like an object. And it goes both ways: It's not just females these days; males feel that as well.

—Rev. Scott Young, Protestant campus minister,
University of Southern California

In Judaism we see sexuality as the pinnacle of spiritual expression, and if you feel crappy afterward, then you're furthest away from where the Jewish perspective wants you to go. It's not hard to find people in college feeling ambiguous, if not crappy, about their sexual life—once you scratch below the surface. They'll be like, "Yeah, I hooked up with this person, yeah, I felt guilty. Was it worth it? Probably not. It was fun at the time, but I feel bad about it now." Why do they feel bad about it? Because there's intimacy without connection. Our need for intimacy comes from a spiritual desire to be connected to people; the bad feeling comes from that connection not being rooted in anything real.

—Rabbi Yonah Schiller,
executive director of Hillel at Tulane University

To engage in sexual behavior without a spiritual connection is essentially a lie. It's saying one thing with your body and your actions that your heart is not in. It's a fundamental violation of the truth. All the messages these students have grown up with tell them it doesn't have to mean anything. But their own experience tells them it does mean something, but it doesn't mean what they thought it would—or that the two of them had different understandings.

—Fr. Larry Rice, CSP,
director, Ohio State University Catholic Center

In Buddhism we have a precept about not using other people, not exploiting sexuality, for example. A lot of sexual acting out has nothing to do with developing or deepening a true relationship with people. It has to do with putting oneself out there to be used or exploiting someone else. To me the precepts are very helpful, because they give you a guide for living a life that is helpful in developing your spirituality. I would imagine that in all the [spiritual] traditions, if your approach to the people around you is one of "What can you do for me?" or "What can I get from you?" then you can't really explore your spirituality—there's a contradiction there. That's why these moral guides exist. They're not rules that we have to follow or reject; they're there for our benefit and for us to be able to grow into the full human persons that we really are.

—Ven. Bonnie Hazel Shoultz, Buddhist chaplain,
Syracuse University

Having sex is so normal in campus life that not having it makes you feel abnormal. I think we have to empower students with knowledge about their faith tradition. We have to explain where these faith traditions are coming from in prohibiting sexual relationships. What is family? What is chastity? What is freedom? Are we free to do whatever we like as long as we don't bother anybody? That's not what our religious traditions are teaching us. Freedom is not only about yourself. You don't own this body. It's temporally given to us as a trust, and we are stewards of what we own. We are taking care of this body on behalf of God. We have some responsibility in this body. Love is not a necklace or a bumper sticker. If you claim that

> *you love God, or anybody, that involves some sort of responsibility and accountability. If you subscribe to that love relationship, that means you subscribe to certain ways of living.*
>
> —Imam Abdullah T. Antepli, Muslim chaplain,
> Duke University

If you end up going further than you planned or your special someone squashes your romantic ambitions by having a different plan from yours, take courage. You're not the first college student to experience a setback. If you're having a hard time handling the consequences, check out chapter 22 to find help on campus. And in case of a real disaster, see chapter 29 on dealing with emergencies like sexual violence.

Megan Foster, of the Rape, Abuse and Incest National Network (RAINN), says, "The best advice I could give to someone starting their first year in college is to know their boundaries and be willing to enforce them. This is incredibly important as far as staying safe and feeling comfortable during your college experience."

THE TAKEAWAY

Make decisions about your standards ahead of time to be sure they're in line with values you can live with and feel good about.

CHAPTER 9

Who Are You?

Survival Strategy #9: There's a tidal wave of new information and experiences coming your way, but don't let your identity get washed away in it. It's easy to lose yourself at college, so once in a while stop to think about the person you were before and the person you're working toward becoming. Somewhere between those two is where you ought to be now.

Everything changes at college. The things you used to do, the people you used to hang with, the externals of your life have all undergone a sudden transformation. You're facing new challenges academically and socially. You're being introduced to new thoughts and ideas in your classes and through the campus community. Dr. Richard Kadison, chief of Mental Health Services at Harvard, says, "Late adolescence is a time of transition, a period of reflection on family values, career aspirations, and lifestyle experimentation. Although this is a normal developmental process, it is a source of great anxiety for many college students." Of course, you're going to grow. Of course, you're going to change. And yet, all the things you know, believe, love, are good at, value, and cherish are still the same.

Over time, college can and should influence, expand, and

inform all those things, but just because *where* you are is suddenly different, that doesn't mean *who* you are should change, at least not quite as abruptly as your surroundings have. You've come from somewhere and you're headed somewhere, and even with all the new stuff you've got to think about, that's worth remembering.

It's the stuff of graduation cards and cheesy movie plots; everybody talks about it, to the point that it's a cliché: "Be true to yourself." What exactly does that mean? And how are you supposed to do that when you've got so many choices to make and new things expected of you? Read on to find out how to do it and why it matters.

College is a time to reinvent yourself, but don't change who you are at your core. Respect comes from others when you respect yourself. Don't give up on the things that are most valuable to you to please others. You'll only end up hurting yourself. One thing I regret about my freshman year is that I failed to respect myself. I changed too much to please the opinions of others. Never again.

—Tim, senior, Stonehill College

The biggest mistake most freshmen make is saying yes to everything and anything to fit in and make friends. Think about the kind of person you want to be—who you want people to see you as. Make choices based on that.

—Darcy, senior, Carlow University

Shed Your Skin but Keep Your Skeleton

At the risk of sounding reptilian, one approach to the "be true to yourself" dilemma is this: Cast off the things you're outgrowing, shed your skin, but hang on to the stuff that really makes you who you are. In other words: Keep your skeleton, the "bones" of your identity. As you enter college life the externals will be changing pretty rapidly. The things you like to wear may be different, your favorite sayings will change, you may pick up some new habits, favorite foods, music, TV shows, activities—things that aren't vital or really life changing. But hang on to your basic framework, the things you've believed in all your life. Your values and your approach toward other people are fundamental qualities that should have some staying power. They may change and grow in time, but if they do, the change should be positive and it should happen slowly.

The trick is finding that same person—your *self*—in this new environment. Another way to think of this process is that rather than redefining yourself, you are refocusing your identity over the course of your college career and figuring out which parts of yourself you primarily want to develop. College is an opportunity to present the new people you meet, not with a new self, but with your *best* self. Don't just chuck the old you and create a brand-new one. That's a recipe for becoming lost and confused. Sift out the best of who you are, the things you and others like most about yourself, and bring that to the surface.

To be a little more concrete: Let's say in high school you were a smart kid—good grades, honors classes. You were funny but sometimes a little mean about it. You also happen to be very good at sports, but the smart kids you hung with had no use for the jocks at your school. When you reassess the high school "you," you may realize that you still want to hang with the other smart kids, but you also want to broaden your social options a bit. Ditch the mean, keep the funny, and maybe you'll join an intramural team. Perhaps this is nothing like the high school "you," but you get the idea: Hang on to the essentials, let the great stuff you've kept hidden because of the limits of high school come out a little, and find your stride.

> ***Online Survival Guide:*** *Who are you? Take our quiz by going to http://TheFreshmanSurvivalGuide.com/chapters/ and clicking on "Chapter 9."*

A word of warning: If you're coming out of a very restrictive environment—say, socially or religiously—or a difficult family situation, you may have a bigger challenge than someone coming from a more moderate or less troubled background. The problem is, the more extreme things were at home, the more you're going to be looking for something new when you hit college. The more stable a situation or reasonable your family, the more organically you'll manage the change. Little by little is a good approach. If you're running away from something at home, you're going to run into trouble at school.

A Different Kind of Examination

Once a week, step back and ask yourself, *What's going on? What choices have I made? Have they been good ones or bad ones?* Try to develop a whole lifestyle of conversation, of both listening and responding, to God, to yourself, and to others. The examen is an ancient practice from the Catholic tradition. It is used to attain an awareness of one's own actions and God's presence in daily life. Here it is adapted for anyone to use no matter his or her faith tradition. Even if you're not a believer, this kind of reflection can really help you get a handle on your life and the choices you're making.

Everyone's Examen

1. Take a moment to be still. As you breathe, become aware of the greatness of creation, life, breath, beauty, friendship, and learning. Take time to be grateful to God.

2. Be aware of being pulled in different directions. There are some forces in the world and in your own life that bring you closer to God and others that move you further away. Take a moment to consider that tension.

3. Next, consider specifically how those forces have been apparent in your new college life. Where have you been led closer to God (the good) and where have you moved further away (the bad) in the last few hours, days, or weeks?

4. Then think about the question *How do I reinforce the good and turn away from the bad?* What specific, practical steps can you take to move toward goodness?

5. The last step is an affirmation of what you've decided. Put these specific steps you've chosen back in the larger context of your everyday life and identity, commit yourself to doing the things you need to do, and be aware that you are not alone in this effort; you are working with God.

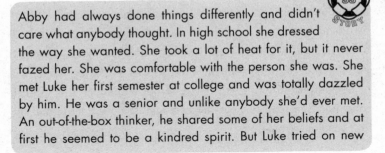

Abby had always done things differently and didn't care what anybody thought. In high school she dressed the way she wanted. She took a lot of heat for it, but it never fazed her. She was comfortable with the person she was. She met Luke her first semester at college and was totally dazzled by him. He was a senior and unlike anybody she'd ever met. An out-of-the-box thinker, he shared some of her beliefs and at first he seemed to be a kindred spirit. But Luke tried on new life philosophies, new activities, and new girls as if it were his job. Abby was always gushing about a brilliant idea Luke had to make the world a better place. He filled her world to the point that she was slowly disappearing and being replaced by a clone of her new friend. Luke used Abby sexually, telling her that he and his out-of-state girlfriend had an open relationship, but keeping the fact that Abby was a friend with benefits a secret. Abby didn't clue in until Luke skipped town on his next adventure. Fortunately for Abby, her old friends came back around to help pick up the pieces.

Online Survival Guide: *Download a free printable PDF version of Everyone's Examen by visiting http://The FreshmanSurvivalGuide.com/chapters/ and clicking on "Chapter 9."*

Sexual Identity

Even though experts say that the core attractions that form the basis for adult sexual orientation typically emerge between middle childhood and early adolescence, individual experiences around orientation vary widely. Many people—gay or straight—"just know" their sexual orientation from early on. For others, coming to understand themselves is a little more of a process or even an ordeal. Especially for people from an environment or a family where being gay, lesbian, or bisexual was not acceptable, college may be the first opportunity to take a serious, honest look at sexual identity. As with every other aspect of identity, we sometimes need other people to help us sort out how we're going to live.

Many campuses have recognized this and have resources in place to support students who are gay, lesbian, or bisexual.

Online Survival Guide: *For additional online resources regarding sexual identity, visit http://TheFreshmanSurvival Guide.com/chapters/ and click on "Chapter 9."*

It may come as a surprise to you that many campus religious organizations are understanding and pastoral on issues of orientation. Your pastor or religious leader at home may have been less comfortable (and perhaps less knowledgeable) about lesbian, gay, bisexual, transgender, and queer (LGBTQ) issues, but students sorting through sexuality issues may be pleasantly surprised to find compassion, support, and genuine help in their campus spiritual leaders.

SEEK → FIND

If a friend or roommate tells you they're gay, remember that they're sharing a difficult truth with you, and they're emotionally vulnerable. It doesn't have to change your relationship, unless you make that decision. You may want to discuss what your boundaries are, so that you're both comfortable and have shared expectations.

—Fr. Larry Rice, CSP,
director, Ohio State University Catholic Center

I think in our time our traditions don't provide enough tools for us to deal with the issues of homosexuality and sexual orientation.

People already know what the Qur'an and other religious texts say on this issue. I take it case by case and try to empower these people—they are still part of Islam, and whatever they do never keeps them out of the boundary of religion at all. What people do in their own personal life is between God and them.

—Imam Abdullah T. Antepli,
Muslim chaplain, Duke University

Discovering one's sexual identity is one of the crucial projects in adolescence / young adulthood. I have had numerous conversations with students about these matters, including several who accepted their homosexual orientation. I believe it is important to disclose homosexual identity to someone you can trust. Communicating (coming out of the closet) to family and friends generally requires a strong support network, if available. The difficulty in public disclosure is often a problem but not the fault of the gay/lesbian student—it is a fearful church and intolerant society that create the obstacles. Most college campuses offer credible assistance in the discovery and communication processes for the gay/lesbian student. I recommend a proactive approach in locating support and resources for this critical dimension of a satisfying life.

—Rev. Scott Young, Protestant campus minister,
University of Southern California

There are many gay men and women who are totally comfortable with being out on campus. There are others who are just beginning to understand that they are homosexual or bisexual or transgendered. We are, each of us, created in God's image: straight, gay, bisexual, and transgendered. We each have a spark of divinity that shines through us. We will be judged by our actions—how we treat each other, how we give of ourselves to make this a better world, how we live up to our greatest potential—and not on whom we choose to sleep with.

—Rabbi Serena Fujita, Jewish chaplain, Bucknell University

Buddhism in the West is quite welcoming of same-sex relationships. Besides the prevalent social stigma, basic challenges remain the same as in any meaningful relationship. A healthy view of love and life is important from the very onset in one's education process. Just [as in] any relationship, cultivating trust, patience, and clarity is of great importance. A healthy view of sexuality is part of becoming a full person, and just [as in] any exploration there is confusion even when one begins to explore sexual preferences or orientations. Attraction is natural, but love requires cultivation. One must have a clear dialogue with oneself or another person, such as a friend or roommate, on this issue.

—Ven. Tenzin Priyadarshi, Buddhist chaplain,
Massachusetts Institute of Technology

College is one big life lesson. In high school, you were only beginning to learn what kind of person you were going to become. In college, it goes way beyond the social pressures and high school drama (don't get me wrong, though, there is still a ton of that). However, beyond the stress, deadlines, and temptations you get to figure out who you truly are, or at least who you'd like to become. Sink, swim, or maybe even float on through, it's all up to you. In the end, only you can make the choice, and it's the choice that defines a great deal of who you are.

—Jen, junior, State University of New York at Buffalo

You've Gotta Grow

Not growing isn't really an option. You're moving out of adolescence and into adulthood. We all know people who never quite made the move. Those forty-year-olds who are stuck in a perpetual immaturity, for example: They're not the people we look up to or want as role models. And "This is who I am, so you need to adjust" is no excuse for being a jerk. You should be growing up in college: thinking less selfishly; becoming more patient, with yourself and others; becoming more forgiving and less impulsive. Exploring new ideas and coming to understand yourself better are the tasks of early adulthood, but they don't just happen on their own. They require actual work, and nobody can do it for you.

Online Survival Guide: Ask our online resident assistants your questions about college life by visiting "Interactive RA" at http://TheFreshmanSurvivalGuide.com and clicking on "Ask."

THE TAKEAWAY

This is like that terrifying moment in elementary school art class when the teacher said you could draw anything you want. Don't just draw what the kid next to you is drawing. This is *your* picture. Choose to stay—and become—the person you will be most satisfied and comfortable being.

CHAPTER 10

Real Stats and Strategies on Mental Health

Survival Strategy #10: Keeping yourself together mentally and emotionally when so much is changing can be a real challenge. Basic self-care—food, sleep, physical activity, managing stress—is your first line of defense. Next comes support: friends, family, community. And if you still can't kick the bad feelings, there are other kinds of help, too. Don't suffer alone.

More than ever, colleges are becoming aware of exactly how stressful starting college—and navigating all the changes that come along with it—can be. Sure, many students handle the shift from home to school with minimal to moderate effort. But, among many new college students, 45.6 percent reported feeling that things were hopeless, and 30.7 percent reported feeling so depressed that it was difficult to function.[1] In the face of numbers like these, many colleges have developed more robust training for their staffs and intensified their efforts to make counseling and crisis care available. There are even national foundations devoted to advocacy and education on the issue of mental health among college students. (Check out http://www .jedfoundation.org, http://www.halfofus.com, and http://www

.ulifeline.org.) If you are worried about mental health in college, you should know:

- You're not alone in this struggle (far from it, in fact).
- You have real options in terms of getting help right on campus.
- It's a sign of strength—not weakness—to reach out for that help.

An Ounce of Prevention

If you're part of the growing number of college students diagnosed with a mental health condition, if you've ever struggled with addiction, or you just know you're sensitive to stress, you probably already know that sleeping enough, eating regularly, and keeping a routine are important prevention measures for you. You already know that people who don't have the same emotional challenges as you can get away with things that might take you down. An all-nighter that leaves someone else a little tired can make everything start to unravel for you. Drinking and drugs for anyone with a mental illness is a bad idea, especially if he or she takes medication. You'll have to be more responsible about self-care than some other students.

If, however, you've never encountered any mental health issues before, the best advice for staying healthy is to monitor the basics— food, sleep, physical activity, stress—and to keep in touch with people from home as you transition into college life.

In Bloom

Late adolescence and early young adulthood can be the blooming seasons for many mental illnesses such as:

- Depression
- Bipolar disorder
- Anxiety disorders

- Stress
- Alcohol and drug addiction
- Cutting and other forms of self-injury
- Eating disorders

The college environment—little sleep, no supervision, a lack of people who know what "normal" is for you—can all add up to danger when it comes to addiction or mental illness. A key to surviving freshman year is listening to what your body and mind are telling you. Understanding how to take care of yourself now that you are no longer under the watchful and caring eyes of your parents is vital to maintaining your mental and emotional well-being. Being stressed about an overdue paper is one thing; finding yourself on the verge of a panic attack on a regular basis is another. Taking the time to assess your well-being can mean the difference between excelling and breaking down. Above all else, you have to be honest with yourself if you want to get through the various difficult patches that college life brings.

Starting to Sink?

Here are a few tips for turning a bad mood around (Note: If you find yourself revisiting this list often, it may be time for the next step):

- Hang out with your most positive friends and try to do something active. Positive thinking plus exercise endorphins can make a bad day better.
- Watch something that makes you laugh—a little comedy can go a long way.
- Temperature extremes can actually reverse a downward slide in mood (weird, huh?). A hot or cold shower can jolt your brain into a different state.

- Indulge yourself a little: chocolate, a *small* purchase, a long phone call with the friend you miss most.
- Lack of sleep is often the culprit, so get some! At night if you can.
- Tell your brain to cool it with the negative thought patterns. If you find yourself revisiting mistakes made, bad breakups, and everything you hate about yourself, shut off the sound with music, a great (uplifting!) movie, or other positive distractions.
- Use the HALT checklist from chapter 25 as a self-care checkup.

Addiction and mental illness are two of the most critical issues for college freshmen, and the failure to address these issues can have deadly consequences. Suicide is the third leading cause of death among fifteen- to twenty-four-year-olds and the second leading cause of death among college students. An estimated 1,100 college students die by suicide every year. By the time they reach their senior year, one in five students (21 percent) report considering suicide.[2] If you find yourself behaving in ways that are contrary to your values, or if you feel as if you're in the bottom of an emotional pit and can't get out, it's definitely time to reach out.

The Signs

How will you know if you, or someone close to you, need help? It is important to recognize the warning signs:

- Persistently sad, anxious, irritable, or empty mood
- Loss of interest in previously enjoyable activities

- Withdrawal from friends and family
- Trouble sleeping or sleeping too much
- Fatigue and decreased energy
- Significant change in appetite and/or weight
- Overreaction to criticisms
- Feeling unable to meet expectations
- Difficulty concentrating, remembering details, and making decisions
- Feelings of worthlessness, hopelessness, or guilt
- Persistent physical symptoms such as headaches, digestive problems, or chronic pain that do not respond to routine treatment
- Substance abuse problems
- Thoughts of suicide or suicide attempts[3]

Advice from the Counseling Office

I would emphasize making priorities. Try to stick to routine for at least the first semester. Practice mindfulness and exercise regularly. I also encourage my students to become well acquainted with their professors, advisors, residential staff and deans, speaking with them early and often to check in and to form relationships. I also have them pay attention to their own behaviors, norms, and any changes. If need be, [they can] even keep a log. Knowing this will help them catch anything that comes up early. I recommend minimal use of social media, especially if the student is easily offended or sensitive. Take advantage of counseling services both formal and informal. The offices often offer seminars and brief groups to help acclimation.

—Katie Pullano, social worker, Keuka College

The Good News

Despite real concerns about mental health on campus, it is essential that students also know the good news: *Mental health problems are treatable and suicide is preventable.* The first step to getting well—reaching out for help—is often the most difficult. "The most painful thing I experience as a clinician is witnessing the amount of suffering that students endure before seeking help," says Dr. Richard Kadison, chief of Mental Health Services at Harvard University. "They often suffer alone, which compounds the problem." The sad irony is that when students decide not to burden family or friends with their problems, the resulting isolation makes the problem even worse. "They haven't learned yet that sharing stress invites others to share their own stresses, solidifies connections, and provides opportunities for new perspectives and solutions," says Dr. Kadison.

"I think it's critical to get students to embrace the idea that they can help themselves or a friend, but we do know that no matter what they do, there are going to be students who aren't going to reach out for help," says Courtney Knowles, executive director of the Jed Foundation, the nation's leading organization working to improve the mental health of college students and to prevent suicide. The foundation has created ULifeline.org, a free, anonymous, and confidential online resource center for college students to learn about mental health and suicide prevention. More than 1,400 colleges and universities currently participate in the ULifeline network, which provides an incredible online resource for students who first want to find out if they actually need help and then connects them with appropriate local services.

Even though mental/emotional issues can often be easily

managed with treatment, issues of shame regarding emotional problems are one of the main reasons students don't ask for help. Other students won't reach out for assistance because they don't think it would help, but ULifeline says, "Between 80 and 90 percent of people who are treated for depression experience significant improvement, and almost all individuals gain some relief from their symptoms."

Online Survival Guide: *Learn more about mental health on campus by going to http://TheFreshmanSurvivalGuide .com/chapters/ and clicking on "Chapter 10."*

Mental Health–The Interactive RA

Don't forget to take advantage of the support groups you have. Your family and friends are always there for you, even if you fight now and again. There is always a counseling center on campus that has trained counselors willing to listen to whatever you have to say. Sometimes, just saying your stresses out loud helps relieve some of the stress. We, the iRA team, are also here for you. Feel free to contact us with any questions you have.

—Megan Stamer, iRA
Ramapo College of New Jersey

Not (Necessarily) Forever

If you are struggling with depression today, that doesn't necessarily mean you will be plagued with mental illness for the rest of your life. There are many students who have a hard time in their first or second semester, then do just fine. Don't avoid getting help because you're afraid of a diagnosis. Mental illness is also more easily managed before symptoms get too severe.

People who get treatment have fewer depressive episodes, and they find those episodes are less severe than those of people who don't get any treatment.

Having struggled with my mental health throughout college, I can give this important piece of advice: Be honest. Be honest with your friends, with your roommates, with your family back home, with [professionals] on campus, but most importantly with yourself. Don't be embarrassed or ashamed. There are countless students on every campus who need help for this type of issue.

—Jillian, senior, Boston College

It is important to surround yourself with people who can help you on a bad day. And if you are having issues, it's okay to go to your health services department at your school. They are there to help. You are an adult now, and it's time to take care of yourself.

—Mindy, senior, Midwestern State University

When Kelly decided to go away to college instead of living at home and commuting, it worried her family and friends. She was already medicated for depression and had an eating disorder. She'd been hospitalized for a suicide attempt in high school, and in spite of pretty intensive treatment she was still not achieving stability in either her mood disorder or her eating disorder. She agreed to write about her experience herself:

I couldn't wait to go to college. Rephrase: I couldn't wait to go away to college. My home situation had made high school a sort of living hell, and I couldn't wait to leave it all behind and start something new. But changing your surroundings does not change the chemical makeup of your brain. I thought that leaving my parents and finally being able to do things for myself would be liberating and free me of all the negative things in my previous life, including my mood disorder.

At first, everything was great. I loved my classes, loved the independence that college life afforded me, and enjoyed not having anyone to tell me what to do all the time. So feeling good means I'm cured and don't need medication anymore, right? Wrong. About halfway through my first semester, I stopped going to classes. I didn't leave my room much, and the tearful calls to my friends and support people back home increased. I was depressed, lonely, and failing every single one of my five classes. College is great—enjoy the experience—but take care of yourself. Set up your supports before you need them, and keep the important people in your life (like your parents) updated so they don't have to deal with heart-attack-inducing surprises. Check if your school has a disability resource center. Get to know your professors. Oh, and most important: Take your medication!

SEEK → FIND

Regardless of our belief system, it is certain that our very purpose of living this life is to discover the best of its qualities, such as love, joy, and happiness. There is nothing [fulfilling] about living a miserable life, and it is self-destructive to hide, suppress, or justify causes leading to misery. Happiness is a healthy state of mind. Most of our prayers and meditations are designed to help us achieve this state. One of my students was suffering from lack of motivation that resulted in severe states of depression. These led to a moment of existential crisis. This is a case in which mental and spiritual well-being are interlinked and need to be addressed accordingly. Students should overcome the stigma that [using the term] mental health *implies something is wrong with their mind, and that they may be perceived in that manner by their peers. Instead [maintaining mental health refers to keeping] a healthy balance of emotions during stressful times. So [getting help is] akin to visiting a nutritionist in order to know what a healthy diet is.*

—Ven. Tenzin Priyadarshi, Buddhist chaplain,
Massachusetts Institute of Technology

The real reasons, the root causes of depression, only come out after several sessions of conversation. A student comes to my room complaining about minor depression, and after two or three sessions you realize that it's not minor depression at all. He's entertaining suicidal thoughts or going through a very deep struggle inside of himself. They come with issues like boyfriends, girlfriends, failing in exams, not being able to focus, etc., but if you dig deep you realize issues such as sexual orientation, death in the family, domestic violence, sexual abuse in the past—things just come—[are at work and the students] have no experience with religious leadership going beyond legal issues [to] try to connect in a deeper way and empower them.

—Imam Abdullah T. Antepli, Muslim chaplain,
Duke University

One of the great awakenings in the collegiate experience is to recognize your limitations intellectually, relationally, spiritually, and emotionally. Acknowledging weakness in these arenas is a credit, not a deficit. Seeking guidance and help is a sign of health. Mental health and emotional intelligence should be as high a priority as obtaining your degree and securing a career!

—Rev. Scott Young, Protestant campus minister,
University of Southern California

*Chaplains, ministers, rabbis, and laypeople can help when some-
one is in need of spiritual counsel, but they are not always equipped
or trained to deal with problems that are emotional or psychological. Although God is present in each and every one, there are those
who are trained to deal with the problems that prayer does not seem
to make better. God works in partnership with people, and it often
makes us more present to God when we seek trained professionals
to help us through a crisis.*

—Rabbi Serena Fujita, Jewish chaplain, Bucknell University

Friends—the First Line of Defense?

Most often, if people are dealing with mental health problems
they turn to their friends first for help. Just as this is usually not
an easy decision for the person asking for help, this is often very
difficult for the person who is being asked. Handling the extra
weight of someone else's problems demands a lot of energy
that can be tough to spare sometimes in college. When a friend
comes to you and unloads her struggles, it's important to make
sure you're taking the appropriate action for both yourself and
your friend.

A student shares her story of helping a friend:

*One of my best friends entered college with diagnosed depres-
sion. The stress of school, wanting to fit in, and feeling a need
to experiment somehow compelled her to stop taking her medications. She fell into a deep depression, didn't want to leave
her room much, started drinking heavily, skipping class, and
began cutting herself. She came to me in tears telling me about
her troubles and asking me to promise not to tell anyone.*

*That was hard. I agreed to hang in with her for a while
without immediately telling anyone as long as she promised to*

get back on her meds and stop hurting herself. But I told her that if there was any evidence she was going against that plan, I was going to need to tell someone for her own good. That was not an easy pill for her to swallow. Gradually, after several tear-filled nights and fights, she was back on her medications.

That helped for a little, but as I got busier and stopped spending every night talking with her, I could see her getting worse again. So finally I sat down with her and laid down the line. If she cared about our friendship, or herself, she needed to go get professional help. And if she wasn't going to do something about it, I was. Luckily she agreed and talked to a counselor the next day. Once she finally got things settled, she thrived and was thankful that I had made her take that hard step.

There is always a fine line you need to walk between doing what your friend asks and doing what your friend needs. *You're not supposed to know how to solve someone else's problems, but you can help them find someone who can.* While honoring your friend's trust as much as you can, try to get him or her to an outside source of help as quickly as possible. If your friend is having trouble admitting he or she needs help, share why you're worried. It's best if you help people help themselves rather than trying to help people who don't want it. Most important, if a friend comes to you for help or obviously needs it, don't turn your back and assume someone else will take care of it. You will never forgive yourself if you ignore warning signs and then something serious happens.

Online Survival Guide: *Visit http://TheFreshmanSurvival Guide.com for additional resources or to ask a question of the Interactive RA.*

THE TAKEAWAY

Mental and emotional distress is a reality for half of all college students. Fortunately these conditions are highly treatable, but not unless you reach out and ask for help. There is no need to suffer alone.

CHAPTER 11

Being a Seeker

 Survival Strategy #11: It's not just okay to ask big questions, it's your duty. Go ahead. God can handle it.

Why? It's the fundamental question many people begin asking during adolescence and young adulthood. Of course, you are already entertaining tons of other questions: How will I like college? What do I want to do with my life? Who do I want to be? Those questions—and many others—are addressed throughout this book.

But *why* questions are different. "Why is that?" you ask. Because they address issues of reason, meaning, and purpose: Why bother with college? Why is it important? Why should I care?

There will be unlimited amounts of information you can learn in college and countless questions you'll want answered, but the questions spiritual seekers ask are the ones concerned with finding ultimate meaning: Why are we alive?

Who Asks Why?

Who are these seekers asking these ultimate questions? All of us! You, your roommate, your RA, the woman behind the counter at the cafeteria, your best friend, your worst enemy, everyone you've ever met, and the billions of people you'll never lay eyes on.

Philosopher, mathematician, and physicist Blaise Pascal (1623–1662) spoke of an emptiness in humans that is commonly referred to as a "God-shaped hole" in each of us. "What else does this craving, and this helplessness, proclaim but that there was once in man a true happiness, of which all that now remains is the empty print and trace?...This infinite abyss can be filled only with an infinite and immutable object; in other words by God himself."[1]

The God Question

Many people believe that all of us are born with some sort of "God question" that we must confront, even if it is only to say, "I don't believe in God." We believe that answering that question for oneself is an integral—and ongoing—element of discovering who we are and who we want to become in the future.

It is a question connected to every aspect of our lives, especially at times of great change and growth—like going to college. The world is a complex place with lots of competing ideas and approaches. It can be confusing, and you may be tempted to resist that complexity by simply settling for answers that were given to you, whether or not they have any bearing on the way you experience the world. In order to live a mature faith/spirituality, you need to be able to honestly confront the world you live in.

Fortunately, the human race has been dealing with questions of faith for millennia, and conveniently, your college probably has representatives from multiple faiths' traditions to help you sort this complexity out. The spiritual component of ourselves is inextricably linked to every other facet of our lives, and different spiritual traditions have been grappling for thousands of years with the very same questions you have now about what a good/moral life is and how to live it. It's a good idea at least to get a sense of what they've learned over the centuries before dismissing them.

Your college experience certainly will force you to grow intellectually, but your physical and spiritual selves will be challenged as well. It is your duty to ask big questions. Questions and doubt are not the opposite of faith. The opposite of faith is fear. Fear doesn't hope. Fear doesn't trust. Doubt—entertaining the questions, seeking answers—is a path to God.

Statistically Spiritual

This God question is one that Americans in general seem to take quite seriously; the United States is the most religious nation in the developed world.[2] In fact, 96 percent of Americans say they believe in God or some form of Supreme Being.

America may be a nation of believers, but more recent studies by the Pew Forum on Religion and Public Life show that we're a spiritually restless people as well:

- Approximately one-fourth of Americans ages eighteen to twenty-nine say they are not currently affiliated with any particular religion.[3]
- Young adults ages eighteen to twenty-nine are more than three times more likely than those age seventy and older to say that they are not affiliated with any particular religion (35 percent versus 11 percent).[4]

Spiritual, but Not Religious

For 20 percent of Americans, this spiritual impatience—no formal affiliation with church or synagogue but nonetheless engaged in spiritual seeking—has come to be more commonly referred to as people being " 'spiritual' but not 'religious.' "[5]

Among people under the age of twenty-five, the numbers are at least as high. An international study released in late 2008 by the Center for Spiritual Development in Childhood and Adolescence revealed that 55 percent of young people ages twelve to twenty-five say they are more spiritual now than two years ago. Interestingly, nearly one-third of the young people say they don't trust organized religion.[6]

Tellingly, "participating in worship services, classes, or other religious rituals" placed ninth in terms of importance for spiritual development, with 60 percent responding that it made their spiritual development "somewhat or much easier."[7]

Miriam Cameron, a professor at the University of Minnesota's Center for Spirituality and Healing, said the results reflect what she has already observed in her classes. "Many of my students equate religion with dogma and spirituality with harmony," she says. Student opinions at the increasingly popular Mindfulness Meditation Club at the University of Minnesota confirm her observation. "I've developed a strong belief in the interconnectedness of the world," said senior David Horn. "It doesn't make distinctions, and religion is all about making distinctions."

Online Survival Guide: Ask our online resident assistants about college life by visiting "Interactive RA" at http:// TheFreshmanSurvivalGuide.com and clicking on "Ask."

I journaled a lot, went on retreats offered, took theology classes (and not just since my major was theology, but because I wanted to grow in my spirituality), talked with theology professors about my questions, went on service trips, and then reflected about what just happened. I made my faith my own...I got involved. That helped. I would tell any freshman to find a mentor in their faith life on campus. I had friends I could talk to about issues of my faith. I also saw how they acted in their faith life. It helped.

—Victoria, senior, Marian University

Why Bother?

"A student told me, 'I've been singing in a choir at this church, but I haven't decided how religious I'm going to be next year,'" recalls Yale's Protestant chaplain, Rev. Ian Oliver. "So clearly she has some of her heart in it, but it's also part of some calculation about her social life and activities and all those pieces she has to put together—and it's just one small piece." If it truly is important to ask big questions in college, you also may want to examine whether spiritual practice in general—and yours in particular—is worthwhile. Is it the ground of your existence? Does it make a real difference in your life, or is it simply another item on a to-do list? Unsure of how to tell the difference?

Test Your Spirituality

Who needs some newfangled spirituality test? We've got one from the first century CE that still works pretty well. To gauge the value of your spiritual beliefs, measure them against the ancient "fruit of the Spirit" as outlined by Saint Paul in Galatians 5. Does your practice yield greater:

- Love
- Joy
- Peace
- Patience
- Kindness
- Goodness
- Faithfulness
- Gentleness
- Self-control

If it does, great, you're on to something—stick with it. If not, you may want to consider why that is so and what you might do about it.

Online Survival Guide: *What are your spiritual strengths? Take our online quiz to find out by clicking on "Chapter 11" at http://TheFreshmanSurvivalGuide.com/chapters/.*

SEEK → FIND—The True Meaning of Jihad

Questioning everything—including the existence of God—is a divine commandment in Islam. It is not only an option but a commandment. We are asked to struggle as Jacob did with God. That is the true meaning of jihad...You constantly negotiate life through the teachings of your religion in order to live an ethical and moral life. You are expected to struggle. This is not a static, primitive, frozen religion invented 1,400 years ago; it is meant to be a language, a tool that every person could use to live an ethical and moral life. Islam is applicable to the twenty-first century. This applies to all religions.

—Imam Abdullah T. Antepli, Muslim chaplain, Duke University

Growing up in a very religious Catholic home, I remember wondering if religion was just a universal "No!" to the world. The formula I was taught seemed pretty simple: Church = Good, World = Bad, Sex = No. If that was the case, then what was I supposed to do with everything in the world that meant so much to me? At that time in my life, I had easily gotten more out of songs by the bands I loved than anything I'd ever found in church. If a decision needed to be made about where my heart truly found greater life, then there was no competition; the world would win by a mile.

Fortunately, around this same time I encountered the Jesuits—a Catholic order of priests dedicated to education who taught at both my high school and college. I was impressed by how they, rather than shutting themselves off from the world, lived in the real world trying to find God and his goodness all around them. They weren't trying to remove themselves from creation; instead they were trying to enter into deeper communion with God's love through the world. What if, instead of seeing things in oppositional terms, God versus World, I could begin to see God in the world? Could God even be found in a song that moved me in some profound way?

Without its ever explicitly being mentioned, I understood that I didn't have to check my brain at the door of the church. I was supposed to bring everything in with me—my hopes, my doubts, my loves, my fears, my questions—God didn't mind. He could handle it.

—Bill McGarvey, Georgetown
University graduate (and coauthor of the *FSG*)

A Vote for Religious Extremism?

Though it is more the exception than the rule, what if you or someone you know wants to go "off the grid" religiously and try to put faith to the test in extreme ways? Living a life of secluded prayer, perhaps? Taking a vow of radical poverty and living among the poor à la Shane Claiborne in *The Irresistible Revolution* or the way Mother Teresa did in Calcutta? Rabbi Yonah Schiller addresses radical approaches to living your faith and adds some caveats:

> *I think there is a place for some people to go and live on a mountaintop or go into some freaky place of learning and spend the rest of their [lives] there, and I think there is a value to that. But that's not for everybody—and probably not for the vast majority of people. The danger is that those people [sometimes] burn out and then ask themselves where they have been for the last five years. "Where were my parents for the last five years, my brothers, my sisters, my friends?" And they'll come away from that experience shattered as opposed to built up, which really misses the point.*

Where?

Each person must find her or his own path to the sacred. But since others have traveled the territory before us, we might as well take along the maps they've made. All the great religious traditions have readings, practices, guides, and disciplines to help the seeker. Here are a few suggestions to get you started:

- Find a mentor, a spiritual director, or a teacher whose faith you admire.
- Participate in worship and a spiritual community. This helps us express faith and challenge it; it guides and nurtures us and keeps us accountable.

- Do some spiritual reading—sacred texts and other spiritual reading will also help you articulate and challenge your faith. (For a list of spiritual classics you should consider reading—or to add your own favorites to our list— visit http://TheFreshmanSurvivalGuide.com/chapters/ and click on "Chapter 11.")
- Practice active compassion, caring for others with intention.
- Develop habits such as prayer, meditation, and fasting (always check with a doctor before fasting). Just as runners get faster and fitter if they run regularly, to maintain spiritual fitness you must regularly work at it.

How?

Below is an excerpt from a column entitled "What Works: Tools for the Spiritual Seeker" by Phil Fox Rose that appeared on BustedHalo.com. This excerpt offers a few simple steps to learn how to meditate, which is using centering prayer.

> *Centering Prayer is particularly good for cultivating surrender to and acceptance of God's Will...but if a different practice speaks to you, or if your friend or [church/mosque/synagogue] offers support in another form, consider that. I discourage you, though, from any practice that's goal oriented, complicated, or overly attached to form. As Thomas Merton said, "Contemplative prayer has to be always very simple, confined to the simplest of acts."*
>
> *[Here's a simple framework to start with:]*
>
> 1. ***Choose a sacred word***, *one or two syllables, with spiritual meaning but not distractingly important to you. Mine is "Oneness."*

2. ***Sit comfortably.*** *I kneel [on] a sitting cushion, or sit in a chair...I don't believe in sitting uncomfortably.*

3. ***Time twenty minutes.*** *Use a method where you don't have to check. I use a timer. You can record twenty minutes of silence followed by a sound, and hit Play. [There are iPhone apps that can do what you need as well.] (If you can't do twenty minutes at first, do less rather than not doing it, but something happens to the stillness around ten to fifteen minutes in that you will miss. That's why twenty-plus minutes is nearly universal.)*

4. ***Eyes open or closed.*** *I keep mine open, unfocused, and glancing down slightly. I learned early on that if my eyes are closed I'm more prone to daydream. Open helps keep me more alert. Others prefer eyes closed.*

5. ***Settle briefly, and silently introduce the sacred word*** *as the symbol of your consent to God's presence and action within.*

6. ***Resist no thought; retain no thought; react to no thought. When you realize you are engaged with your thoughts, including sensations and feelings, return ever so gently to the sacred word.*** *This is what it's all about. You may drift into not needing the word, just "resting in God." Or you may stay in this attachment-surrender loop the whole time. As Fr. Thomas Keating, the founder of Centering Prayer, says, ten thousand thoughts means "ten thousand opportunities to return to God."...The goal is not emptiness. As Cynthia Bourgeault says, "Striving for emptiness is a surefire way to guarantee that your meditation will be a constant stream of thoughts."*

7. ***Remain in silence*** *at the end of the period for a couple of minutes.*[8]

Online Survival Guide: *Visit "Chapter 11" at http://TheFreshmanSurvivalGuide.com/chapters/ to download a PDF guide to centering prayer.*

THE TAKEAWAY

You've been given a good brain for a reason, and college is the perfect place to put it to use. Take responsibility for your life, beliefs, and practices. Go ahead, ask all the questions you like. Just keep in mind that over the past few thousand years countless smart people like you have asked the same questions. In formulating your answers, be humble enough to at least take what they've found into consideration.

CHAPTER 12

Go to Class!

 Survival Strategy #12: Whenever you need a little more inspiration, admonishing, or encouragement, come back and reread this chapter (then go to class).

If you're not on campus yet, this may seem like strange advice. *Of course* you'll go to class. That's why you're going to college. But if you're reading this after you've been at school a while, it probably won't seem odd at all. In either case, you probably know at least one person who's dropped out—or was kicked out—because he ditched class once too often.

Thirty percent of freshmen drop out,[1] and only a little more than half who stay (53 percent) ever graduate.[2] Next to finances, the main reason students who've left school give for dropping out is academics. Your first line of defense against academic failure is to show up. It's a big temptation not to. No one's there to make you go. You oversleep, your paper isn't done, you're hungover, it's a huge class and nobody takes attendance—there are lots of reasons to skip class. But none of them will be very comforting at the end of freshman year if you've got a year's worth of college bills and little or nothing to show for it.

Go to class! My freshman year I failed to go to class and failed a lot of classes. After my first semester I went to classes and raised my GPA by 2.5 points.

—Senior, University of Iowa

Experts agree: The number one predictor of academic success for freshmen continues to be regular class attendance.

Professors can be touchy if they don't see your shining face at class each session (see chapter 15). Being absent is a clear signal that you don't care. Professors are much less likely to give you the benefit of the doubt when you need an extension or are ill and need to reschedule a presentation. Showing up is the best way to make sure your professors know who you are and that you want to do well.

Keep in mind that the professors and teaching assistants are often people who have dedicated their lives to the subjects they teach. Many of them (though clearly not all) will be among the most interesting people you will ever meet, and the material they teach you can be incredibly inspiring, life-changing stuff.

True, some of your classes may be in vast lecture halls where nobody takes attendance. You still need to go! Missing instruction is a waste of money, and that friend you're counting on to take good notes for you (1) may not be a great note taker, and (2) is definitely not a highly qualified expert on the topic. You're shortchanging yourself and probably missing way more than you think—how can you even know if you're not there?

"Students need to be there for the first week in my class," advises Dr. Amir Hussain at Loyola Marymount University. "In the first week of class, we go over process, not content. So this is one of the most crucial weeks to be there, as we go over how we will talk about the issues that will arise in the course during the semester. If you miss this week, you will be more than one week behind."

> *Don't think you can goof off the first week of classes just because you assume there's not much work and you can catch up on it later. That usually comes back to bite you.*
>
> **—Christine, senior, Northwestern University**

Skipping class will make you feel less connected, another common reason for dropping out. Conversely, showing up will send a signal—not just to your professor, but also to your classmates—that you're serious about this venture. Nobody wants to be in a work group with the guy who may not be there when it comes time to divvy up the work or to present. There are a lot of other factors that add up to success, but ditching class is the first skid along the slippery downhill slope of slacking. Showing up is not the only step, but is a vital *first* step in connecting and staying connected.

James had chosen a small and pricey private college. He had the grades (and the smarts) to get in. He was a great kid, but even in high school he liked to party more than he should have. Consequently he'd been really anxious to get out from under his parents' critical eyes. Shortly after he entered college, James was struggling. The problem wasn't just the drinking. He was also having a hard time academically. Rather than seek help, he dove deeper into the party scene to escape. When he ended up back home in community college the next year, he was angry with himself, more frustrated than ever to be living with his parents again, and unhappy that they had this to hold over his head as well.

One thing I regret about my freshman year is skipping my animal biology class way too much. I got a D in the class. I went to high school from 8 A.M. to 3 P.M. every day, so I didn't think I'd have a problem. Wrong. The most common mistake people make their freshman year is not going to class. Mom and Dad aren't there to make you go, and the principal doesn't call your parents to tell on you. Don't skip class—lectures included.

—Jacqueline, senior, University of Iowa

5 Reasons to Go to Class!

1. Learning is relational, not just reading a book or completing an assignment. The enterprise of education involves active listening and engagement of others—fellow students and professors.
2. A college classroom is a professional environment—it's why you're there on that campus!
3. You're paying for this course. Get your money's worth!
4. The class you miss may be the class that will change your life forever.
5. If you're not there, everyone's learning experience suffers.

—Prof. Lee Chase, Saint John Fisher College

The $140 Nap

The national average cost of attending a four-year public college is over $28,000 per year, and at a four-year private college it's $59,000.[3] At five classes a semester and twenty sessions per class, you're passing up a $140 ticket (for private school it's $259) you've already paid for every time you sleep through a class. Pretty expensive nap.

Class Struggle

The most common reasons why freshmen miss class and what to do about them:

Problem: Oversleeping.

Solution: Figure out why. Are you simply staying up too late? Is it too noisy in your dorm to get good sleep? Give yourself a regular bedtime. Try white noise—a fan, ocean sounds on your iPod—or earplugs. Watch caffeine intake late in the day; if you can't settle down at night, the culprit may be that can of Monster you drank after dinner.

Problem: Partied out.

Solution: Take it easy (see chapter 24 on alcohol and substance abuse). On many campuses there's a party every night, especially in the first few weeks. Save parties and their accompanying hazards for the weekends. Think of it this way: If you can avoid drinking your way out of college this semester, you'll be rewarded with three more years (at least) of college life.

Problem: A bad professor.

Solution: It may seem as if there's nothing worse as you head off for an hour or two of boredom, but there is—bombing the class and having your GPA take a dive because of that professor who tortured you all semester. Don't let him or her win. Go to class anyway and rely on the reading. Even "bad" professors will sometimes choose good material.

Problem: A challenging subject.

Solution: Sometimes when you're struggling it's hard to force yourself to go to class. It's like eating a vegetable that you hate. Find someone who loves the subject who can get you past the hard parts. If there are any links or media mentioned in the syllabus, take the time to check them out. Sometimes a different medium can make clear what has been murky for you.

SEEK → FIND

 You're here to learn how to learn. You get to learn for your entire life, [but now] you've got a concentrated period of time around a bunch of learners that know how to learn so...learn how to learn.

—Rev. Scott Young, Protestant campus minister,
University of Southern California

Problem: The class is just too early.

Solution: A two-step solution: First, remember this for next semester and if you can avoid it, don't go for the 8 A.M. offering of the class. Second, try waking up even earlier than usual so you're functioning by the time you have to get to class.

Problem: The homework isn't done.

Solution: Bite the bullet and make yourself go anyway. The more you give in on this one, the more anxious you'll be about going if you're not prepared. It's better to tough it out than to start piling up absences.

Connect with a study group or find a classmate who's on top of the work to help push you along.

Online Survival Guide: *Ask our online resident assistants about college life by visiting "Interactive RA" at http:// TheFreshmanSurvivalGuide.com and clicking on "Ask."*

THE TAKEAWAY

The one thing you have the most control over regarding academic success is showing up for class. Skipping class is one of the quickest roads *out* of college. Whatever it takes, no matter how bad you feel, how tired you are, whether or not you've done the reading, or how much you can't stand the professor, *go to class*!

CHAPTER 13

How to Be a College Student
Studying and Time Management

Survival Strategy #13: Organizing and effectively using your time can be a struggle. Give yourself time to get used to this new learning environment, and don't expect to figure it all out yourself. There are resources to help you learn how to get it all done and still have time to kick back and relax.

The time you spend, and the way you spend it, can make or break you academically. Even if you never considered yourself a great student in high school, you *can* learn the habits and skills that will help you become one in college. You wouldn't have gotten in if the college administrators didn't think you could make it. If you've always done well, you may find that college is a little more challenging than high school was and you need to sharpen your skills. Whatever the case, take the time to develop the skills you'll need to get through first semester and beyond.

Don't be intimidated because there are people who are smarter or more organized than you. Instead of letting this fact shake your confidence, seek out students who are skillful and imitate them. You've heard the expression "Don't work harder, work smarter"?

In college you have to do both, but there are things you can do to make your academic life easier and your grades better.

Research the help that's available on your campus. Online assistance, resources in the library, learning centers for different subject areas, and special classes for freshmen that teach study skills are available on almost every campus (see chapter 22 for other possibilities). Many campuses have an office for first-year students that can connect you with the help you need. And you can always ask older students what's been most helpful for them.

Office Hours and Other New Terms from the College Glossary

If you already know what terms like *office hours*, *syllabus*, *teaching assistant*, *learning center*, and *study group* mean, skip ahead to the next section. If these terms are new to you, it's good to know how each of these resources can work to your advantage.

Most colleges require professors to keep *office hours*—a set time every week when professors are in their offices and available to students. This guarantees you a time and place to speak with your professors if you need them. In high school your teachers were on campus and available during every school day...not so with college profs. Their office hours are generally relatively limited. Most will not have time to talk right after class, so don't let this precious resource go to waste. You're paying for it with your tuition whether you use it or not.

At the first class, every professor will give you a *syllabus*, a printed summary of the course (or they will direct you to one online). Guard it with your life and rely on it throughout the semester. All the information you need to do well in that class is there—expectations, attendance policies, grading, tests, assignments, and contact information for your professor. Some professors will drift from it a bit, but many use it as their own outline for teaching the course.

Depending on the size of your school and your major, in some classes you may have a *teaching assistant*, or TA, often a graduate student or upper-level student, as an instructor. They can be a mixed bag. If you have a TA who's solo-teaching your class, she may be overwhelmed and disinterested, or she may turn out to be your savior. TAs know their subjects and what the professors are looking for, and they can be a great resource when a busy or confusing professor is less than helpful.

Learning centers (or labs) are tutoring centers staffed by graduate students and advanced students in the major. A learning center often offers sophisticated help that can cater to your precise needs as a student.

This last term is pretty self-explanatory, but just in case... *study groups*, sometimes formal, sometimes informal, are gatherings of students who help each other in a subject. If one doesn't already exist for a class you're having trouble in, take the initiative and start one yourself.

As you can see, many resources are available if you're struggling in a class. Dr. Thomas O'Brien of DePaul University recommends making an appointment with your professor, as he or she can talk through your options with you and point you in the direction of assistance. You should *never* be embarrassed to ask for extra help. All these resources were put in place before you got there because other students needed them, so clearly you're not alone.

MOOCs

Okay, truth be told, this term is pretty new to almost everyone on campus. *MOOC* stands for "Massive Open Online

Course." Technology has revolutionized nearly every aspect of twenty-first-century life and higher education is no exception. MOOCs are part of a very dynamic educational landscape that is using online technology to make knowledge and learning available to everyone.

Numerous online learning centers and universities—including some of the most elite schools in the world—are aggressively committing resources to this new approach to education. People can learn math basics online at Khan Academy, or take a crash course in app programming at Udacity, or learn about almost any subject at Coursera or edX. Harvard University and MIT founded edX in 2012 as an online learning destination and MOOC provider. Through their partnerships with some of the best universities in the world, learners everywhere can take high-quality courses—usually without any cost. It is the only leading MOOC provider that is both nonprofit and open source. "An ambitious, motivated, curious learner will find that there are a myriad courses offered online...time and curiosity are the only limits," says Ana Trandafir of HarvardX. "Browsing these platforms can offer one a taste of courses offered at various places and the teaching styles of various professors and scholars."

It is impossible to predict what online learning will look like in the future, but there are online opportunities available right now that can help prepare you for college or complement courses you are already taking.

Pace Yourself

Use a planner—digital or paper, whatever works best for you—to avoid surprises and keep all-nighters to a minimum. The first week of class, sit down with your laptop and the syllabus for each of your classes and bookmark each of your teachers' websites. If there are websites that go along with your textbooks, bookmark them, too. Then, no matter where you are and whether or not you've got your notebooks or textbooks with you, you can always access the info you need quickly. Write in your planner when each paper, project, or presentation is due; then create and enter your own deadlines to space work out and avoid having to do it all in the same week (or night).

Online Survival Guide: *Ask our online resident assistants about college life by visiting "Interactive RA" at http:// TheFreshmanSurvivalGuide.com and clicking on "Ask."*

Don't take too many classes. Sure, you were able to take five classes in high school, but in college one hour of class equals three hours of reading and study time needed to pass. So a three-hour class is nine hours of reading and studying each week.

—Graduate, California State University, Monterey Bay

Start studying for tests at least three days before the exam. It may be tempting to hang out with friends and put studying aside until very late at night, but you will regret it and it will show in your grades. If you start things early and get enough sleep, there will be no problem with stress, because when other things come up, you can deal with them because you have plenty of time.

—Rachel, sophomore, Stonehill College

To Drop or Not to Drop–The Interactive RA

Once you have been to class, taken a look the syllabus, and possibly completed an assignment or had a quiz, it's a great time to review your current load of classes. If you think that the material may be too much for you to absorb, if you think you have taken on too much, or if you think the class load will hinder your academic success, now is the time to consider dropping a class. The best scenario is to drop the class without it having a negative effect on your transcript. You want to make decisions that will not affect your chance to graduate on time or to graduate with a higher grade point average.

Dropping a class is all about timing. The registrar's office will have specific dates that you must adhere to in order to successfully drop a class. Sometimes the steps are quite easy and will simply allow you to just drop the class. In other classes you may have to obtain a signature from the professor, an advisor, or even the dean. The second factor to consider is how the drop will appear on your transcript. Your preference is for the drop not to appear on your transcript at all; this, of course, is the best-case scenario and will be the earliest deadline. The later the deadline is in the semester, the more detrimental it will be toward your grade point average.

Dropping a class is not necessarily a bad thing. It is a mature decision that almost all students have to face at one point in their academic careers. Dropping a class also should not be a way to avoid hard work. As you progress through your academic program, your courses are designed to become more challenging and push your complex thinking to the next level. Shying away from hard work or a more challenging professor will not prepare you for your professional field or life after college. Consider the course is only twelve to sixteen weeks and in the end you will benefit the most from it. So before you do it, consider your true intentions behind dropping the class. Meet with your advisor and discuss the class and the ramifications. Consider getting a tutor or seeing if the professor offers one-on-one sessions or has any other resources to help you be successful. If you find that the class is just too much for your current load, you can also consider retaking the class next year or finding a suitable replacement.

Dropping classes is a great option to have as a student, but before dropping classes ensure that is the best solution in the long run. Making a quick decision should not have long-lasting effects on your academic career. Consult your advisor, exhaust all of your possibilities, and make the best decision.

—Danielle Shipp, iRA
Community Manager, Greystar Student Living Communities

Study Skills: Where? What? How? Why?

The single most important element of study skills is setting aside the time for homework, but there are other components as well: finding a good place to get work done, removing distractions, and understanding your own work style and how you learn best. As you work on each of these elements, you will add to the effectiveness and efficiency of your study time.

Where?

If you have a considerate roommate and a relatively quiet dorm, your room can be one of the best places to get work done. You don't have to worry about packing up everything you need, then forgetting one vital textbook or folder of notes. Plus your music, snacks, and bathroom are all close by. The downside of studying in your room is that all those same comforts can turn into distractions. And if you're in a suite or a noisy hall, frustration can build up and steal your work time.

Explore the library, lounges, and computer labs, and try a few places that might work for study spots. What looks like a quiet corner might be traffic central at certain times of the day or night. Don't overlook the coffee shop in town with free Wi-Fi; you may find just the degree of solitude you need.

Make sure you have *some* work space in your room, because there will be days when you need to work there. One day you may be too sick to move but have to get a paper done. Or a storm may keep you inside but midterm studying can't wait. Laptops have freed us from having to sit at a desk to work, but sitting on your bed can turn study time into nap time. Figure out what works for you, but make sure you have options.

If too much solo work drives you nuts, find a study buddy or join a study group for every class you can (the more challenging the class, the more valuable this will be).

What?

Some students come to college with excellent study skills: They know how to take notes, read for retention, write papers, and prepare for exams. But others—more than you might guess—are sorely lacking these vital skills. Many, if not most, colleges have put services in place to teach any skills that might be missing. Use them!

How?

Download the "Freshman Survival Guide Study Budget" PDF from http://TheFreshmanSurvivalGuide.com/chapters/ (click on

"Chapter 4"). It will help you organize your time and keep track of exactly what needs to be done—and when. Also consider making a pact with a friend and hold each other accountable for study time. It's way too easy to let other things distract you and let your study time slip away.

Why?

In some classes you can squeak by without doing the reading, but the benefits of doing that reading really outweigh the time spent. "Many students say reading all course material isn't worth the time, but in my experience it makes class participation much easier and cuts study time in half," offers RA Michaela McDonald from Providence College. "Read at night to unwind, and always use a pen or highlighter to keep yourself interested and to burn it into your memory." Doing the reading will make you more confident about speaking up in class discussions and reinforce what you're learning, improve your retention of the material, and ultimately improve your test grades.

Sam was always quick with a smile, warm, friendly, and a bit of a class clown, so it came as a surprise to most who knew him that he spent almost every night in the library his first semester. He'd been nervous about how hard he'd have to work compared to high school, so Sam really gave it his all. When he got his grades, he was pretty pleased with his resulting 3.7. "I don't think I'll spend *so* much time studying next semester," he told his friends, flashing a smile. "But I'm really glad I worked my butt off for my first. Now I know I can do it and have an idea what it takes."

Online Survival Guide: Share your best study tips online. Go to http://TheFreshmanSurvivalGuide.com/chapters/ and click on "Chapter 13."

SEEK → FIND

There may be other students in your class with higher IQs, fatter bank accounts, wider travel experience, and more impressive secondary school credentials than you, but no one has more days in the week or hours in the day than you. Twenty-four/seven means equal opportunity for all.

—Rev. William Byron, SJ, former president,
Catholic University of America

Time-Saving Tip

Cut down on travel time. If you know you have a busy day and a lot you need to accomplish, don't plan to go back to your dorm to pick stuff up. Just bring your work with you. Walking back and forth can be a big waste of time, not to mention the fact the most easily distracting space is your dorm, where all your stuff, friends, and time wasters reside.

Good Students Know…

- That if you can, you should avoid checking your e-mail or social media when you first sit down to work. It can be a time waster. Reward yourself when you're at the halfway point with twenty minutes of self-indulgence (or as long as you want once your work is finished). Check out chapter 17 ("Online Is Forever") for info on apps students are now using that allow them to set a timer to block their access to anything they choose on the Internet, especially distracting websites or social media.

- To watch out for other time wasters (see our list in chapter 14 on procrastination) and learn to give clear signals if a friend stops by to kill time: "I've gotta get this paper [reading, studying, project] finished. Can I call you when I'm done?"
- That they should seek balance—some work, some recreation every day.
- To find friends who support their goals. Want good grades? Hang with people who want that, too.
- That busy people get stuff done—a full schedule forces you to dedicate specific times to certain activities and avoid the trap of "I'll do it later."
- That you should always let your syllabus be your guide. Your professors have already told you what they expect and when they expect it—look ahead to avoid all-nighters.

 Online Survival Guide: *Ask our online resident assistants about college life by visiting "Interactive RA" at http:// TheFreshmanSurvivalGuide.com and clicking on "Ask."*

10 Ways to Steal Back Time

When crunch time hits, you may have to "steal time" from your own schedule. You can't do it every day, but when you have to, follow these emergency time-snatching measures:

1. Stay away from TV, and turn off all distractions.
2. Skip a meeting or have someone cover for you.
3. Skip the shower and just wash up—the hat and the pony-tail were invented by college students.
4. Go to bed early, skip the late-night caffeine, and get up earlier.
5. Eat in your room. Protein bars are your friend; now's the time to splurge on pizza delivery.
6. Prioritize, and finish what you can.
7. Don't be a perfectionist. It doesn't have to be perfect. Get it done to the best of your ability and then let it go.
8. Ask for help! Have an organized friend who's already finished or a family member with time on her hands? Ask him or her to proofread your paper.
9. Put the between times to work. Instead of killing time between your classes, stay in the classroom or head to the library after class to get work done.
10. Be careful about skipping one class to finish work for another. Know your professors and what you can get away with, and keep track of your own attendance. (How many times have you missed your eight o'clock? Twice? Four times?)

 Online Survival Guide: Have more helpful ideas? Share them online; go to http://TheFreshmanSurvivalGuide.com/ chapters/ and click on "Chapter 13."

THE TAKEAWAY

Find the resources on your campus to help you learn the skills you need to be a college student. Practice the skills until they become habits. Surround yourself with friends who share your goals and will help you stick to the promises you've made yourself.

CHAPTER 14

Thrill Seekers, Avoiders, and Other Procrastinators

Survival Strategy #14: Procrastination can turn into an academic disaster. Learn strategies to fight it and save yourself from stress, sleeplessness, and self-sabotage.

"But I do my best work under pressure." If you have ever uttered this sentence, you're probably a procrastinator. Yes, every once in a while, the down-to-the-wire thrill of waiting until you absolutely have to get it done *can* cause a creative rush. But for the most part this is something we procrastinators tell ourselves to rationalize our bad behavior. We lose sleep, freak out, drag down our GPAs, and miss out on other things we'd like to have done but couldn't because we didn't plan well and/or we let ourselves get distracted when we should have been working.

One American Psychological Association study showed that people overwhelmed with choices had impaired self-control and increased levels of procrastination.[1] It is hard to imagine a group of people faced with more new choices than college students. There are lots of reasons we put things off: We may be afraid of not doing well; we would rather do something we enjoy; we are a little—or a lot—distractible; maybe we don't have great study habits; or maybe we are smart enough to fake it most of the time and so, usually, can get away without actually doing the work. Most people, especially college students, procrastinate at some point. In fact, Dr. Timothy Pychyl of Carleton University says about 25 to 70 percent of college students do it. His website, Procrastination Research Group, has been around since 1995 and has a great self-help section.

Procrastination expert Joseph Ferrari, PhD, associate professor of psychology at DePaul University in Chicago, identifies three types of procrastinators: *thrill seekers, avoiders,* and *decisional procrastinators.* Thrill seekers love the high and the drama of the last minute. Avoiders are afraid of being judged and are also afraid of failure (and sometimes they even fear success). And decisional procrastinators dodge responsibility for outcomes by refusing to choose.

Whatever your particular proclivity when it comes to waiting until the last minute, now would be a great time to ditch the habit. As they say, the first step to recovery is admitting you have a problem. From there you can start using different tactics to break the habit and get the darn work done.

Procrastinating might not seem like a big deal at first, and taken individually, skipping one assignment doesn't hurt that much. The problem is that it gets easier to keep skipping and it really adds up fast, much faster than most people expect it to. Watch out for the Internet. It will kill more of your time than you ever thought possible. You just go online to check your friends on Facebook and four hours later, you still haven't started on your paper.

—Sophomore, Iowa State University

Put Procrastination in Its Place

Researchers point to five ways we procrastinators trick ourselves:[2]

1. We think we have more time than we do.
2. We think the thing we're putting off won't take as much time as it actually will.
3. We assume that at some point in the future we'll feel more like doing it.
4. We think that to succeed at it we need to feel like doing it.
5. We think that it's a waste of time to do it when we're not feeling motivated—that we won't be as effective.

It may be going too far too say we're lying to ourselves, but each of these misconceptions can seem pretty convincing when the immediate gratification of a snack, a video game, time on the Internet, or hanging around with a friend is right there tempting us. Procrastinators are also pretty good at self-deception, so we can also trick ourselves into getting work done. Here are some strategies.

Give Yourself an Allowance

Whatever your game system, favorite app, or digital distraction, be very careful. That harmless-looking little Xbox or PS4 can be your education's worst nightmare. It should stay in the closet and come out only on weekends after your papers are written. If you're not confident you've got enough willpower, you should consider leaving your game system at home. It's a great destressing method, but it can also mean your academic doom. Next time you go home for a visit, if you are still dying to play you can bring it back to school, but giving yourself a chance to experience college without this distraction may pay real dividends academically and socially.

Anything addictive or familiar right now is going to be more attractive than getting your work done. TV, Netflix, your favorite social networks, and just surfing the web can all be nice stress fighters, but they're a slippery slope. You start out just finding a little comfort or harmless distraction, and before you know it you've stayed up all night, not written your paper, and missed a couple of classes because you didn't sleep.

Self-discipline is a bigger challenge for some of us than others, but one of the biggest tasks in life is setting your own limits. If you're struggling, give yourself an Internet, television, or gaming "allowance" each day and stick to it. Nobody can multitask when it comes to combining work and fun. All it does is slow you down and keep you up later. When you're doing homework, don't let anything or any*one* steal your study time. You could even post on social media that you're studying or writing your paper so friends and family know not to message, call, or text. Chapter 17 ("Online Is Forever") has info on apps that allow you to set a timer to block access to anything on the web, social media, and so forth so your laptop isn't a source of potential distractions. If you have to talk to someone, chat or text for fifteen minutes and then get off. Silence your phone—or better yet, shut it off—and get your work done. Afterward you can stay up and chat without the worry of the unfinished work hanging over you.

Get Up, Don't Stay Up

Another trick for procrastinators is the "get up, don't stay up" rule. Our self-regulation is lowest when we're tired or overwhelmed, especially late at night after a long day. But, first thing in the morning, we've actually got a better shot at completing a task with minimal distraction. Consider going to bed early, which might mean 11 P.M. rather than 3 A.M., and then wake up, grab a cup of coffee, and get the job done.

Get Away from It All

Find a place to study that's distraction free. Crank up your productivity by getting away from the place where you sleep and hang out. Head to the library and find a quiet corner. Having a study spot away from your living space tells your brain *Now it's time to focus* and pushes you more quickly into work mode. Plus, you'll be much less likely to be interrupted there by someone dropping in to see if you want to play Frisbee. If your friends can't find you they can't distract you.

> *The library is a terrible place to study.* Everybody *studies there, especially near exam time. Instead, try to find out-of-the-way places like weird lounges in old buildings. They're quiet, and nobody will bother you.*
>
> **—Rich, University of Vermont**

Just for Five Minutes

This strategy is for the project or paper you can't seem to make yourself begin, for the class you detest or the professor who bores you to tears. You've known for a week you should be working on it, but you always end up working on something else. This tip is an easy one: Get started but promise yourself it's "just for five minutes." You'll crack the book, read over the assignment, or spend five minutes researching online. It sounds stupid, but if you do it once or twice a day for three or four days, suddenly you've accumulated fifteen, twenty, maybe forty-five minutes on a project you couldn't get started on. Still stuck? Keep reading...

SEEK → FIND

The more communication students have with their instructors in class, [the more] they will know what is expected of them, and that allows them to keep up with the work. If student[s] have a problem distributing their time and workload equally, it is directly proportional to the amount of stress they have. The more well-distributed their time is and the more able they are to catch up on work in time, the less stress there will be in their lives.

—Ven. Tenzin Priyadarshi, Buddhist chaplain, Massachusetts Institute of Technology

---

Chop It Up for Cash and Prizes

One effective strategy is dividing up work into achievable increments and then rewarding yourself when you reach each mini-goal. For a short paper or project, maybe you do the research one day and the outline the next, and day three has you writing a first draft. After each step do something nice for yourself: Take yourself out for coffee, watch your favorite show, call a friend, or just take a well-deserved nap. Human beings are actually pretty unsophisticated when it comes to motivation. It doesn't take much to trick us (and we can even trick ourselves) into getting things done. Divide, reward, and conquer!

Just Start

A practical tip for writing a paper is to simply start typing. Some people wait until they have a complete idea of what their papers will be before they begin. Try instead to skip to one of the body paragraphs you know will fit into the paper somewhere and just start writing. It will get you started and will help you flow into the rest of the paper.

Make a List

One way to fight the "I'm so overwhelmed I just have to escape" feeling is to write down everything you need to do. The simple act of making a list can be one of the biggest stress busters in college. It's almost as if you've actually begun the work. Hang on to the list and cross things off as you finish them to give yourself a visual on what you've actually accomplished. Putting the easiest things to accomplish first can help give you a sense of progress and push you further along.

 Online Survival Guide: *For more tips about procrastination and time management, click on "Chapter 14" at http://TheFreshmanSurvivalGuide.com/chapters/.*

From Actual Students Who Have Lived to Tell the Tale

You may be a procrastinator if:
- You've had to turn in a paper via e-mail and tried changing the clock on your computer to make it look as if you turned it in earlier.

- You've hidden behind someone so the professor you owed a paper to didn't see you.
- You've made more cups of coffee than you have complete sentences.
- You don't start writing a paper until 2 A.M. of the day it is due.
- You've stayed up past sunrise writing a paper . . . three days in a row.

Online Survival Guide: *Ask our online resident assistants about college life by visiting "Interactive RA" at http:// TheFreshmanSurvivalGuide.com and clicking on "Ask."*

Matt was freaking out. He had three weeks of work to do in twenty-four hours. He'd been sick and was already behind when he got the flu, but now he had two projects, a presentation, and a paper to get ready and was in total panic mode. He was the opposite of lazy and could outwork most people, but he wasn't always superskilled at looking ahead. In the past he frequently responded to stress by pretending his to-do list just didn't exist, especially if he lacked confidence about a subject. This time he called a friend he knew could talk him down from his anxiety ledge. She helped him prioritize and figure out which professors to appeal to for extensions and which ones he had to deliver on time for.

<u>*The Power of Lists—The Interactive RA*</u>

The start of something new can be a great time to make changes and resolutions. But how do we keep those changes? The way I have found *most* helpful is to make a goal list. Use a planner, Post-its, an app on your iPad, whatever works for you. There are lots of variations. One of my favorites is the Post-it list. You can use Post-its to write down the goals; stick them all to a small poster, and then you'll be able to switch them out when they are completed.

Another great way to keep to your resolutions, especially if they are related to coursework, is to set up an Assignment Checklist. This is just a simple table that lays out the due date, assignment, and whether or not it is completed.

Just make sure that you break up the goals into manageable pieces. Take the semester day by day. Setting a goal to be fluent in a language by the end of the semester, without setting smaller goals along the way, won't happen.

—Megan Stamer, iRA
Ramapo College of New Jersey

4 More Reasons to Stop Procrastinating

1. It's a confidence killer. Wasting time can erode your confidence. Once it becomes a habit, you may start to believe you're not really capable of college-level work, which isn't true—otherwise you wouldn't have been accepted.

2. You can bump up your grade. Starting early will improve the quality of your work. The extra day (or even few hours) to review and revise can crank you up a whole letter grade.

3. You deserve better. Your level of enjoyment and satisfaction in friendships, campus life, and the things you're learning

will increase dramatically if you can break the habit of waiting till the last minute. You'll have time to do the things you want to do. The activities you choose to do when you're finished with work are usually not the same time wasters you use to put it off.

4. You'll be better prepared for crisis management. When you finish early, you're in better shape to handle an emergency: You can't find a working printer, the campus e-mail system has crashed, you have an allergic reaction, and your eyes are swollen shut. If your paper's already done, what would have been a crisis is no big deal.

Procrastination—everyone does it. Recognize it and learn to counter it with productivity. Just think, if you do the thing you have been putting off doing now, you will have free time when everyone else is freaking and losing their sleep. (I wish I could take my own advice!)

—Graduate, California State University, Monterey Bay

THE TAKEAWAY

Trick yourself, reward yourself, tie yourself to your chair—but use whatever means necessary to get your work done in a timely fashion. You'll have more fun and less stress, and you may just pass freshman year.

CHAPTER 15

The Care and Feeding of the College Professor

 Survival Strategy #15: Understanding the difference between high school teachers and college professors will make a big difference in your academic success.

No matter how well (or poorly) you did in your classes back home, or how pleased your high school teachers were with you and your work, you'll find that the college professor is a whole different animal. Behavior, expectations, communication, and attitude vary widely between the two species. Understanding the distinction between your high school teachers and your college professors this fall can mean the difference between making it your first semester and failing.

The Hard Facts

You will surely encounter some fantastic and very engaging instruction on campus, just as surely as you will have teachers who can bore you to sleep in the first ten minutes of class. College can be a mixed bag when it comes to the quality of teaching.

Though many professors make an effort to keep student interest piqued, there are also many who take the attitude of "not my problem."

> *Don't pay too much attention to what other students say about professors. I have had great professors who had awful reputations on campus for being too hard or unclear. And I have had horrible professors who had great reputations. Take the courses you want, do the work, and it will be fine. Too many freshmen think that the professors are going to prompt them and remind them about assignments. Most of them don't. You are an adult and they are going to treat you like one. Now it's your responsibility to manage your schedule and decide how much time goes into studying, social activities, and class time.*
>
> **—Junior, Providence College**

Whose Job Is It?

Back in high school, if you were struggling in class or an assignment was missing, you'd usually be invited to stay after school to chat with your teacher. The change from senior year of high school to freshman year of college is a huge shift in responsibility—theirs to yours. Last year the teacher kept track of how you were doing and what work was missing; this year that's your job.

"If you do not turn in an assignment, I will not ask you for it. I will assume that you are content with a grade of zero for that assignment," Loyola Marymount professor Dr. Amir Hussain tells his students. He offers extra help but also reminds students, "Contact me when you first have a problem. If you wait until it is too late, then it is too late!"

Patti was a good student in high school. She was smart and worked hard but had always managed without too much effort. When she got to college the story was a little different. Patti's advice to freshmen? "One of the worst ways to handle college stress is to think that you're never going to get past this small issue (because honestly, most of the things are small) and have a mental breakdown over one paper or one bad test grade. Most professors have seen it before and usually have a backup plan to help good students who have had a tough week." Patti earned her master's degree in forensic molecular biology at George Washington University and now works as a DNA examiner.

"Take the initiative and take ownership of your education," advises Michelle Goodwin, associate director of the University Catholic Center in Austin. "Be prepared and participate. If you don't understand something, ask questions, e-mail [your professors with] concerns, or set up an appointment. Office hours are there for a reason. Meet your professors and help them put a name to a face. They'll never get to know you at all unless you make the effort both inside and outside the classroom."

How Do You Keep a College Professor Happy?

Keep in mind that not all profs will be offended if you don't show up, get your work in, or get to know them. Many are too busy to care and assume that since you're paying for it, it's your education to waste. Conversely, a little bit of class participation (asking a question, offering an answer in class), coming to a special event hosted by the department, and showing up during office hours can go a long way.

SEEK → FIND

College professors are sensitive sorts. They take it personally when you express manifest disinterest in their lecture, course, subject, discipline, or person. Care and feeding of your professors is important. Talk to them. It is amazing how many first-year [students] don't get their money's worth from their professors. Make them work during office hours. Many of them actually like students.

—Fr. Rick Malloy, SJ, University of Scranton

Professors' Pet Peeves

Everyone gets irked by something, and your college professors are no exception. Most hate it when people carry on side conversations; some don't like you to bring food to class. Be on your best behavior. Don't arrive late or leave early (common professor irritants) and *be sure* your cell phone doesn't ring during class. Some professors kick students out for that offense. Remember that in many, if not most, of your classes you are learning about a subject from someone who has dedicated his or her life's work to it. Showing a little respect for that dedication is wise.

Students might think they can browse on their phone and pay attention at the same time, but in truth, it's just not possible to effectively listen and multitask. Everyone also thinks they can check something subtly without a professor noticing. They always notice. I've had professors say they'd prefer students leave the classroom in the event that they really need to use their phone.

—Jenna, Boston College

Classroom Etiquette Tips

- Turn off (or set to silent) any electronic devices such as watch alarms, smartphones, laptop/tablet notifications, etc.
- If you come in late, leave early, or need to leave during the class, do so with minimal disruption. Open the door slowly, and close it slowly behind you. Don't make a lot of noise packing or unpacking your things. If you are coming in late, it's a good idea to take off your coat and open your book bag or knapsack in the hallway.
- Don't start to put away your things until the class is over.
- Don't interrupt when someone else is speaking.
- Good manners will go a long way, but pay special attention during the first few classes. Most professors will tell you right off the bat what makes them crazy so you can avoid an academic faux pas.

Online Survival Guide: Have a quirky professor with some crazy classroom rules? Share your stories online by clicking on "Chapter 15" at http://TheFreshmanSurvival Guide.com/chapters/.

Starting from Scratch

Know that you will have to prove yourself to your professors by showing up, jumping into class discussions, learning the material, and turning in the required work completed to his or her specifications. It won't always be easy, and sometimes it'll be a tremendous effort. But if everybody could do it, they wouldn't award degrees for it.

Dr. Thomas O'Brien of DePaul University says it well: "No matter what your friends tell you, college is hard work, and you owe it to your future self and to your family to focus on your studies for the next four years. If you really need an adventure, then take a year or two off between high school and college. Don't treat college like it is going to be your adventure. It is not designed to be an adventure, and there are penalties for not realizing this. It is designed to be a learning experience, and there are substantial rewards for understanding this."[1]

Prof Points

There are professors who will make you wonder how they ever got the job, but for the most part professors are really interesting people, experts in their fields, and some of your best resources on campus. Here's our checklist for making the most out of this opportunity:

- Utilize office hours to ask questions about papers and exams and to discuss the current subject material.
- Attend events put on by the department and the receptions afterward.
- Invite your prof to dinner or lunch.
- Go to class and participate.

Old-School Strategies

As streamlined and high-tech as much of the college learning experience has become, some studies have shown that there are analog strategies from days gone by that actually have better results in terms of academic success.

Taking Notes

Researchers at Princeton University have found that while laptops are an indispensable tool for the college student, taking handwritten notes in class is actually far more effective in terms of retention of information and synthesizing information. "Our new findings suggest that even when laptops are used as intended—and not for buying things on Amazon during class—they may still be harming academic performance," says psychological scientist Pam Mueller.

In the study, college students watched TED Talks on subjects that weren't common knowledge. The students were either given laptops (disconnected from the Internet) or notebooks, and told to use whatever note-taking strategy they normally used.

Thirty minutes after finishing the test, they had to answer factual-recall questions and conceptual-application questions based on the lecture they had watched. The results showed that:

1. Both types of note takers performed equally well on answering questions that involved facts; laptop note takers, however, performed significantly worse on the conceptual questions.

2. Laptop users' notes contained more words and verbatim overlap with the lecture than the handwritten notes.

3. Overall, students who took *more notes* performed better, but so did those who had *less verbatim overlap*, suggest-

ing that the benefit of simply taking more notes is canceled out by "mindless transcription."

4. One week later, handwritten note takers still beat laptop note takers on recall when both groups were allowed to review their notes before taking the recall test. Again, the amount of verbatim overlap correlated negatively with performance on conceptual items.

5. Even when researchers explicitly instructed the students to avoid taking verbatim notes, they saw similar results. This suggested that when typing, the urge to take verbatim notes is hard to overcome.

"It may be that longhand note takers engage in more processing than laptop note takers," the researchers wrote, "thus selecting more important information to include in their notes, which enables them to study this content more efficiently."[2]

Where You Sit

Researchers in 2007 compiled studies that correlated student performance with where they sit in class. Students sitting front and center (middle) of the classroom tended to achieve higher average exam scores. These findings were consistent even when the instructor chose the seats for students. The study suggests that it isn't simply a function of the notion that motivated students tend to sit in the front and center of the room. Instead, the higher academic performance of students sitting front and center is most likely due to the fact that there are actual learning advantages to sitting front and center, such as:

• Better ability to see the blackboard
• Better ability to hear what the instructor is saying

- Better attention to what is being said, because there are fewer (or no) people between the student and the instructor to distract them
- Making continual eye contact with the instructor—potentially increasing students' sense of personal responsibility to listen to, and take notes on, what their instructor is saying[3]

A College TA Has Her Say

As a teaching assistant who is assigned mostly to first-year students, I am often dismayed by the behavior that greets me the first semester. Here are tips gleaned from watching first-year classrooms carefully:

- **No skating.** If you were able to skate through class in high school, don't expect to do it in college! Professors know shoddy work when they see it. The standards are likely to be *much* higher. Be serious about your work.
- **Proof.** Take your time with your writing; don't write anything ten minutes before class. Finish every assignment at least the night before, so you can proofread it the next morning before turning it in.
- **Draft day.** If possible, give your professor a draft of your paper to look over a week or two before it's due. This is not cheating. It's smart study behavior. She or he will usually give you a lot of feedback that will help your writing, and it may bump you up at least a letter grade just for making the effort. (Not every prof will do this, especially at larger colleges, but many will, and it's worth checking.)
- **Turn off.** For heaven's sake, don't think you can send a text message under your desk and not be noticed. Put that phone away!

- **Front row.** Sit up front. You'll be less likely to space out (or fall asleep!) during long classes.
- **Write it down.** Taking notes communicates that you're paying attention.
- **Do some research.** Google your professors' names before you take their classes! Find out as much as you can about their areas of interest or specialty. You'll often find that you're lucky enough to be taking a class with an expert in the field. For potentially big bonus points, read their articles or books, and use them as reference sources when you have to write a paper.
- **Duh!** Of course everyone already knows this, but don't even think about copy-pasting anything from the Internet. If you can find it, so can your professor, and even the tiniest offense can get you kicked out permanently. Don't risk it.

When you attend a large university it is easy to become just a number. It is really daunting to be in large lecture halls! It's easy to slip away from class, not do your homework, and to give up when you don't understand the subject matter. Do not be afraid to ask your professors for help. In fact, even if you don't need help, it's a good idea to make use of their office hours anyway. Introduce yourself, tell them you wish to strive academically (without sounding pompous, of course!), and say you look forward to their class. This way the professor puts a face to the name. If you need help later in the semester or have an extenuating circumstance, it will be easier to communicate with them. Plus, it will hold you accountable to go to class if you think the professor knows you.

—Rebekah, University of Kansas

THE TAKEAWAY

If the college professor seems like a strange new breed, don't be frightened; millions of students encounter them every year and live to tell the tale. There is no standard behavior among this exotic species, however, so paying close attention to what they expect from you in their class is your safest bet.

CHAPTER 16

The Fastest Way to Get an A

 Survival Strategy #16: At the risk of sounding repetitive, go to class! Get to know your professors, and take advantage of all the resources your college has made available to you.

"Go to class—and take notes. It's the fastest way to an A," says University of Wisconsin professor Dr. Christine Whelan. It's not only about picking up the material; you'll also come to know your professors and their expectations, which makes writing papers and taking tests less of a guessing game. Just showing up and taking notes won't guarantee you a good grade, but it will definitely put you much further down the road to success. Running late? Go anyway. Better to be there for part of a class than miss the entire class. But don't make a habit of it; latecomers are a common professor pet peeve.

In Mississippi State University's student retention program, Pathfinders, students who miss as few as two classes first semester are contacted by program staff. Based on over eight years of research and thousands of college students, the program has found that *two absences* are a red flag for a student starting to have a problem. Whether or not your college has such a focused save-the-student mentality, you can save yourself. Go to class, and if you miss one, take it seriously. Follow up with your professor, get the notes from another student, do the reading.

> *The most difficult thing for me freshman year was waking up in the morning to go to class. [But] I managed to care about the stuff I was being taught. An interest in the subject goes a long way.*
>
> **—Elias, graduate, Fordham University**

By second semester many of the things that seemed like a tremendous effort at the start will become second nature. Starting college is like going to a foreign country: You've heard stories and read about some of the customs, but until you're there it's hard to truly understand the cultural differences. In this strange new land it pays to spend time with the people who know.

Once again, meet your professors and do your best to be sure they know who you are. Ask questions and participate in class, stay after class to talk, and use office hours. You'll have access to information beyond what gets imparted in class. Remember these people are experts in their respective fields and are wells of information. Dr. Whelan offers this insider tip: "The students that came to my office hours learned study tips and received further explanation and instruction from me. But most of the time, no one showed up. Just think of all the students who could have gotten better grades if they'd come by in the time allotted. Being there for class and then taking that extra step to get to know your professors and letting them see your interest can make the difference between a B and an A (or a D and an F) and may earn you a little wiggle room if you need it later on."

SEEK → FIND

First, take only as many classes as you can handle. Second, spend as much time with the professors and TAs as possible. Third, know what the workload is. Sometimes people go into a course they think they will spend ten hours on per week when the course actually demands twenty-five.

—Ven. Tenzin Priyadarshi, Buddhist chaplain, Massachusetts Institute of Technology

The most common mistake freshmen make is partying too much and not going to class. Freshman year [the professors] usually go easier on you than later years, and if you can't make it to class then, you're toast. I have always made an effort to get along with my professors, and it really pays off. I'm not always the most responsible student, but since they know and like me they will often give me a break.

—Vreni, freshman, School of Visual Arts

One of the smartest things I did first semester was get involved in a study group for organic chemistry class (my major is chemistry). It made studying more fun, helped me do well in the class, and helped me make friends with the same major. You'll be more likely to study if there's a group holding you accountable. You'll learn the material better, because studying will consist of more than just reading through your notebook. In some cases, you can split up the work (for example, if you need to know fifty definitions for an exam, each person can look up some of them and share). It gives you another opportunity to get to know people well and make friends.

—Julia, senior, Northwestern University

Year after year, stories of freshmen who didn't make it almost always begin with "I had problem X...and so I stopped going to class." Problem X could be almost anything: too much drinking, exhaustion from being overcommitted, falling behind with the work, depression over a breakup or loss, feeling overwhelmed academically, the beginnings of a mental health issue. Whatever the problem, it's always followed by "And so I stopped going to class." It doesn't necessarily happen all at once, but three or four absences over eight weeks is often enough to fail one class. Once a student has stopped feeling successful, he or she usually misses more. Because outside accountability doesn't come into play until after the semester is over, you can feel tempted to just slink along (or party along, as the case may be) in denial of the inevitable disaster. But so many people are hoping for your success! Let the knowledge of their love and support push you along on the days you don't feel like pushing yourself. Even if you don't have that support, you owe it to yourself to take action if you're running into trouble. You are the person who will benefit the most if you make the effort.

If you have missed a class (or multiple classes), how can you get back on track? Dr. Albert Matheny, head of academic advisement for the University of Florida, gives this advice: "Early intervention is the key. If they come in to see us already failing, we don't have much to work with. But if they come in early enough, we can get them to meet with each of their instructors to get a firm estimate of their academic chances." Course-specific tutoring and academic advisement can mean the difference between a bad semester and flunking out. Seek out help as soon as you start to struggle. It's a little like quicksand: The further in you get, the harder it is to get out.

I was too embarrassed to admit that college wasn't as wonderful as I thought it would be and that I was struggling, so I just shut myself up and never sought help my first year. There is always someone out there—family, friends, or school counselors—who can help you. You have to take the first step and reach out. I got help from my professor when I was struggling in math class. Even better, I was talking to other students in the class. They gave me some good tips that brought my grade up to an A. I learned that I didn't have to do everything all alone.

—**Emily, junior, Tulane University**

From a Professor's Perspective

Four more reasons to go to class:

1. Lots of professors expect that at least some of the learning will come in dialogue and discussion. Missing class means missing out on valuable learning opportunities, even if the professor is not lecturing.
2. Many professors keep attendance and base the participation grade entirely, or partly, on that data.
3. Missing class regularly can demonstrate a lack of interest in or curiosity about what is being taught. (Not exactly the message you want to send if a good or an excellent grade is your goal.)
4. Missing class is a waste of money. Do the math. You may be shocked to discover how much money you are throwing away every time you blow off class.

Finals!—The Interactive RA

Finals will always be the hardest time of the semester for students, because you have term papers to write, tests to study for, projects to create, speeches to memorize, PowerPoints to recite—the list is seemingly never ending.

There are no ways to make preparing for finals magically easier. A lot of hard work and commitment is required in order to pull out a good grade. But here are a few ideas from personal experience that may help you cut a few corners here and there and make the finals process a little bit less stressful.

Eat right, sleep well, and take breaks. Simple as that. Eating right gives you proper nutrients and brainpower to focus on studying those exam questions. Sleeping well makes you a lot less stressed and helps you maintain a proper schedule. Taking breaks gives your brain some leisure—because, believe it or not, cramming for nine-plus hours with no breaks overnight, with no sleep, eating nothing but fast food isn't healthy.

Whatever you do, *don't* miss the review session. Interestingly, many people seem to think "review session" is synonymous with "Wow! No class, I learned all this already!" I think the exact opposite. I hear "review session" and think *Wow! A window into what the final is going to look like!* And I am right about 99 percent of the time.

Pay attention to how professors structure their classes. If all the past tests have been multiple-choice, more than likely so will the final. So prepare accordingly. If the tests or midterm have always had two essay questions at the end, more than likely so will the final. Time to put that essay thinking cap on! Also, listen when the professor or TA says something along the lines of "This might be a good essay question on the final." That is, generally, a pretty good indicator to what the essay question on the final is going to look like. Personally, I always highlight a giant neon star next to those notes.

During finals, *breathe*. Before I start any final, verbal or written, I remember to take a giant deep breath and calm down for ten seconds before actually starting. If giving a speech, those ten seconds give you enough time to feel a bit more comfortable in front of the audience so you don't become a babbling mess due to your nerves. Same goes with a test. Take a breather before beginning and then dive in. Starting off calmly actually helps your mental state.

—Josh Martin, iRA
Director of Residence Life, Culinary
Institute of America at Greystone

Online Survival Guide: *Have a question or need some extra ideas? Go to "Interactive RA" at http://TheFreshman SurvivalGuide.com and click on "Ask."*

THE TAKEAWAY

Go to class. This is your life. If things are going wrong, take action and take it early!

CHAPTER 17

Online Is Forever

 Survival Strategy #17: The ongoing explosion in communications and social networking technology has helped connect people in profound new ways. But, like power tools, communication devices need to be handled intelligently and carefully.

One of the biggest challenges during your first year in college is making sense of the new world you've entered. You may feel like a foreigner in terms of the social, academic, and institutional cultures you're encountering, but in one key area you'll probably feel more at home than many of the professors and administrators you come across. Students starting college now are *digital natives* who grew up in a world where digital technologies already existed and were in common use. As a result, you adapt very easily to technological changes. You're far more adept at using this technology than *digital immigrants* like your parents and some of the older faculty and staff on campus, because it's always been a part of your life.

The immense potential for connectivity has transformed the way people learn, share, and process information in college. Keep in mind that there is also a shadow side to all this connectivity. Privacy issues, addiction issues, and potential long-term consequences in terms of jobs, internships, and grad schools make the social networking universe a place you'll want to approach with some intelligence and caution.

Even though you might be more tech savvy than your elders, they still have a lot more experience in the offline—"real"—world than you. Their judgment in terms of what's appropriate and what could have bigger repercussions down the road is worth paying attention to.

The Digital Upside

The revolution in digital technology over the past twenty years has allowed students to engage with their academic material in much deeper ways than was ever thought possible. For starters, though the debate regarding Wikipedia continues to take place on campuses, there is some evidence that it may not be as unreliable as many people originally made it out to be. The British journal *Nature* found that Wikipedia is about as accurate on science as the *Encyclopaedia Britannica*.[1]

Early on, Wikipedia gained a reputation among academics as the work of amateurs who created entries that contained erroneous information at times. Since then, Wikipedia has tried to repair their reputation by including better safeguards and reaching out to a lot of colleges. According to a 2014 *Los Angeles Times* article, "Once the bane of teachers, Wikipedia and entry-writing exercises are becoming more common on college campuses as academia and the online site drop mutual suspicions and seek to cooperate." The piece goes on to note that in 2014 students were given assignments to create or expand Wikipedia entries in at least 150 courses at colleges in the United States and

Canada. The list of schools includes the University of California, Berkeley; the University of California, San Francisco's medical school; Boston College; and Carnegie Mellon University.

Wikipedia has also created an educational outreach that includes "Wikipedia Ambassadors" who advise educators and student editors and ensure that class assignments for creating content adhere to the site's technical demands. According to UC Berkeley's Kevin Gorman, the nation's first "Wikipedian in Residence" at an undergraduate institution, Wikipedia "has essentially become too large to ignore."[2]

All that being said, you still need to be very careful. We don't recommend using Wikipedia as a reference material in a paper. Use it to familiarize yourself with upcoming material or prompt further exploration in a given subject. For example, if there is a section in a coming class on a poet you are not familiar with, go to Wikipedia for a brief biography and examples of some of the poet's work. You may also want to explore links to other potentially credible sources about the subject. This only helps to enhance in-class discussion and participation. Many colleges have policies/suggestions regarding the use of Wikipedia. If your school doesn't have a clear policy, your professor will…make sure you know what that policy is.

The benefits of technology also extend to various forms of online communication. Classes no longer meet just for the hour that students and professors are together in a physical space—they can be carried beyond the walls of a building. Although nothing beats a fiery debate in the midst of class, e-mail and course blogs can help bring this debate into an ongoing forum. Students can e-mail or post concise and well-thought-out responses to a topic whenever they want. They can now engage even beyond the semester. Professors can e-mail updates in a given field to students they may have taught a few semesters prior, reinforcing the connections learned in years past. They can also highlight a specific passage in a text via e-mail the night before a reading is due to clarify or further elucidate a specific point.

Finally, modern technology can help you find a fruitful internship or even a lifelong career. Applications can be sent out across the country to a job that fits your interests. Consequently you could find yourself spending a semester on a boat at sea, or on a tropical island one summer doing research. If you use modern technology in a mindful and positive way, the possibilities for healthy growth are endless.

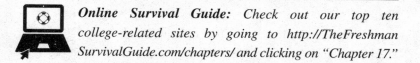

Online Survival Guide: Check out our top ten college-related sites by going to *http://TheFreshman SurvivalGuide.com/chapters/* and clicking on *"Chapter 17."*

The Digital Downside

If instant access to professors, classmates, and incredible scholarship are the benefits of being a college student in the digital age, issues of privacy, isolation, and unintended consequences are the liabilities. The information and tips offered here will help keep you aware and on track.

Privacy

There are people who love drama and think their lives are a reality show. If you give them the ammo (and sometimes even if you don't) they can turn your life into one, too. Getting mixed up with these folks adds an ugly new layer to the term *web*. Be careful what you say online. A rant about a professor or someone you just met, whether on Facebook, Twitter, or even over e-mail, can suddenly be copied and posted or forwarded to more people than you can count. What was a private conversation can suddenly become campus news.

Now that almost everyone carries around a camera with them—in the form of a phone—pay attention to who you're with and what they're doing, especially on Friday and Saturday nights. If someone whips out her cell or camera when you're in a compromising position, turn your back, cover your face, step outside, or leave the party. Let friends know that you think photographing drunken escapades is stupid and creepy. And don't do it yourself—even stupider is participating in drunken escapades.

Sexting

Do we really need to tell you that taking sexually suggestive or explicit pictures is a bad idea? We do? Okay, consider yourself told. A study by the National Campaign to Prevent Teen and Unplanned Pregnancy, a Washington-based advocacy group, found that 20 percent of teens had sent or posted nude or seminude photos of themselves electronically.[3] A more recent study of college freshmen from the *International Journal of Cyber Criminology* (2014) put the number at closer to 30 percent. *Sexting*—broadly defined as "the sending and/or receiving of sexually suggestive images or messages to peers through a cell phone"[4]—can have serious legal repercussions, not to mention potentially damaging social, emotional, psychological, and spiritual effects. The guy or girl you're with now may turn out to be a jerk who turns your shared intimacy into posters to hang around the dorm. You have *no control* over where those pictures will end up. Google *sexting* and you'll discover some real-life horror stories.

Take some time to read over your Facebook profile or personal website. Does it accurately reflect the person you are now? If you're not happy with it, take it down, change it, or protect it. It's not about being paranoid, just about keeping yourself emotionally safe and having the choice to reveal only the things *you* choose to reveal to all these new people in your life.

Does your profile accurately reflect who you want to be? Often you will now be Facebook friends with people at college before you meet them, and certainly before you get to know them well, so make sure that the person you're presenting yourself as on Facebook is really the way you want people to think of you freshman year.

The Post That Keeps On Giving–The Interactive RA
Facebook, Twitter, Instagram, and so much more

Take a second and Google your name. What did you find? Pictures, links to your Facebook, a full history? In today's technological age you have to be careful with the brand you create for yourself. The Internet has made it extremely easy to market yourself, but it has also made it harder to hide minor indiscretions from your youth.

If you can see it, others can see it, too. Believe it or not, employers (internships, volunteer opportunities, and more) take time to research social media websites to make sure the person that you represent is the person you are actually representing. Pictures containing alcohol, drugs, or sexual innuendos will not be favored by companies or organizations offering you an opportunity. Poor displays of judgment are the easiest way to eliminate yourself from the competition.

Social media websites encourage users to express who they are, voice their opinions, and share the details of their daily life.

As a savvy user you have to determine how you will represent the real you without compromising who you are or jeopardizing your future. Select pictures that are tasteful yet show who you are, what you like, and how you express yourself. Write posts that allow you to provoke thought, but do not allow [thoughts that will lead others] to question your integrity or your character.

Social media websites are fun, but they are also a platform for your future. Use the sites responsibly, and remember you never know who could be watching you. Use them wisely and know the power they could hold.

—Danielle Shipp, iRA
Community Manager, Greystar Student Living Communities

Addiction, Isolation, Depression

One of the great paradoxes of the digital age is that you can instantly be connected to billions of people on the planet from the privacy of your tiny dorm room. You can *friend* other people, get *tagged*, and join groups and communities without ever physically interacting with another human being. All of this has made college students particularly vulnerable to the threats of addiction, isolation, and depression.

Though it is one of the most powerful communications tools ever invented, research has shown, ironically, that the Internet can actually decrease a person's sense of social well-being.[5]

Excessive Internet use seems to be an increasing problem, depriving people of true relationships and interaction with others. A 2006 Stanford University study found that one out of eight Americans suffers from Internet addiction. A 2014 study found that 16 percent of eighteen- to twenty-five-year-olds are involved in compulsive behavior regarding Internet use (almost all of the 16 percent admitted to spending over fifteen hours a day online).[6]

The survey looked at five signs of possible net addiction:

- Spending hours online
- Becoming irritable when interrupted during web use
- Feeling guilty about how much time is spent online
- Isolation from family and friends due to excessive online activity
- A sense of euphoria when online and panic when offline

Another study published in *CyberPsychology and Behavior* found that people who suffered from loneliness or lacked good social skills could develop "strong compulsive Internet use behaviors" that actually made their problems worse and negatively affected other significant activities such as work, school, or significant relationships. The study also found that problem Internet usage is associated with more frequent interpersonal and academic conflicts as well as some physical/health-related issues.[7]

"Science has already established that early or excessive use of screens and digital devices affects us neurologically, some people more than others." says Dr. Catherine Steiner-Adair, a clinical psychologist. "It's different for everyone, and you need to understand your own wiring. Beneath it all is the deeper damage that tech and Internet dependence can cause. Excessive use can become a source of chronic tension, compromised physical health, emotional distress, decreased performance at work and school, and an obstacle to emotional intimacy."

Do you have a problem with an online addiction? Take our quiz to see where you stand. If you find yourself having problems, go to chapter 22 for helpful resources that are readily available on campus.

Are You an Internet Addict?

1. Do you feel preoccupied with the Internet (think about your previous online activity or anticipate your next online session)?
2. Do you feel the need to use the Internet in increasing amounts of time in order to achieve satisfaction?
3. Have you repeatedly made unsuccessful efforts to control, cut back, or stop Internet use?
4. Do you feel restless, moody, depressed, or irritable when attempting to cut down or stop Internet use?
5. Do you stay online longer than originally intended?
6. Have you risked the loss of a significant relationship, job, or educational or career opportunity because of the Internet?
7. Have you lied to family members, a therapist, or others to conceal the extent of involvement with the Internet?
8. Do you use the Internet as a way of escaping from problems or of relieving a dysphoric mood (e.g., feelings of helplessness, guilt, anxiety, depression)?[8]

If you answered yes to five or more questions (over a six-month period and when not better accounted for by a manic episode), you may suffer from Internet addiction. The first step toward getting this problem under control is to try using time-management techniques that moderate how often you are online. If you find yourself loitering on Facebook for countless hours every day, set yourself the goal of reducing it to thirty minutes total per day. Then consciously begin weaning yourself down in ten-minute increments daily until you've hit your target.

If there are a host of sites that you are compulsively visiting, you may want to try cutting off your visits to one of those sites each week and limiting your time on the other pages each day until you've gotten things under control. If there are subscription sites you belong to, you may need to seriously consider dropping your subscription or at the very least not renewing it.

There's an App for That?

Students are now using apps like SelfControl for Mac and Freedom for PCs that allow them to set a timer to block their own access to anything on the Internet, especially distracting websites or social media. Once the timer has been set, there is nothing the user can do (except restart their device or delete the app) to escape the blocked access. Students struggling to focus are finding these apps and others like them are very effective for reducing their use of Facebook/Twitter/Instagram while trying to get work done.

If the problem seems more severe and none of the above strategies seem to be helping, you may need to get in contact with a counselor on campus who can help you (see chapter 22 for helpful people on campus).

I wish I was more of my own person. My freshman year I tried to be the person that everyone liked and, for the most part, it worked. I had accumulated five hundred Facebook friends in one year. The problem was they were just Facebook friends. I didn't have any real connections because I knew so many people superficially. The deep connections are the ones that count. I was so envious of the people I knew that had a group of three or four really close friends. Don't sacrifice quality for quantity. Take time and build friendships.

—Rebecca, Saint Louis University

Online Survival Guide: *For more online cautionary tales from college students go to http://TheFreshmanSurvival Guide.com/chapters/ and click on "Chapter 17."*

Unintended Consequences (Online Really Is Forever)

Here's the dichotomy of the Internet: What feels like a private note to friends or a living-room conversation is actually a billboard. Just because nobody has driven past that billboard yet makes it all seem private until very suddenly it's not.

SEEK → FIND

As both a priest and a computer scientist, it has been fascinating to witness the development and use of social-networking technologies like Facebook and Twitter. They help facilitate a hunger young adults have for community and relationships. These technologies provide an easy means to initiate and maintain relationships across distance, time, and breadth. They counter that great fear of loneliness. However, on the flip side, they can stunt our ability to relate with others to develop intimacy and real, mature connections. Living in a false virtual intimacy through the Internet, people may work less at physical and deeper encounters, resulting in a new unsettling loneliness and depression. Given the importance of our bodies in defining our being and sharing of our being, nothing replaces the dynamics of face-to-face interactions.

—Fr. Ivan Tou, CSP, Catholic Center,
University of California, Los Angeles

"It's not illegal for a company to Google a prospective employee, and it's not illegal for them to look you up on Facebook, LinkedIn, or anywhere else online," cautions human resources expert Kimberley Mauldin. "Keep in mind that everything with your name on it or linked to you on the Internet is in the public domain. If you have a LiveJournal or other blog linked to one of your social media accounts, anyone can make the connection. Even if you casually mention that you post on a certain message board, it takes no more than a few minutes of idle clicking to connect the dots to your other profile."

Any kind of online speech—blog posts, wall posts, comments, shared jokes—that are sexist, racist, antigay, or in other ways discriminatory or inflammatory make you considerably less attractive to a prospective employer. Even the groups you join on Facebook can say a lot more about you than you realize. It might be a joke around the dorm to join satirical sites, but an employer—either in the future or one who hires you for a part-time job while you're in college—who checks online activity may not find it so funny.

You can't completely rely on privacy settings to protect you from unexpected eyes. Profile settings are helpful in providing a measure of privacy, but they are not an ironclad system. Obviously a better mentality than "Don't get caught" is "Don't do anything that could destroy your reputation."

Online Survival Guide: *Read a companion article, "When It's Online, It's There Forever," by visiting http://The FreshmanSurvivalGuide.com/chapters/ and clicking on "Chapter 17."*

The new summer internship Jim landed sounded like a huge opportunity. The work he would be doing was relevant to his major in college and would look great on his résumé. But Jim's great opportunity turned into a big setback requiring embarrassing explanations to his parents. He lost his internship when his new employer found online pictures of him stumbling drunk—pictures he'd posted himself. He ended up back at the same restaurant job he'd done for years.

Another student, Susan, was a bit smarter. She "scrubbed" her online presence when she was hired for a high-security job, taking down all but the most basic information.

7 Steps to Scrub Your Online Info

1. Delete any photos that show you falling down, drunk, holding alcohol, drugs, or drug paraphernalia. Delete anything you wouldn't want your grandma to see.

2. If you are tagged in a photo by a friend and it contains any of the above, ask your friend to remove the photo. Untag yourself in the meantime.

3. Set up privacy filters. Each social-networking site should have guidelines on how to do it. Many also have privacy levels so only certain people can see certain things. Take advantage of these filters, and set your profile so that people you don't know can't browse your page without making a friend request.

4. Do not post negative things about your current workplace— especially if you identify yourself as an employee.

5. If you have more than one social-networking site, do not post links to the other ones. Don't make it easy for people

to look you up! Never post links to any kind of inappropriate website.

6. Keep it clean. If it's online, it's there forever.

7. Finally, Google yourself. Try variations on your name. If
something comes up that doesn't seem right, contact the
website and get it removed. If you have a common name,
put in your full name and the cities/schools/groups you're
associated with. If you're looking to go into a government
job, Google your family and closest friends. All of them
will be checked if you need security clearance.

Online Survival Guide: *Ask our online resident assistants
your questions about college life by visiting "Interactive
RA" at http://TheFreshmanSurvivalGuide.com and clicking on "Ask."*

The Savvy Social Networker

Don't Be a Stalker

Texting plus Facebooking plus tweeting people constantly might
just equal stalking or is at least really annoying. Let one form of
communication suffice. In an emergency you could Facebook *and*
text, but don't leave your new friends feeling smothered or nagged.

Keep Your Secrets

For a while anyway, keep private your biggest regrets, most
embarrassing moments, and traumatic events from your past. No
one is entitled to know them, and there are people who use information as power. People can tell *your* secrets to gain allegiances.
Protect what's already online and don't make blog posts about
things that should stay private.

Be Yourself–All the Time

There's nothing a snake loves more than catching someone in a compromising position and then telling half the campus about it. How many teen movies do we have to see before we believe it?

But You Don't Have to Reveal All

You may look really hot in a bathing suit, but set your privacy settings so that no Facebook creeps can download and make that shot his or her wallpaper.

Get a Job

Based on your Internet photos, comments, and current group listings, would you hire yourself to intern for your company, do the accounting for your business, teach your kids, or run for office? Keep your future in mind as you're posting.

Online Survival Guide: Visit us at https://www.facebook .com/FreshmanSurvivalGuide.

THE TAKEAWAY

As a digital native you're well acquainted with how to connect online. It's an incredible tool, but be smart about what you post and keep in mind that, for all the connections you can make digitally, nothing can ever replace the relationships and communities you develop in person offline.

CHAPTER 18

Get Involved...but Not Too Involved

 Survival Strategy #18: Service, clubs, activities, and Greek life can be really important parts of the college experience. Just remember to keep your priorities straight and find a good balance.

Building a new network of activities and relationships is a big job. As a new college student you've got a lot of choices to make, and one of the biggest is how you'll spend your time and energy. College is, of course, first and foremost about academics. But it is also about becoming the person you want to be. You may be at your number one–desired school, with the best program and faculty, but campus activities can help you build a life.

Maybe you're concerned about how much time your academic work will take up—if you are, good! Keep paying attention to that. You *will* need a break from classes and studying, though, and all the people you hung out with and things you used to do are suddenly not there. It's unlikely that schoolwork alone will fill that void; college can be an opportunity to try things you never would have tried at home and meet an entirely different group of people.

I have heard a lot of freshmen say they are worried about getting involved in extracurricular activities because they aren't sure how much time they are going to need to spend on schoolwork. While schoolwork should come first, get involved as soon as possible. Everyone needs a break from work sometimes—people to talk to when things get tough, and people to laugh with.

—Lindsey, senior, Youngstown State University

Free Time and What to Do with It

What did your schedule look like at home? If you were a busy kid, sports, dance, theater, clubs, church, volunteering, or work probably filled in the gaps. Parents and friends and all those commitments, activities, and responsibilities were there to lay claim to your free time, take over your life, and keep you active and out of trouble. It may seem as if you would have *less* free time in college because the academic demands placed on you will be greater, but because you're suddenly without all those elements that used to be part of your routine, you may find you've actually got more time on your hands, and definitely more choices to make about how you'll spend it.

Getting involved through campus-sponsored clubs and activities is the best way to make your college experience a home away from home. Enjoying an activity that is a common interest is a great way of meeting new friends and sharing experiences with others. Retreats and club or intramural sports will change the perspective of any hesitant or uneasy college freshman.

—Brian, junior, University of Scranton

Choosing Wisely

The most wonderful, and sometimes most daunting, part of college is the fact that you can get involved with anything you choose, and more and more colleges are making it easy by providing a vast and ever-growing variety of clubs and organizations you can join. From the Quidditch Club (no, we're not kidding) and the Anime Society to the juggling club, food club, knitting club, and beyond, there is a club for everything and anything on campus. This makes the activities fair a hectic mess sometimes, but it also means that you really do have the opportunity to explore almost anything while you're in college. Take the opportunity to do so. Often if a club doesn't exist, you can create your own (although that probably is not something that needs to be on your agenda the first semester of college).

If you missed the boat on the activities fair, you can look online for student activities; though not every group will have a great online presence, there should at least be contact info. Ask upperclassmen and your RA what they are involved in, what's worth spending your time on, and where the action is. Try to choose at least one familiar thing—especially if you're a little lonely or intimidated—and choose one thing you've never done before. You've already been through high school; no need to play it safe or worry about being judged here. Take a chance and try something new.

Take advantage of the opportunity to make a new name for yourself. College is a new beginning, and most people don't know who you were in high school, so take every opportunity to be the person you've always wanted to be. Get involved in anything you find interesting, and if it turns out you don't like it, then don't do it. But try new things all the time. I was able to discover myself as a whole person and really feel comfortable about who I am.

—Kyle, sophomore, Loyola Marymount University

On a big campus, getting involved in clubs and activities related to your major can connect you with a group of familiar faces and deepen relationships that will become increasingly important over the next few years. Look for smaller clubs and activities that help "shrink" the campus and make it less overwhelming. On a smaller campus (or in a smaller department), you may want to choose activities that are entirely apart from your major so that you're meeting different kinds of people. At a small school, look for activities that will stretch you beyond the campus boundaries into volunteer opportunities such as tutoring or Habitat for Humanity.

Double Bonding

Keep an eye out for groups that have faculty involved—your advisor's pet project or the big fund-raiser on campus—to pump up your campus connections and build mentoring relationships that can sustain you when the going gets tough. Give special consideration to service groups. Whether the groups serve in the local community or travel to needy areas, you'll find yourself working side by side with other students, often in environments outside your usual haunts. The challenge helps form strong relationships based on common experience plus the sense of accomplishment that comes from serving together.

Online Survival Guide: *Visit http://TheFreshmanSurvival Guide.com/chapters/ (click on "Chapter 18") to share your most rewarding extracurricular experiences.*

Setting Limits

Campus activities and clubs will make school feel less strange and offer opportunities to build relationships, but don't try to do everything. "Sometimes I see freshmen who sign up for everything under the sun," says Dave Nantais, campus minister at the University of Michigan, "and by mid-October they're already burned out from being too involved." Keep in mind, the more things you try to do, the less of each one you get to do. Go ahead and sign up; get information on as many clubs, events, and activities that look good to you. Then start choosing. Remember you've got four years (maybe more) to sample everything, so relax and enjoy a few activities, get to know the other students involved in them, and don't try to be a superhero—at least not this semester.

Becoming Well-Rounded–The Interactive RA

As a student you want to aim to have a reasonably balanced college experience. Too much emphasis on academics may not let you give enough attention to developing social skills, and too much emphasis on extracurricular activities may not let you give necessary attention to academic demands.

There are hundreds of clubs and organizations to pique your interest in what extracurricular activities have to offer. Honor societies, fraternities, sororities, special interest clubs, and academic clubs are all options that will be available to you. Each club or organization offers different benefits for membership, but all require that you get out and network with other students. Networking will be an important part of your extracurricular life on campus, and this is how you will learn of activities and events happening on campus.

Whatever the case may be, there should be a club that sparks your interest. Anime, dance, community service, racquetball, and more are all available on campus through the Student Activities office. If you have a special interest and the club does not exist on your campus, there is a relatively simple process of starting your own club on campus.

It is also a chance for you to gain interest in things in which you may not have previously had an interest. Your campus will offer a variety programs and activities. You should challenge yourself to attend at least one program in each category per year, or at least one each before you graduate. Enjoy the talented peers you have in your class; you never know what will become of them and how your paths may cross in the future.

There will be plethora of things to choose from: plays, symposiums, concerts, parties, lectures, athletic events, novelties, comedians, musicals, dance recitals, art gallery showings—the list goes on and on. Even if you are not extremely intellectual, not the artsy type, or do not understand football, still try to attend an event at least once. This is the time for meeting new people and gaining exposure to unknown territory for free or relatively cheaply. Students gain admission into many university-sponsored events for free, at a special rate, or at a discount.

Another way to get involved on campus is to talk with your RA. Your RA can assist you with getting involved in the hall and residence hall complex. The residence halls offer a variety of programming and leadership opportunities. The residence halls sometimes offer hall councils and a hall government; a place where you can program and make changes within the halls. Residents that become involved in the halls often lead to employment in the hall as an RA or front desk worker.

When graduation comes and it is time to look for job opportunities, employers look at candidates that can bring a well-rounded college experience to the table. Being well-rounded means you have successfully completed the requirements of your major, you have successfully worked with others, and you have successfully participated or planned activities outside of the classroom. Employers look for a nice balance between classroom and nonclassroom experiences. To join or not join is the challenge as the new student.

—Danielle Shipp, iRA
Community Manager, Greystar Student Living Communities

Online Survival Guide: How many hours do you really use in a day? Find out by visiting "Chapter 18" at http:// TheFreshmanSurvivalGuide.com/chapters/.

5 Signs That You're Doing Too Much

1. You wake up in the middle of the night wondering what you forgot.
2. You don't have time to sleep anymore.
3. There's no one left on campus that you're not on a committee with.
4. You haven't seen your roommate in two weeks.
5. Your friends make you a T-shirt that says, I CAN'T, I HAVE A MEETING.

Get involved in something besides academics. It will keep you sane. There are many valuable skills to be learned being involved in organizations, and the leadership roles they provide will set you apart from everyone else.

—Patrick, Rensselaer Polytechnic Institute

3 Thoughts to Ease Your Conscience When You Have to Drop an Activity

1. If an event crashes and burns because you weren't there to support it, that's a sign that the rest of the group needs to carry their weight. But if your semester crashes and burns—well, no one else will have to pay the price the way you will.

2. Are you resenting a certain meeting a little more each time you go? That's probably the activity to drop. Your extracurriculars have to pass a pretty rigorous test to stay in your schedule—they should be fun, they should energize you, and they should be something you look forward to.

3. Overcommitment is really common among freshmen. Cut yourself a little slack and admit to being human. It doesn't make sense to have a meltdown over voluntary activities when the required ones will probably be pretty challenging to begin with.

Online Survival Guide: Need help saying no? Visit "Chapter 18" at http://TheFreshmanSurvivalGuide.com/ chapters/.

Greek Life

Friendship, leadership, service, support: These aren't words that fit the stereotypes of fraternity and sorority life as it's depicted in *Neighbors* and *The House Bunny*. But many students find Greek life an important part of college that helps them academically and socially. A lot has changed in Greek regulations since the time of *Animal House*, and although there are probably still some Delta Tau Chis out there, Greek organizations have done a lot to make their organizations safer for their members and pledges, as well as more dedicated to the foundational ideals of their organizations (which usually have more to do with fraternity, scholarship, and philanthropy than drinking and parties).

Like any other activity, getting to know a new group of people can be a tremendous benefit, and becoming part of a Greek community magnifies that by getting you hooked into the entire Greek life network on campus, and often a nationwide fraternal organization. Add in the opportunities for leadership and service as well as the mentoring systems many Greek organizations have, with upperclassmen looking out for freshmen, and it's a pretty convincing argument to consider pledging.

> *Get involved! Do as much as you can, but more important try to find something you love, something you are passionate about, and go for it. That includes Greek life. Don't be afraid—give it a shot. I found a service opportunity and fraternity that I love, and they made all the difference over the past four years.*
>
> **—Andrew, senior, Saint Joseph's University**

Are there wild fraternities on some campuses? Sure. Are some sororities drama-filled estrogen dens? Frighteningly, yes. But that doesn't mean you have to join those houses. Ask around and see what others say about the different chapters. Or better yet, find out for yourself. Rush (the process of mutual discernment when you decide where you'd like to go, and the fraternity or sorority decides whether you're a good fit for their organization) can be a hectic and emotion-filled time for both sides. Taking time to get to know members of the different organizations and seeing if you get along with them beforehand (preferably in a nonparty setting) is a good idea. Stereotypes are just that, so just because one of your floor mates thinks Delta Such and Such members are all nerds or Alpha Chi Whatever is the *only* house to join doesn't make it true; you need to determine this for yourself. As with any other campus groups, you need to decide whether a particular sorority or fraternity matches up with who you want to be and how you want to spend your time.

> *Many of the problems that can come from college, such as classes, professors, and dating, can be a lot easier when you have a group of friends who can support you. I can safely say that had I not joined my fraternity, I would have transferred schools or even dropped out. My fraternity has given me a chance to become a leader in our house and out of our house.*
>
> **—Jesse, junior, Rensselaer Polytechnic Institute**

A Greek Life Glossary

Rush: Also known as *recruitment*, rush includes events and activities designed for members and potential members to learn about each other and the organization. There is formal rush, which is a more organized, structured set of activities where you are divided into groups and helped by a rush counselor to explore all the fraternities or sororities on campus. And there is informal rush, which has no formal schedules and is driven by your choice. You pick which houses you feel like rushing and go to their parties and other fun events. Different campuses do rush at different times depending on their Greek life office. On most campuses, rush, both formal and informal, has been declared "dry" to avoid the problems with underage drinking that had become part of the bad reputation surrounding Greek life.

Rush Infraction: Since fraternities and sororities had developed a bad reputation for "dirty rushing" (drinking with freshmen or other off-limits rushing strategies), the North-American Interfraternity Council and the National Panhellenic Conference (the organizations that internationally govern Greek life) have set up a number of rules that fraternities and sororities have to abide by during rush. Depending on the campus, these rules can be pretty strict, so often Greek members are hesitant to talk to rushees outside of rush-sponsored events. They fear they will get their house a *rush infraction*, indicating they've broken one of the rules, which can put sanctions on the organization and hurt them during the process of recruitment.

Pref Parties: After the first few parties of formal rush, and often even informal rush, there are invite-only parties where the small group of people being considered for bids are invited back to get to know the organization better. After a pref party during formal recruitment, rushees are asked to fill out *pref cards* that rank their preferences of the houses they've been invited back to.

Bid: This is an invitation, given at the end of a rush period, to join a fraternity or sorority. Most organizations have a limited number of bids they can hand out during each rush process. Unfortunately this means not everyone the organization wants, and not everyone who wants into an organization, will necessarily get a bid.

New Member (aka Pledge): After a student receives and a fraternity/sorority accepts a bid, the pledge process begins. During this time you learn about the history and rituals of the chapter you've chosen and get ready for initiation, when you become a full member of the organization.

Tips for Going Greek

- Even if you are sure you want to be in a certain house, you may not get a bid from its members. That doesn't mean they don't like you; it just means that you may not be the right fit for that organization. Or they may really like you but just don't have enough bids to offer you one. That doesn't mean you can't still be friends with the members (in fact, you should definitely maintain friendships), and that doesn't mean your Greek life career is over. Often people don't get into their dream house and get a bid from another chapter, and it ends up being the perfect fit for them.

- Rush is a hectic time for both the rushees and the Greek organizations. Especially during formal rush, there are lots of rules in place about when and how current members of Greek organizations can talk to you. Don't think you're being snubbed if someone leaves the room at a party when you walk in or says he or she can't come meet you at your dorm. There are lots of ways rush infractions can get current members into trouble, so don't take it personally.

- You don't have to join where your friends are joining. You can, and should, still be friends with someone no matter what organization she joins. So follow your own gut when it comes to narrowing down which houses you may want to pledge. The great thing about going Greek is expanding your circle of friends, not limiting it, so if you find a chapter you seem to fit, even if you don't know many people involved in that organization, don't count it out.

The Pros and Cons of Going Greek–The Interactive RA

I took an informal survey on campus about going Greek. Hopefully these stories will help you see if it is right for you.

"I went Greek during the spring of my freshman year and since then, there have been a lot of pros and cons. Pros: I've met so many people when I joined my fraternity and I just keep meeting more and more. Being in a fraternity also gives you a connection with tons of other people from around the country in other colleges, active members and alumni (obviously this depends on if the fraternity is national). Greek life also introduced me to other things on campus such as community service, Greek events, and even parties. The cons? Pledging... I hated it. Also, there is a lot of stupid drama in Greek life that I hate. Finally, dues are way too expensive and you have to pay them every semester."

"I never thought of myself as a sorority girl, but seeing the amazing women of my sorority changed my mind. I decided it was a right fit for me. It had a lot to do with fate and just plain luck. I am so glad I went Greek."

"A friend dragged me to meet the Greeks freshman year. I didn't have any reason as to why I was against it; I just thought Greek life wasn't for me. But when I met the women of my sorority, I felt so comfortable around them. Now, I'm proud to call them my sisters. Going Greek was probably the best decision I've made at college."

"I debated going Greek for a while in my first years at school. I know my friends all enjoy their experiences but going Greek just didn't seem to fit my already busy lifestyle. While it would have looked great on my résumé and have been the 'icing on the cake,' I realized I did just as much to make my résumé stand out without being Greek, than some students do by being Greek. My decision was right for me."

—Megan Stamer, iRA
Ramapo College of New Jersey

 Online Survival Guide: Ask our online resident assistants about college life by visiting "Interactive RA" at http:// TheFreshmanSurvivalGuide.com and clicking on "Ask."

THE TAKEAWAY

In one sense you're fresh meat for every organization on campus. They need membership, and you're energetic and idealistic—just what they like. But they're also what you need in terms of relationships, connection, and recreation. You're the only one who will be able to decide if your time is being spent wisely or not.

"Growing Up" Your Religion

Survival Strategy #19: Don't settle for what you learned as a kid. Explore the riches of your own tradition and broaden your horizons to find out about others' as well. If religious practice was part of your childhood experience, it may remain in your mind a childish thing. Move beyond that and "grow up" your faith.

If all the math you ever learned was what you knew in fifth grade, if you finished your history studies at age thirteen, and if you never learned any more science than what you knew before you started high school, you'd be in pretty sorry shape. Just as a middle school knowledge of science, math, history, and so forth would not really hold up in the world, it's not a surprise that college students find the things they learned in Sunday school inadequate to meet the challenges of college life. Dr. Stephen Prothero, chair of the religious studies department at Boston University, points out that while Americans are the most religious people in the developed world, we are also the most religiously ignorant.

Fewer than 50 percent of Americans can identify Genesis as the first book of the Bible, and only half can name even one of the four Gospels.[1] According to the Pew Research Center on Religion and Public Life, atheists and agnostics are among the highest-scoring groups on a survey of religious knowledge. On questions about the core teachings, history and leading figures of major world religions, they outperformed evangelical Protestants, mainline Protestants, and Catholics.[2]

The studies, says Prothero, show there is hardly any difference between the biblical knowledge of younger teens (seventh through ninth graders) compared to that of older teens (tenth through twelfth graders).[3] A study of one thousand high schoolers found that just 36 percent know Ramadan is the Islamic holy month; 17 percent said it was the Jewish Day of Atonement.[4]

"College is a place to learn from professors, but lots of what you learn there is from other students. And you can't engage them intelligently on all sorts of issues (politics included) if you don't know something about your own religion and the religions of others," says Prothero. "Knowing something about your own faith will allow you to answer other students' questions, and to correct their misperceptions. Knowing something about other faiths will allow you to ask intelligent questions of your own."

And college students *do* talk to their friends about faith. A recent UCLA study of college freshmen showed 80 percent are interested in spirituality, 80 percent talk to their friends about it, 79 percent believe in God, and 76 percent are searching for meaning and purpose in life. And 81 percent say they attend religious services.[5] As your faith begins to bump up against the academic rigor of college and collide with the big life questions of early adulthood, knowing more than just the basics will become increasingly important.

What You Think You Know

When asked about Westerners converting to Buddhism, Ven. Bonnie Hazel Shoultz, Buddhist chaplain at Syracuse University, says, "From a Buddhist perspective, His Holiness the Dalai Lama always encourages people to explore the tradition they grew up in. The point is not to give up your spirituality or abandon your religious tradition but to explore it more fully than you were ever able to before."

Of course, there is wisdom in requiring people who want to convert to examine and reconcile their relationship with their original faith tradition first, but it's also worth doing even if you know you want to keep practicing the religion of your childhood as an adult. If that's the case, you need to educate yourself more about it and your experience of it. Simply continuing to go to services and getting out the hymnal at the appropriate time for the rest of your life could very well be the equivalent of *practicing* your religion as an adult with the comprehension/mentality of a child or an adolescent.

You're growing up—your faith needs a chance to grow up, too. This is a great time to reconcile your anger or dissatisfaction with the tradition you were born into. (If you don't think you have any, look a little closer—just about everybody has at least some.) It's also a good opportunity to examine which parts you really value. A lot of people leave church because they "don't get anything out of it." Faith doesn't work that way, though—you've almost always got to put some effort in to get something out of it.

If you've worshipped in the same community all your life you might be surprised—in both a good and a bad way—when you come across different understandings or approaches within your own tradition. You may be tempted to back off;

instead, try moving closer. Get a deeper, more mature look at the faith of your childhood. If your experiences were not great or your participation was inconsistent, college may be one of the best opportunities of your life to explore. The chaplains and religious professors on campus are ready for your questions, expecting them, thrilled to have you ask even.

Imam Yahya Hendi, Muslim chaplain at Georgetown, says this about Muslim students questioning their faith: "If they don't believe, I would say, 'Listen, let's talk about it. What is it that you don't like in Islam?' I encourage discussions about whatever issues they want to talk about. Usually people really change after a few sessions of discussions about whatever subject, and they say, 'Oh, that's not the way I heard about it back home.'"

Hendi doesn't press. "I give people that right and I encourage them to go out and research for themselves. Go and talk to some Jewish people and Christians or even be willing to be secular. But I also encourage them to not deprive themselves of the right to be open." This kind of "make your own choice but be informed" approach is a pretty common one across denominations. Hendi, like many other college chaplains, invites students to leave the door open. "Some people say, 'I don't like religion.' I say, 'Okay, but don't deprive yourself of the [chance] that you might discover religion can also be good.' You've got to be open to other things."

A Bad Name

It can be embarrassing, frustrating, and faith shaking when someone from your own faith tradition makes the news for doing harm or peddling hate. Between sex scandals, extremism, violence, hypocrisy, and bigotry, it seems almost as if we're having a contest to see who can behave the worst in the name of God. And we have to face the truth that damage has been done in the present day and throughout history in the name of religion.

But there have also been periods in history where the churches, temples, mosques, and monasteries were the bastions of scientific knowledge. These were the places where literature, history, and the arts were preserved and passed on. Rabbis, priests, imams, monks, and vowed religious men and women were some of the most highly educated and intelligent members of society. A person seeking knowledge would join the church. Scholarship was prized and seen as the imperative of any religious person.

Smart, faith-filled people do still exist. The folks at the extremes make for more exciting TV, but don't let them cheat you (or disgust you) out of an adult understanding of faith. At this moment in history—at least in Western culture—religion has become one of society's favorite scapegoats. Unfortunately, all too often the ineptitude and moral failings of some religious leadership are to blame. None of the major religious traditions espouse hate or bigotry, but at times the most vocal people cloak themselves in religion to justify questionable speech and action.

Here's another hard truth: Some of the people practicing your religion are hypocrites. You can count on this because they are all human. Some of the people practicing every religion are hypocrites. You can ignore them, forgive them, blind yourself to them, whatever, but don't write off the whole belief system just because some distort it—even if their voices are the loudest ones. Some of the most sincerely faithful people alive have the quietest voices.

See what truly practicing religious people have to say. And

don't think they have to have all the answers or that you do: That's not what religion's supposed to be about. It is not a matter of having the answers as much as it is getting comfortable with the questions.

Seek out the masters in your own tradition even as you seek out the masters in your field of study. Find the scholarly parts of your faith tradition (go to http://TheFreshmanSurvivalGuide. com/chapters/ and click on "Chapter 19" for "Spiritual Classics" from different traditions) and see what the educated people of faith have to say before you give it all up as superstitious or hypocritical bunk.

This May Happen to You

You've been at school a few days and already met most of the people on your hall when one of the guys you haven't met yet stops by your room to introduce himself. He seems like a really great guy, friendly and open. He asks where you're from and how you like things so far. Then a mere three minutes into the conversation he pops the question "Have you accepted Jesus Christ as your personal Lord and Savior?" This is a question you want to answer very carefully. Christian or not, you may find yourself entangled for the next hour or two debating theology, scripture, and defending, or attempting to defend, your beliefs against an onslaught of accusations from Friendly Guy.

If you were raised in a tradition that speaks openly about the love of Jesus and how you're doing in your walk with the Lord, you may be comfortable having this conversation. Carry on. Be ready for the inevitable invitation to Friendly Guy's upcoming Bible study.

Online Survival Guide: *Need help living with differences? Go to "Interactive RA" at http://TheFreshmanSurvival Guide.com and click on "Ask."*

If your experience of religion has been a more private one, or you don't really know Jesus from Adam, this guy's questions may leave you confused about your own beliefs and genuinely wondering, *Well, where* would *I go if I died tonight?*

Don't get too upset. Friendly Guy has been trained in this script to unsettle you enough in your own beliefs, or lack thereof, that you'll be more likely to accept his invitation to learn more. Take that as a wake-up call, if you want, to learn a little more about your own faith, but don't feel too guilty about a lack of religious knowledge. You're in good company. On campus you'll be encountering:

- People of different faiths from all over the world: Christians, Jews, Muslims, Hindus, Buddhists, and others
- Folks recruiting for Jesus, some of whom are sincere if slightly intense, and other groups that could be classified as cults (see our checklist at the end of this chapter to find out if your new fellowship group actually falls into that category)
- Nonreligious and antireligious peers and professors ranging from the "live and let live" crowd to those who would eradicate every mention of God from public life

Online Survival Guide: *Ask our online resident assistants about college life by visiting "Interactive RA" at http:// TheFreshmanSurvivalGuide.com and clicking on "Ask."*

Attending a Jesuit college, we're required as undergraduates to take philosophy and theology, which to many of my friends sounds like a pain and waste of time, but which turned out to be one of my best college experiences. I was lucky enough to get to take a class that combined both subjects with a service component, and the things I learned were so invaluable, in that they taught me how to think about myself, life, society, everything, in a reflective and impactful way. I think an important point to make beyond learning the essences of every religion is learning how to think about what you believe and who you are—something I think is really supplemented by studying how others have approached and reasoned through life.

—**Jenna, Boston College**

Not All Bible Studies Are Created Equal

There are Bible studies offered on every campus, but stop in at the campus ministry office to get an overview from someone on the staff before you attend. If you can't find one from your own tradition, make sure the one you choose doesn't hold teachings contrary to your own beliefs. Different Christian denominations have quite different understandings of scripture. If you go and hear things that sound wrong to you, again, campus ministry or your own pastor from back home can be a great resource with whom to sort things through. Most people in ministry are real scripture nerds and love it when they get a good Bible question! Also check out more spiritual reading resources at http://www.TheFreshmanSurvivalGuide .com—click on "Chapter 19."

As a high schooler Josh always wanted to know *why.* Why people do this or believe that. Why do people use this symbol or that ritual? He was not a fan of metaphor or mystery. He was a concrete thinker. To him, the story of Jonah was just a story about a big fish, rather than a story of God helping a man to overcome his own prejudices and see that God's mercy extends even to undeserving people. The story of Noah was just a story about a flood, rather than one of faithfulness, mercy, and promises.

As Josh moved into adulthood and began to realize the stories from his elementary education had perhaps a different set of meanings, he began to feel a little bit as if he'd been lied to. In college a few Christian fundamentalists were his friends, and whether through irritation with them or real internal struggle, he began to get snide and condescending about the things he saw as ridiculous in scripture and in the church. Though he doesn't participate in church anymore and believes that the absence of religion in the world would solve most of our problems, he is still deeply engaged in the discussions and questions of faith. He still raises lots of questions and still wants to know *why.*

God in the Classroom

Despite the stereotype that college professors are an atheistic bunch hell-bent on making sure nobody leaves college with an ounce of faith, a recent study has revealed that professors are a surprisingly spiritual group. Four out of five describe themselves as being "spiritual persons." Three out of five consider themselves to be religious, and a similar number (61 percent) report that they pray/meditate.[6] A new study that takes a closer look at professor's religious attitudes and affiliations shows that professors' belief in God varies considerably across the type of institution and disciplinary fields. "Our general finding is that although many professors are religious, few are religious traditionalists." They also found that, like the general public, 80 percent of the professors agree with the statement that "American colleges and universities welcome students of faith."[7]

"Faculty oftentimes have religious convictions of their own that they would love to talk about but don't talk about in class. I think all this is opening up because our traditional ideas of the secular wall that excludes religion entirely are changing," says Rev. Ian Oliver, Protestant chaplain at Yale University. Oliver believes that American notions of separating issues of faith from academics are not universal. "We're inviting students from all over the world who don't have any of those presuppositions. We have to be ready for conversations that don't presume this radioactive wall between the academic and spiritual life. It's messy but it's reality."

Rev. Oliver has found younger professors to be highly motivated to bridge this apparent divide. "I find that a lot of younger faculty…want to find a way to integrate this [discussion] because they realize that for some students these are highly motivating issues. If their education is walled over here and it never interacts with their motivating principles, then what's the purpose of the education?"

That said, some devout students dealing with an antireligious professor can face a different kind of challenge. For some people, academia and religion don't go together. You will find peers and professors on campus who have strong feelings against organized religion and some who hold that a belief in God is foolish and ignorant. While they are entitled to their own opinions, don't feel responsible either to engage in debate with them or to defend your own faith. You might like to mix it up a little with a nonbelieving peer. After all, college is about testing out your own ideas and seeing how they compare with others'. Still, professors should be handled a little more cautiously. Usually you'll have little to gain by trying to argue religious ideas, and an antagonistic prof can really put you on the spot. (Remember he or she has had this discussion a lot more times than you have.)

Decide, Don't Just Slide

If you've ever gone to church, especially on a regular basis, it's likely your parents, at least to some degree, helped form your beliefs (or lack of them). Now you've got to decide how you're going to form your own beliefs. A recent UCLA study found many college students drift away from their religious upbringings. In the study, 52 percent of the students said they attended religious services frequently the year before entering college, but by their junior year attendance had dropped to 29 percent.[8] Maybe you're thinking that whatever religion you grew up with just isn't fitting with the person you have grown into or want to become. Maybe it's just easier to sleep in on Sundays or head straight to the party on Friday or Saturday night (choose the case that applies to your holy day).

Whatever you choose, don't just slide out of your beliefs—make a conscious choice about religion. Inform yourself, then decide. Even if your decision is "Not now," consider that in the future the question of religious identity may (and probably will) come up again. Religion can be a really vital part of your identity, past, present, and future—it's definitely worth digging a little deeper, whether you're sticking with what you know or taking a hike.

I found two friends from my track team to go [to church] with. We would eat dinner Sunday nights in the dining hall and then go straight to the chapel. If one of us missed one week, the other two wou 'd get on him to come the next week. Together we all did our best to go to Mass every weekend, and the three of us actually became much closer because of it. That Sunday trip to the chapel recharged me in a way. The Sunday feeling, however, does not last for the rest of the week, during which I found it helpful to take a minute before I went to sleep for silent meditation/prayer. Just a minute at night helps me to remember what I believe in.

—**Tim, freshman, Nazareth College**

Stressing the Spiritual–The Interactive RA

Your campus will offer a host of options for you to stay in touch with your faith. If you are not faithful to a particular religion, the campus will offer a plethora of options for you to explore. If you are looking for a more formal faith interaction, your campus may host a weekly church service. There may also be a local church that offers special services to the students on your campus. Some services may include a shuttle service, dinners, and scholarship opportunities. If you would like to engage in less formal services, explore the student organizations that your campus has to offer. Both of the options provide you the opportunity to continue to develop your faith and stay spiritually connected. Attend meetings and campus events to become more familiar with the values and beliefs of the organization. If your campus does not offer the organization that aligns with your spiritual beliefs, you have the option to create your own organization. Find others with like beliefs, and create an organization that will help to get you on target. Creating your own organization is definitely a way you can leave your mark on campus.

Are you afraid to explore faith alone? Take a friend along with you. Ask around your residence hall, perhaps with a classmate, or coworkers. Although branching and exploring religion can be scary, once you arrive you will be welcomed by others excited to share more about their faith with you. As you continue to visit and grow within your faith you will find people with similar interests and mind-sets.

During the semester, you will experience increased levels of stress. Some of your peers will turn to substance abuse, some will opt to sleep, others will exercise, and some will give up. As you approach this stressful season of your life, developing and strengthening your faith can aid you in staying calm and peaceful during this time. While your peers venture to find unhealthy ways to manage their stress, you will be able to guide them and offer support to them.

Regardless of where you are on your spiritual journey, your campus will offer you a way to stay connected and ways you can continue to grow. Explore the options that are available to you on campus or in the neighborhood. Being away at school does not mean you have to step away or lose who you are spiritually.

—Danielle Shipp, iRA
Community Manager, Greystar Student Living Communities

Remember Two Things

Imam Yahya Hendi says:

- People grow in their faith. What you were yesterday is not what you will be tomorrow, no matter what. People grow in their understanding of faith, spirituality, religion, identity. People grow in their intellectual interests, emotionally, in the way they see politics. People change. It is natural for them to see those changes, to expect changes, and to have the ability to adapt to a new way of life.

- The best way to handle yourself is really to be in the right company. To attend religious services. It's good to go to a local mosque, church, or synagogue. It's good to engage with people who are older, who will give you some of their own experience with how to deal with these changes.

Religion is sort of like a gift-wrapped present. No matter how attractive or unattractive it looks from the outside, you have to unwrap it before you can decide if it's something you want to own. Don't give up; go to people you know and trust who still practice your religion. Ask them, "Why are you still _____?" Maybe your faith community is really conservative but you aren't, or vice versa. There's more room there, though—every faith has a left and a right. It may take some looking, but they can be found. Give campus ministry a chance. Their programs, speakers, and services are geared toward you and where you are, not toward your parents and where they are.

SEEK → FIND

 I encourage people to study their own religions. This guy came to me and said, "I want to convert to Islam." I said, "Why?" "Because I hate Christianity. I don't like it in any way, shape, or form." The more I spoke with him, the more I realized he really did not like his priest and his diocese. So I introduced him to one of the Jesuits and he came back to me a few months later to thank me for helping him become a better Catholic. Now after all that, if someone studied Islam or Christianity or Judaism and

he feels drawn to Islamic spirituality, I would have him become Muslim—but that would not be my goal [with every student I meet].

—Imam Yahya Hendi, Muslim chaplain,
Georgetown University

There's a real discrepancy between people's spiritual drive and their language to apply anything meaningful to it. Their concept of literature and science is significantly more evolved than their concept of a Jewish God. The tension is that the students haven't become less spiritual because of it; they've just become more confused. A lot of my work is trying to bring a language to that kind of spiritual intuition.

—Rabbi Yonah Schiller,
executive director of Hillel at Tulane University

THE TAKEAWAY

Understanding sacred writings in the context of scholarship, understanding religious practice in the light of great religious minds, and exploring the teaching and mysticism found within your own tradition are all adult endeavors. These are the steps that anyone should take before they choose to accept or reject a religious tradition. These are the steps that can change religion from being just one more thing you do because you feel you should into something that can help you make sense of the most difficult things you'll face and offer meaning, solace, and challenge in the months and years ahead.

CHAPTER 20

When You're the First:
First-Generation Students

Survival Strategy #20: First-generation students face challenges other students don't, but help is available. Tap into the resources your college has put in place, and rely on the help and advice of other first-gens to help you succeed.

Did your parents go to college? If not, you are what's known as a first-generation college student. According to the *Washington Post*, of the 7.3 million students in four-year public and private colleges and universities across the country, about 20 percent are first-generation students.[1] First-generation students sometimes face challenges that other students whose parents went to college might not have to deal with. According to the *Post*, often—though not always—first-gen students are less economically well off than their counterparts; about half are low-income. Nearly 50 percent of first-gen students also come from minority backgrounds. Colleges have started to recognize that it can be an uphill battle for students who are the first in their families to make the college journey. More and more schools have special resources and programs available to help these students and level the playing field when it comes to college success.

One challenge first-generation students face is that it can be harder for them to find the information they need. Parents may not know where to go for help on a particular issue. They're unfamiliar with the different offices and structures. Not knowing the college jargon or even what resources are available can be alienating. If you're a first-gen, you may have to advocate for yourself more than other students do. It can be tiring, but it can also be a point of pride as you become more acquainted with your campus and the resources offered there. Many first-gen students find that connecting with their RA, especially in the first few weeks, can be a good way to overcome that experience gap. As you meet more people around campus or older students in your major or activities, they can become great sources of information, too.

Many colleges have at least one staff person, but sometimes a whole department, whose job it is to help solve problems and overcome hurdles for first-gen students. Connect with them! Know where that office is, and get to know that person who will be your go-to problem solver. Even if you don't have a specific issue or problem that needs solving, make an appointment and ask that person's advice. If you run into trouble later on, it will be easier to get help, because you already have a relationship.

Less Well-Off

Graduation rates for first-generation students who are also low-income are a depressingly low 11 percent.[2] Many of these students are also working and have extra demands on their time besides "just" being a student. Not only that, many of the high schools that these students have come from often have fewer opportunities available for students to prepare academically for college: fewer AP classes, less rigorous courses overall, and lower expectations. All these factors add up to students who often find themselves not as well prepared as they should be for the demands of the college environment. If these are challenges you are facing, you can improve your chances of success by joining study groups, visiting the writing and math centers (sometimes called labs) on your campus, and tapping into the people and programs on your campus. First-gen students may see asking for help as a sign of weakness, but knowing when you need help and flexing your self-advocacy muscles actually shows the kind of strength that you'll need to be successful in college.

Family

First-gen students sometimes get mixed messages from their families about college. The money, time, and commitment that college demands of you can be a source of stress and worry for your family. Going where your parents have not gone can also leave you with a sense of division, almost like you're leaving your family behind. At the same time there's a sense of pride and accomplishment that you have this opportunity. Help your family feel like they are a part of your college journey. Invite them to campus family events, and take pride that this opportunity comes because of the support they have shown so far.

I Don't Belong Here

You may feel like an imposter at times. First-gen students often report feeling like outsiders on their own campuses. Racism, classism, and just plain ignorance on the part of other students you are interacting with simply highlights the fact that not everyone has grown up with the same advantages or taken the same path. It can be discouraging. There may be times that you feel like explaining or taking the privilege blinders off someone else's eyes, and other times you just don't want to bother. Don't feel as if you have to be the ambassador for your racial or socioeconomic group all the time. If you feel yourself getting discouraged or disgusted, find some support with other students facing the same problems or with a mentor who has traveled this path ahead of you.

Online Survival Guide: *Ask our online resident assistants about college life by visiting "Interactive RA" at http://TheFreshmanSurvivalGuide.com and clicking on "Ask."*

When we asked the first-generation students at Saint John Fisher College in Rochester, New York, to put together their best advice for other first-gens, they had a lot to say. Here are their top ten tips for first-generation students from first-generation students:

1. Don't be afraid to ask questions at any level, from the college application process to graduation. If your parents don't know the answer to a certain question, there is someone out there who does. This could be your high school counselor, college admissions officer, academic advisor, and many others.
2. You are not alone. There are many more first-generation students out there, too, going through the same process you are.
3. You are on equal ground with all other freshmen. Just because your parents didn't go to college doesn't make you inferior. All other students are still trying to figure out college, too.
4. Take pride in being a first-generation student. Make your own path, no matter what path your family took, and do so

with confidence. This is your opportunity to set an example and create any kind of life that you want.

5. Involve your family in any on-campus activities that you can. Remember, this is their first experience with college, too, so you can help to educate them. They were your support system growing up and continue to be, so be supportive of them as well.

6. Take full advantage of every opportunity that you can and fight for everything that you want. Don't take the easy way out. Get involved in everything that you can to really achieve all of your goals, but remember that it is okay to say no. Don't stretch yourself too thin, though. Pick the opportunities that will better shape you as a person.

7. Don't base your college decisions on cost and financial difficulties. Don't rule out your dream school, because there are financial-aid opportunities that can really help you. Look for scholarships, grants, and any other aid to assist you.

8. Engage in the community. Give back and become a resource to other potential college students to empower others to go to school and receive a higher education.

9. Nobody said that this was going to be easy, but it will be worth it. It is okay to fail, but you must always learn from your mistakes.

10. Always have a positive mind-set and outlook. Don't put too much pressure on yourself, but rather take a step back and focus on what is important. Enjoy the time that you are here at college; it goes by quick, and you get only one chance.

Be a pursuer of information. Read about first-gen students, talk to other college students you know who were the first in their own families. The website I'm First! (http://www.imfirst.org)

has stories of other first-gen students and a blog with tips and resources. Visit the chapters in this book about academic and social help and then become an expert about your own campus so you can find help when you need it.

> *Be proud of being a first-generation student, and use it to be an example to others. Maybe you have a younger brother or sister, a niece, a nephew, or younger friends; show them that they can go to college and earn their degree. You are the first in your family to go to college, but do not be the only [one].*
>
> **—Tyler Wheelock, first-generation scholarship coordinator, Saint John Fisher College**

THE TAKEAWAY

There are many, many resources available to you, especially as a first-gen student. Your college has an interest in your success, so take advantage of those offerings.

CHAPTER 21

Come Early, Stay Late: How to Do College as a Commuter

Survival Strategy #21: If you're commuting and you're feeling short-changed or like you're missing out, step up. You're entitled to just as much of the college experience as anyone else. You may have to fight for it, but you'll be glad you did.

When you're a commuter, it's really easy to feel left behind and isolated. If you're like a lot of commuters, you've stayed home and are going to a local college. Many of your friends have left town for a college far away. Even if you're in a new place, people sometimes make the mistake of telling you that you are "missing out on the college experience" by not living on campus. The fact is, though, that you're not alone. One in five freshmen, on average, commuted or lived off campus in fall 2013,[1] and a third of the nation's college students are commuters.[2]

It can be hard to separate the fantasy of living away from home—finding a new group of friends, becoming a new person, being away from parental supervision and having the freedom to make your own choices—from what is actually right for you.

But remember education is not a one-size-fits-all operation. People make the choice to commute for different reasons. Maybe you're at community college or close enough to home that the expense of living on campus just doesn't make sense. You may have made the decision to commute because the idea of living in a dorm just doesn't appeal to you, or health or family issues are keeping you close to home. And while you may miss your friends that have left, or worry that you're missing out in some other way, there are serious benefits to commuting.

Being a commuter reduces the amount of "new" that you have to deal with as you begin college. Being a college student is a big adjustment, and not having to deal with a new roommate, new food, new city, new rules, homesickness, and all the other nonacademic newness can really help you focus on your studies. Many college students are eager to get away from their families and strike out on their own, but that's not the case for everyone. If your family is a positive support, and they give you opportunities to balance freedom and responsibility, then living home and commuting can be great.

Then there's the money. College costs continue to soar. The *Christian Science Monitor* recently reported, "Tuition and housing costs rose 439 percent from 1982 to 2008, compared with a 147 percent increase in median family income."[3] Starting at a community college and transferring after two years to a four-year school can save you approximately 40 percent of your college costs.[4] Whether you're commuting to an expensive private school, a less expensive state school, or a community college, the choice to be a commuter is saving you a bundle of money. Based on 2014–2015 college costs, you're probably saving a sweet 10K annually on room and board.

I can tell you that I wish I would have gone to community college first! First, because of finances. It would have made a lot more sense to stay at home and get my basic coursework out of the way while avoiding high dorm or apartment costs. Second, I feel like I could have used a couple of more years to dip my toes into a more uncontrolled atmosphere responsibly rather than jumping right in and getting sucked into the party life.

—Gerald, State University of New York at Fredonia

I'm a commuter student and knew right away I had to become involved. It wasn't really a choice. Everyone had a roommate to be friends with or a hall where they could make friends. I didn't have those ties. It began with chapel choir and has become a million different activities, from orientation to retreats to student government. Sometimes I feel really overwhelmed, but it has helped me feel like I am part of the community. It has given me amazing friends I know I can always count on emotionally and even for a piece of their floor. They're amazing in every sense of the word.

—Ashley, sophomore, Stonehill College

Just because you're saving money on your college experience, though, you should never sell yourself, or your college, short. You deserve the same opportunities to get involved, try new things, meet new people, and be challenged as a whole person that resident college students have.

You may not be living on campus, but that doesn't mean you shouldn't be a part of the campus community. Get involved in campus activities—it's a great way to meet new people and feel more connected to what's going on on campus. Hit the activities fairs, and scour your student handbook and your school's website for activities and clubs you'd like to connect with. Even though you'll be busy as a new college student, try to choose at least one campus activity beyond classes to try out.

- Use your school's resources, study groups, library, and writing and math labs. Professors' office hours are there for your use.

- Maintain your relationships—fight the isolation that can sometimes be part of the commuter experience by scheduling time for friends. (Yes, I said *scheduling* and *friends* in the same sentence.) Since you won't be running into all your friends every day like you did in high school, set up times when you can see each other either in person or online.

- If you can, set up your schedule so you'll have some time on campus a few days a week. If you're also working, it can be tempting to pack your classes in the morning so your afternoons and evenings can be spent off campus. If at all possible, though, consider leaving some gaps in your schedule so you'll have time built in to hit the offices (financial aid, academic advisement, the registrar), go see your professors, visit the library, or attend student activities.

One of the biggest headaches for commuters is parking! Especially during your first few weeks of classes, get to campus half an hour early. Unless you're at a teeny-tiny college, and sometimes even then, parking can be difficult or impossible. Parking on the far side of campus and sprinting to class makes for a miserable way to start your day. Give yourself the extra time. Check ahead of time what you'll need to do to park on campus without getting ticketed or towed. Most campuses are very strict about who can park where when. You usually need to purchase a parking pass for the semester (or year) and pay attention to designated lots for students.

Good shoes are a must to go along with your far-flung parking spot. Expect to walk a good distance between the lot and your class, and if you're going to school someplace where the weather isn't always sunny, warm good boots, a warm coat, and an umbrella can make life much more pleasant.

Commuters can usually purchase a meal plan and eat in the same dining halls as resident students. Find out if that's true at your school. It can be pricey, but it's one way to reduce the feeling of being an outsider at your own school that sometimes comes along with commuting.

At my school there is a commuter lounge called J.Lee's. This place has couches, a TV, a pool table, and video games. There are tables and free popcorn. This is a great place to relax in between classes. So find a place on campus that you can relax in between your courses, or find a friend to crash with in case of late classes or downtime. Having a place that's your own on campus will help you feel comfortable and get you focused on studying.

—Megan, Ramapo College of New Jersey

Commuter Packing List

You may not have had to pack up your whole life and fit it in a car, but it still pays to pack for the day. Be prepared—whether your commute is ten minutes or two hours, you want to be sure you have everything you need for the day when you leave home. Monica from Monroe Community College advises the following:

1. Your student ID. Not all places require it on you to get into school, but many do. It also acts as your library card

(again, most places). It's important that you always have it with you.

2. Your school's Class Cancellations page, bookmarked and checked daily. There is nothing much worse than hauling yourself there and finding a "no class today" note on the door. Or my personal favorite: the dark locked room with no note at all.

3. Small water bottle (about 16 oz.). *And* a travel mug with a good seal that won't leak in your bag. Something without handles is best. It is much easier to get through class with something to drink, hot or cold. (Just be sure to find out first if food or drinks in class is irritating to your professor.)

4. Appropriate layers. Some lecture halls are frigid and some are steamy.

5. A serious backpack. The giant purse and tote bag combination can seem more appealing than carrying a "freshman pack." However, hobbling through the hall like that makes you look like a peasant from ancient times.

6. A budget. While you do save a considerable amount of money by commuting, there are lots of different and hidden costs. The $4 you spend on a giant caffeinated, chocolaty, sugary cup of goodness to get you through class may very well be worth it. But charts and graphs may make you think about how many times a week you indulge. Check out https://www.mint.com for some help managing your money.

7. Food or money or both. If you'll be on campus for mealtime, have a plan. It's hard to focus on the lecture when your stomach is rumbling.

SEEK → FIND

Commuter life is often challenging. Talk to club and activities leaders and student government about what works best for you to be more involved in activities. There's always a way to slightly adjust the schedule. Our commuter student association is heavily involved in campus ministry and runs our Agape Latte Coffeehouse Speaker's series. There are lots of partnerships to be had, but you have to be a bit more assertive to present how you can best get involved.

—Mike Hayes, director of campus ministry, Canisius College

Justin was disappointed when he realized that the student aid he'd been counting on to get him away from home and living on campus wasn't going to be enough and that, even though they wanted to, his parents couldn't bear the financial burden of putting him in the dorms. At orientation he felt like he was missing out as people connected with their roommates and all seemed to know each other from their dorms. He was a little shy, and it was already hard to get to know people. They had a special session for commuters the second day, though, and he met some other students in the same boat. He also met Jill and Shawna, students who were commuting because it was their first choice. Sure they wanted to save money, but they also knew the stability of living at home would give them the academic success they were looking for. "It's why we're at college, right?" said Jill as she dragged Justin to the commuter lounge full of comfy chairs and vending machines.

One commuter recommends, "Always remember to have some extra money in your backpack, just in case! Even if it's only some spare quarters, you never know when you might need it!" Another swears by his headphones. "Get a small set of earbuds. Since you may not have an area of your own to study, something that you can just pull out of your pocket can be useful for being courteous to others and concentrating on your work. It also allows you to watch videos in places like the library."

Talk with your family about how being in college will impact your role in the family and what you may need from them. You may need quiet for studying, or you may just have less time for chores or family connections. Have a backup plan for transportation in case there's car or public transportation trouble.

Real Advice from Real Commuters: The Top 10 Commuter List!

1. **Get involved!!** Come early. Come often. Stay late. Don't just come and go around classes. It's easy to stay for the noon or afternoon club meetings, but stay for the late-night ones, too. There are more cool people to meet and interests to share. Ask questions and make connections with peers, faculty, and staff. Be open-minded and try new things.

2. **Use on-campus resources.** The library and computer labs are there for you, and people can be a resource, too! Connect with classmates you can study with and find a mentor—an older student in your major can be just the resource you need.

3. **On-campus jobs are a great option.** Stay on campus and get paid to do it. You'll save gas and time, and it will give you more ways to connect to the campus and the people there. Campus employment will work with student schedules where some off-campus employers may not.

4. **Participate in orientation.** It's too easy for commuters not to participate in on-campus orientation, but it gets you connected with new people and will help you find activities, clubs, and organizations that you want to participate in.

5. **Find a routine.** Start early in your college career and establish a schedule for fitting it all in—your daily life, activities, and responsibilities. Take into account parking and traffic. Bring all your stuff for school so you don't have to make emergency trips home. Find a place to hang out during downtime, maybe a place with couches. Adding up all these little pieces will help make you more comfortable.

6. **Keep your family involved, too.** Don't skip family or siblings weekends just because you see your family more often. Keep them involved.

7. **Give yourself *you* time.** Yes, you're busy with school, friends, activities, and family, but you need time for yourself. Go to the gym or do things that you want to do just for fun.

8. **Get a meal plan.** It's easier than having to run off campus or pack your lunch every day, and there's the social aspect of eating together. A meal plan is usually healthier, too. You can fall into the fast-food habit or end up making unhealthy food at home because you're rushing to leave or getting home late. Pop-Tarts and ramen are okay once in a while but not every day.

9. **Take care of your ride.** All of your college friends, academics, clubs, and *fun* rely on that motorized box on wheels, so change your oil and keep your car maintained. Drive safe and give yourself a time cushion; don't get into accidents because you are running late. Know your public transportation schedule and routes.

10. **Find other commuters and take pride in being a commuter.** Don't feel inferior because you're a commuter—commuters make up a large portion of campus! Just because you do not live on campus doesn't mean you are less special. Maybe another commuter lives near you and you can carpool!

Online Survival Guide: Ask our online resident assistants about college life by visiting "Interactive RA" at http:// TheFreshmanSurvivalGuide.com and clicking on "Ask."

THE TAKEAWAY

The college experience goes way beyond simply showing up for class and getting assignments in on time. Commuters may need to be more deliberate in their efforts to get involved in campus life, but make no mistake: The lectures, social events, service opportunities, and sporting events that occur practically every night on campus are there for you as well.

CHAPTER 22

Help Is All Around

Survival Strategy #22: You're on your own but you're *not* alone. All colleges have resources to help you deal with the inevitable challenges you'll face—it's never a bad thing to ask for help.

For most students, freshman year is the beginning of some of the best years of their lives. Beyond what you'll learn in school, the opportunities, experiences, and people you'll encounter will be unlike anything you've come across before. Still, there will also be rough times where you may need some help. Depending on your past experience with student services, your expectations may not be too high. The level and quality of services at high schools across the country can vary widely. Fortunately, college is usually a different story. The faculty and staff providing support to students on college campuses are generally highly degreed, experienced, and effective.

Being at college is like having a spa for your brain, body, and spirit. The quality of all the services and support—academic, psychological, physical, and spiritual—may surprise you (and most of it is already paid for with your tuition dollars).

The Myth of Independence

You may feel as though you shouldn't need help. You're supposed to be an independent college student, right? Well, yes and no. Yes, you *are* an independent college student; you even have a new bedspread and microwave to prove it. You made it in. You're taking classes. But nobody expects you to go it alone. College staffs have realized over the years that throwing people into the deep end without a lifeline doesn't get the best results.

If you're struggling, it's pretty common to feel you're the only one with problems. When you walk around campus, you might get the impression that everyone is keeping it together. You may even feel ashamed to have to admit, even to yourself, that you need help. The truth is that everyone struggles. Even some of those perfect-looking people will seek out some kind of help. Chances are there's an office on campus for nearly any problem you might encounter. Find it and use it.

Online Survival Guide: Ask our online resident assistants any questions you may have about where to find help on your college campus by visiting "Interactive RA" at http:// TheFreshmanSurvivalGuide.com and clicking on "Ask."

Kate had decided she didn't need help. Or more accurately, that she *shouldn't* need help. She came from a family that valued independence...a lot. Somebody needing counseling was joked about, and extended family members who'd gotten help through counselors were ridiculed behind their backs. The idea that she might run into a struggle she couldn't handle on her own was simply unacceptable.

But Kate was having trouble staying focused and getting her work done, and she finally confided to a friend who mentioned different resources available on her campus. Finally Kate agreed to hit the writing lab for help finishing the paper she was wrestling with, and she promised to at least introduce herself to the chaplain that weekend. Both kinds of help turned out to be important first steps that really made a difference for her and led her to other helpful people.

SEEK → FIND

 My best advice has to do with the student reaching out and asking for help. We don't want them getting into such a state of despair that they no longer feel they're worth helping. That's why chaplains are there, that's why mental health counseling centers are there—because it's very common. It's a human thing for all of us to go through these types of journeys into despair, depression, feeling inadequate, or not knowing where to turn. If you can get through [those issues], you will find greater strength within yourself than you have ever been aware of before.

—Ven. Bonnie Hazel Shoultz, Buddhist chaplain,
Syracuse University

Reach Out

"Many of the students we see struggling are students who *could* succeed," says Dr. David McMillen of Michigan State University. "They've got the scores and the grades. But nobody's watching them to see if they get up in the morning; they might stay up all night playing video games, or they get involved in underage drinking. [Their behavior] can have a lot to do with who they start hanging around with when they first get to college." The way you perceive your college experience initially is heavily influenced by the people you spend your first year with. It's also common early on to think that these are "your people" for the next four years. Making friends is a life thing, not a freshman-year thing. If the friends you make early on have helped you to develop some bad habits that are thwarting your chances to succeed, it's time to seek out new, healthier relationships.

Common Problems / Uncommon Resources

So you've realized you might need some help. Need to work out academic issues? Struggling with depression? Where do you go? Your residential life advisor or faculty advisor is there to answer your questions, and if they can't help you it's their job to find someone who can. Following is a short, general list of the problems you may come across and the people who can help. If you're embarrassed and you want to learn more a bit anonymously, a little research on your school's website should yield good results.

 Online Survival Guide: It's always better to know where you can go for help before you actually need it. Our scavenger hunt for help on campus will give you the chance to learn this essential information ahead of time. Go to

http://TheFreshmanSurvivalGuide.com/chapters/ and click on "Chapter 22" to download a PDF listing the different resources found on college campuses. Fill in the contact information and location for those resources on your campus in the blank spaces provided.

Problem No. 1: Housing or Roommate Issues

If you have an issue with your dorm, floor, or roommate, it can affect your mood, your ability to get your work done, and your overall satisfaction with college life. Your dorm room is your home away from home, the place you return to each day to relax, unwind, and get ready to face the rest of the world. This is a problem worth addressing because its impact can be big. For hall, dorm, and roommate issues, see chapter 3, then talk to your residential advisor, who is usually an older student who lives on your floor.

The RA is trained to deal with all sorts of problems in freshmen life, and he or she is there for you to talk to. The RA can work with you to try to fix your problem, like figuring out your floor dynamics or mediating a discussion with you and your roommate. If your problem continues, your RA can assist you in talking to the office of housing or residential life to inquire about switching rooms. This is a drastic step, but important if you are truly unhappy in your current situation. Your room is your home and the last place you need to stress you out.

Problem No. 2: Academic Issues

College classes are much more demanding than high school classes, and you may find that you are struggling to finish work in all your courses. Adjusting to both the quantity of work and the new level of academic rigor is often one of college's biggest challenges. Talking to your professors can help with individual classes (see chapter 15 for more on profs), but there are also other resources available to help you handle the workload. Learning labs, first-year or freshmen retention offices, as well as library staff can all help.

Rather than wait for disaster to set in, it's in your best interest to get familiar with these places on campus early on. If you weren't able to visit those places before trouble struck, fear not. Dr. Albert Matheny, head of academic advisement for the University of Florida, suggests getting help as soon as you start to struggle. According to Matheny, the academic advisement office can connect you with tutoring, course-specific help, study skills, and support services, and help you work with your professors to catch up or keep up. Set up a meeting with an academic advisor, a member of the faculty specifically assigned to you or your major, to discuss what classes you should take and how you can manage them.

Students at Boston College's management school create a four-year plan as freshmen. This allows them to take stock of all the course requirements as well as make their hopes for the future more tangible (e.g., studying abroad or taking on a second major). Being able to refer back to this plan every year has been an invaluable asset to their students and something that could benefit every student regardless of their major.

If you don't have a major yet, some schools assign academic deans to each class—make an appointment to talk to them about your plan and class schedule. Many schools also have workshops and peer mentor programs run by students who can help you figure out what to do from their own experience. Paper writing is a very different thing in college from what it was in high school. Getting a writing tutor to look over your first paper is a must.

> *Something I should have done more of was taking advantage of office hours and the professors. It would definitely be a good idea to form relationships with some of your professors so that later, when you need recommendation letters and the like, you have people who are familiar enough to write something terrific. Professors are also a great resource for advice on careers and internship opportunities in their field. Take advantage of that! That's what they're there for!*
>
> **—Christine, senior, Northwestern University**

Problem No. 3: Health Issues

For all sorts of physical problems, from a twisted ankle to the flu, visit your campus student health or wellness center. The health center is close by and its staff is used to dealing with college students. Keep the number in your phone, and if you feel sick or get injured, call to set up an appointment. Call ahead if you can so you're sure to get a spot. If your health center can't fit you in and you need help right away, consider the local hospital. For emergencies, your school may have its own emergency medical service—always keep the number in your phone as well. If you've got a chronic health condition, especially one that is affected by stress, you probably already know that managing your health in college will be challenging. There may be services on your campus to help.

Problem No. 4: Emotional/Psychological Issues

Maybe you just feel as if you're having a hard time. Maybe you have all three of the problems we've just talked about; maybe you have none of them. Either way, something isn't quite right. It doesn't matter whether you've gone to counseling before, talking to someone about your situation really helps. Often college campuses have their own counseling and therapy offices to provide help from professionals who understand your school's culture. Call or visit the website to set up an appointment.

Some 77 percent of students who responded to a survey conducted by the University of Idaho Student Counseling Center reported they were more likely to stay in school because of counseling and that their school performance would have declined without counseling.[1] Another study found retention rates of 85 percent for those in involved in counseling and 74 percent for the general student body.[2] You may be reluctant to tell a stranger your problems, but when you consider the benefits you could reap—a calmer, more productive, less anxious you—you may decide to gather your courage and give it a shot. One appointment won't hurt, and you may find that talking through what stresses you out and strategies to fix your problems is just what you need.

Dr. Richard Kadison, chief of Mental Health Services at Harvard, says, "My view is that the emotional well-being of students goes hand in hand with their academic development. If they're not doing well emotionally, they are not going to reach their academic potential."[3]

Problem No. 5: Spiritual Issues

Some students feel lost to the point where they don't know themselves anymore or are wondering why they ever wanted to go to college. The campus ministry or spirituality center can be a great place for meeting like-minded students and finding caring staff whose specialty is guiding people on the journey of college life. On a lot of campuses, these centers can also just be nice places to hang out. If you're stressed out, most campus ministry centers have a TV, games, snacks—something to remind you of home.

It's okay to embrace your faith. I became so much closer to God during my college years. There will be people there who can help you and guide you. Go to your [clergy leader] and get involved with your college church group. And remember: God forgives. We all make mistakes, we all fall down.

—Bethany, Pennsylvania State University

One Step Ahead

If you've had issues in the past with depression, anxiety, nutrition, eating disorders, self-esteem, and so on, it's a good idea to contact the counseling center and/or campus ministry pretty soon after you get to campus. Even if you're doing fine, the pressures of college and work are a lot to handle. Stressful times might trigger a downshift in your emotional state. If you start developing a relationship with a new counselor early on, when you're doing okay, he or she will know you well enough to be able to help you more effectively if you do run into trouble. Often the biggest challenge is being able to acknowledge to yourself when you aren't doing well. Having someone who knows you and can be there as a resource is a great way to set yourself up.

And More...

Many campuses also have:
- Addiction treatment, including twelve-step groups
- Information and support for LGBTQ students
- Conflict resolution services
- Extra supports for students with disabilities or low income, minority students, first-generation college students, international students, and women

If you need it, there's a good chance your campus has it. These are services that your tuition helps pay for and that make or break academic success. Don't shy away from putting them to good use.

Remember 3 Things–The Interactive RA

1. **Remember what you are here for.**

    I have lost count on how many freshmen I meet that lose track as to why they are at college in the first place. They get caught up with their friends, trying to be popular, partying, drugs, and laziness. College is not like high school. You are responsible for yourself. Your RA will not wake you up for class, make sure you study, or get your prescriptions when you're sick.

    Take control of your education and be responsible with your choices. What you do on a Friday/Saturday night may come to haunt you the next day, week, or month, or years later. The choices you make now will affect you the rest of your life.

    What I am telling you comes from personal experience. I have seen alcohol and drugs cause students to fail classes, get arrested, drop out—or most likely fail out—of school. I have seen the student who does not study or go to class, and those students rarely make it to their sophomore year.

So please remember why you are at college. Make smart choices.

2. **Ask for help.**

College is not like high school. Your classes will not be easier, and you will have to study (gasp). You may find out that you do not even know how to study, since you never had to do it in high school. Well, then, ask for help. Talk to upper classmen, tutors, professors, or your RA.

Asking for help is not a sign of weakness. I had to learn this the hard way. You don't want to be the person who failed an exam or a class because you did not ask for help. You don't want to look back and think, *I could have passed that class if I went to my professors' office hours.*

Asking for help is not limited to the classroom. In the dorm your RA is placed on your floor to *help you.* So if you are having roommate issues, do not wait till you are ready to murder each other. Bring your RA in. Roommates who have been having issues since September have contacted me, and now it's March and they cannot stand it any longer. And I am always confused as to why didn't they tell me sooner when I could have actually helped.

3. **Don't stress.**

Unfortunately, stress and college often go hand in hand. Perhaps it takes the form of an assignment due tomorrow and you haven't started yet, or your roommate's music is driving you crazy, or maybe your parents are hounding you about that grade you got on your biology test. Stress is all around; how you deal with it makes all the difference.

Talk to a friend, an RA, a professor, or a counselor. Taking time for yourself is important, whether it is working out, spending time with friends, playing video games, reading a nontextbook, or just hiding out in your room.

That one class you are struggling with really won't make a huge impact on your life as a whole. Try not stress over the little things and enjoy the ride.

—Kailynn Cerny, iRA
West Virginia University

Online Survival Guide: For more resources on any of these issues, visit "Chapter 22" (go to the "Chapters" drop-down menu) or "Interactive RA" at http://TheFreshman SurvivalGuide.com.

THE TAKEAWAY

If you're struggling, get help. Be smart enough to know that utilizing the resources before you is like eating the food that someone has put on your plate when you're hungry: It only makes sense, and it will leave you recharged and ready to do what you need to succeed.

CHAPTER 23

Am I Safe?

Don't Be Paranoid, Just Be Smart

Survival Strategy #23: Taking safety seriously is mostly common sense, but it's not always common practice. Develop smart habits around keeping yourself and your stuff safe.

If you grew up locking the front door, the car, and your bike, then basic safety precautions may not even be a concern: You already do those things as a matter of habit. But if you've never had to be safety conscious before, either because of where you lived or because someone's always done it for you, then getting into the habit of locking everything up and being aware of your surroundings can be a pain. What are ordinary precautions for some may seem strange to others.

But looking at the numbers—88,444 crimes were reported to college and university campus police in 2012[1]—serves to remind us that crime on campus does happen. Basic safety precautions not only reduce your risk of becoming a victim, they also give you some peace of mind knowing you're doing everything you reasonably can to stay safe.

Your Stuff

According to the Office for Victims of Crime—sponsored by the U.S. Department of Justice—over 96 percent of the crimes reported on campus in 2012 were property related. It may be annoying to always lock up and to constantly keep an eye on personal items, but not as much of a pain as replacing your ID, your bank card, and everything else you'd lose if your wallet or purse or laptop is stolen. The extra thirty seconds it takes to lock and unlock your door is well worth the trouble.

It might seem a little summer campish, but don't be afraid to label your stuff. Write your name on the tags of your clothes, toiletries, and personal items (missing towels, anyone?) to increase the chance of things getting returned to you if you leave them behind somewhere. That sticky-fingered girl up the hall will be less eager to snatch your favorite shampoo if your name is written up the side of the bottle. And the pair of jeans you left in the dryer might just come back to you if someone can figure out who to return them to.

Why do we love laptops? They're portable, lightweight, and easy to move quickly. All those wonderful qualities, and the fact that they're pretty expensive, make them a really attractive target for theft. Never, never, never leave your laptop unattended in a public place. Not even for just a second.

Bait Bikes?

National Bike Registry and campus police say bicycle theft is the number one type of property theft on college campuses. To combat the issue, universities across the country are placing "bait bikes" with GPS-tracking technology in prime locations around their campuses. The program has led to a decline in bicycle thefts and an increase in arrests at numerous schools, including Arizona State University, Tulane University, Winthrop University, the University of Wisconsin–Madison and the University of Texas at Austin. Tulane's bait-bike program has decreased thefts from three to four per week to one or two each month.[2]

Of course, it isn't just "stuff" that some thieves are after. According to the *Financial Times*, "College students are five times more likely to be a victim of identity theft than the general public."[3] The primary reasons college students are so vulnerable is that they live in close quarters and they aren't sufficiently protecting their information.

In 2013, 39,335 consumers between the ages of twenty and twenty-nine were victims of identity theft, which constituted 20 percent of the total reported complaints of identity theft that year.[4]

The 2015 Javelin Strategy and Research Identity Fraud Report found that college-aged adults fell victim to identity theft more often than other groups. In addition, it took twice as long for college-aged adults to begin repairing their identities once they realized that they had fallen victim to identity theft.[5]

According to Steve Weisman, author of *50 Ways to Protect Your Identity in a Digital Age: New Financial Threats You Need to Know and How to Avoid Them*, there are numerous precautions students should take, including:

1. Don't carry your Social Security card in your wallet or purse. Lock it up.
2. Lock up all your important papers with personal information.
3. Don't download attachments or click on links unless you are positive that they are legitimate.
4. Install security software and antimalware software on all of your electronic devices and keep them current.

5. Keep your computer, smartphone, tablet, and all electronic devices locked when not in use.

6. Use strong passwords and different passwords for all of your devices.[6]

Weisman has a ton of other great suggestions and information about how to protect yourself that we'd love to reprint here, but that, apparently, would also be theft. Check out his book or his articles yourself online.

Students may end up at colleges with very different geography, weather, language, history, or culture than they're used to. Being ignorant of these differences can have real consequences. One student shared this story: "I went to college in a rural, cold environment and most of the students from warmer climates were not ready for the cold. We sadly had one student get lost in a storm right near campus and die. It was a tremendous tragedy on our campus and shook our sense of safety for months." Whether it means watching out for heatstroke in a hotter climate or remembering to bundle up and keep a snow shovel in your trunk, talk to the natives about the region you're attending, and pack—and act—accordingly.

Always, and I mean always, lock your door when you leave. And never leave stuff in public areas on campus. Leaving something there is just like putting a big sign on it that says, STEAL ME. I can't count the number of e-mails about stolen laptops that people have left in the lounges unattended while they went to do something.

—**Paul, Rochester Institute of Technology**

Yourself

Especially when you're new on campus, choose caution over courage. Is it brave to walk home alone at 3 A.M. through an unfamiliar part of campus? Maybe, but most experienced students would tell you it's just stupid. Don't leave a building alone after dark. If you feel as if someone is following you, get to a well-lit place, go back to where you came from if it's nearby, or call campus security from your cell. Keep numbers for campus security and the emergency ride system (if there is one) in your cell. You may never need them, but if you do you'll be glad you've got them.

When you go out, always go with a buddy, or better yet a group, and keep an eye on each other. Stick to public places for early dating experiences, make sure your drink stays in your hands so nothing gets slipped into it, and if you plan to leave campus make sure someone knows where you're going and when you plan to be back (see chapter 7 on dating for more safety advice). Always have a backup plan for getting back to the dorm.

> *Your parents always told you never to talk to strangers, and there's a college corollary: Making new friends from class, the residence hall, or around campus is a good thing; however, don't fully let your guard down. Don't assume the worst of everyone, but don't be naïve, either. Go with your gut. If something doesn't feel right, don't do it. No one should ever make you feel bad about yourself. You should never feel obligated to compromise your values for friendships, grades, or for the next party. If you don't feel safe going to a party, hanging out with a certain person, or walking around late at night—don't do it.*
>
> **—Zahrah, Fordham University**

Random Acts of Violence

The violence in recent years on college campuses has given *freshman survival* a disturbingly literal meaning. The events on those campuses changed forever terms like *campus safety* and introduced a new term to campuses: *lockdown*. These events shock us and make us worry about our own safety and the safety of the people we love. These acts of violence loom large precisely because of their unpredictability.

But consider this: Approximately 19 million students were enrolled in college in the fall of 2014,[7] and only a tiny fraction of those were victims of random acts of violence. Still, if you do have a concern about a specific person on your hall or in one of your classes, talk to your RA, campus security, or a professor. After the Virginia Tech shootings in 2007, the campus put together a staff and faculty guide to help students identify potentially dangerous individuals. More and more campuses are taking steps to aid students who are overwhelmed by college life and educating people on campus to identify students who might be at risk for violent behavior.

The place to really put your concern is where the trouble is. If you're wondering what you should be concerned about, what problems you are most likely to struggle with your freshman year, random acts of violence should be waaaay down at the bottom of the list. Many more freshmen get into trouble with using drugs and alcohol, skipping class, or struggling with depression than come to harm because of random violence. In fact, add drugs and alcohol to the mix, and there's nothing random about the majority of violence on campus. According to estimates from the National Institute on Alcohol Abuse and Alcoholism, each year:

- 1,825 college students between the ages of eighteen and twenty-four die from alcohol-related unintentional injuries, including motor-vehicle crashes.
- 696,000 students between the ages of eighteen and twenty-four are assaulted by another student who has been drinking.
- 97,000 students between the ages of eighteen and twenty-four report experiencing alcohol-related sexual assault or date rape.[8]

Making choices about what you do and who you hang around with has a much greater influence on your safety.

Big pitfalls for incoming freshmen are drinking and drug problems. It's no secret that college makes it very easy to start drinking, and a lot of kids aren't used to having that kind of freedom. They end up needing their stomachs pumped on their first night in the dorms.

—Andy, Virginia Tech

Try not to live in fear. It's reasonable to be cautious but unreasonable to be thinking about the possibility of harm all the time. If you find yourself obsessed with danger, get some help (see chapter 22 for help on campus). There's a good chance you're misdirecting your anxiety about other college issues onto this one.

"Unfortunately, school shootings, bomb threats, and acts of terrorism are all a part of our lives now. Be vigilant without being a vigilante," recommends Michelle Goodwin, associate director of the University Catholic Center in Austin. "If on a website, in a conversation, or shared writing assignment, you find something disturbing, share it with a professor or staff member. In spite of the media's perpetuation of the myth, very few people with mental illnesses are actually violent. Know the signs and know how to get help. Don't be paranoid, just alert."

Commonsense Safety

- **Lock it 1.0.** Lock your doors, car, dorm, or apartment every time you leave. Make it a habit, and soon it will feel weird not to.
- **Lock it 2.0.** Lock your bike. Even on a "safe" campus, crime still happens and opportunity is the invitation. A four-year student cyclist has at least a 17.75 percent chance of losing his or her bicycle to theft.[9]
- **Locker it 2.5.** If you have a locker the same principle applies, even if your stuff doesn't seem that valuable to you. Keep it safe. You'll have a greater sense of control—becoming the victim of a crime undermines a sense of safety.
- **All eyes.** Keep your eyes *always* on your cell, your laptop, your phone, your backpack, your purse.
- **Trust your instincts.** Be aware of your surroundings. If somebody makes you uncomfortable, put some distance between that person and yourself, leave, or ask a friend to stay close.
- **Group travel.** To avoid potentially sticky situations, travel in groups and have a shared signal or code word to use if it's time to get out.

Want the Crime Stats on Your College?
The Department of Education has a very helpful online resource called the Campus Safety and Security Data Analysis Cutting

Tool, which enables users to look up crime statistics for individual institutions. It can be found at http://ope.ed.gov/security/.

SEEK → FIND

You're no more in danger on campus than anywhere else today. In fact, because college campuses tend to be somewhat insular, you're safer from violent crime on most campuses than off. There's no point living in constant fear; pay attention to your surroundings, and go on with your life. Ten people who live courageously are more powerful than a hundred who live in fear.

—Fr. Larry Rice, CSP, director, Ohio State University
Catholic Center

Smart, Safe, and Secure–The Interactive RA

Campus safety should be a concern of everyone; parents, administration, and, most important, you the students. Safety is one thing that cannot be guaranteed. The university and university housing department will take precautions and attempt to mitigate risks and hazards. It is also the responsibility of the student to make sure they are implementing safety practices into their daily routine. Criminals prey on the innocence and naïveté of students. Being aware of your surrounds and familiarizing yourself with these safety tips below can help you avoid unsafe situations.

1. Program the campus police phone number into your phone. Also, add the RA on-call phone number and the front desk phone number so they are handy in the event of an emergency.

2. Program three to five people in your phone as ICE (In Case of Emergency) contacts. In an emergency situation, someone can easily identify whom to call if you need help.

3. Report all suspicious persons, vehicles, and activities to campus authorities. Many universities have emergency phones installed throughout campus; do not be afraid to use the phone in an emergency.

4. Use the buddy system and watch out for your neighbors.

5. Keep your doors locked, especially whenever you find yourself alone in an apartment/room.

6. If you see someone being victimized, get involved and notify the police.

7. Avoid traveling alone at night. Travel with a friend, walk with crowds, or request an escort from campus police.

8. Walk on well-lit, regular traveled walks and pathways. Avoid shortcuts and keep away from shrubbery, bushes, alleyways, or any other areas where someone could be hiding.

9. Avoid big, open areas like the athletic fields and tennis courts after dark.

10. Do not accept rides from casual acquaintances.

11. When walking to your vehicle or residence, have your keys ready in hand.

12. When being dropped off by taxi or private vehicle, ask the driver to wait until you get inside.

13. When getting out of a car, take a look around to make sure that you are not being followed.

14. If you think you are being followed, call for help and run to safety. Draw as much attention to yourself as possible by enlisting the aid of a passerby, flagging down a car, or pulling a fire alarm.

15. When walking at night, look up and look around; do not wear earbuds playing loud music in both ears, and walk as quickly as possible.

—Danielle Shipp, iRA
Community Manager, Greystar Student Living Communities

Online Survival Guide: *For more on campus safety, talk to the Interactive RA by visiting http://TheFreshmanSurvival Guide.com/chapters/ and clicking on "Chapter 23."*

THE TAKEAWAY

Try to let go of worry over things outside your control. Keep fear in check by maintaining your perspective. Take action on the things you can to reduce your risk. Standard precautions, awareness, and commonsense safety will go a long way toward keeping safe on campus.

CHAPTER 24

Too Much of a Dangerous Thing

Alcohol and Drugs on Campus

Survival Strategy #24: Alcohol and drugs: It can seem as if everybody's doing it, but it's not a simple matter of do or don't. You have an array of choices in front of you–choices you need to make, not just fall into.

Many people take it for granted that alcohol, and lots of it, will be part of the college scene for them, and the statistics bear that out:

- 80 percent of college students drink.[1]
- 41 percent of college students reported binge drinking at least once in the prior two weeks.[2] (*Binge drinking* is defined by the National Institute on Alcohol Abuse and Alcoholism as a pattern of drinking that brings blood alcohol concentration levels to 0.08 grams per deciliter. This typically occurs after four drinks for women and five drinks for men—in about two hours.)
- More than 50 percent of young adult men exceeded the recommended daily drinking limit, as did 40 percent of young adult women.

Even people who choose not to drink at all are still some-times surprised to discover the degree to which alcohol saturates their social lives at college. Either way, it's simply unrealistic to think you won't come into contact with alcohol and drugs in college. You can (and will have to) make choices. In this chapter you'll find some facts and figures about the reality of the situation on campuses. Most important, beyond the statistics you'll hear from students and professionals whose real-life experiences can help inform the choices you'll have to make.

Options

It's not as simple as *Yes, I will drink* or *No, I won't*. While choosing not to be a part of the party scene is a legitimate option, it can take some effort to find other students who've made the same choice to hang with on Saturday night. The fact is, most students don't make that choice. And for students who choose to party there's a wide spectrum, from "going but not drinking" to being the guy passed out in the corner. Some parties are simply a chance to meet people, and alcohol is an accompanying factor. Others parties are peopled with a harder drinking or drugging crowd that can be dangerous. Learning to handle yourself and deal with people under the influence is important. Learn your limits, draw your boundaries, and decide ahead of time whether or not, how much, and with whom you're going to drink.

Your choices about drinking will be influenced by who you're hanging out with. In the first few weeks, pay attention to the friends you've chosen. Listen to their attitudes and assess their actions. Do they just seem to want to get messed up as quickly as possible? Do you end up in situations or with people who go beyond the boundaries you've set for yourself? Is there a lot of pressure to keep up with their level of consumption, or are you free to make your own choices without being judged?

If you have never drunk alcohol before, I can assure you that you are not prepared for college parties. You need to ease into drinking. And a lot of people make huge mistakes by thinking they need to prove themselves to others by drinking all the time, or more than they can handle. Don't try to be someone else; be yourself. A lot of people think that this is a time they can change who they are, but being yourself will make you feel better and have a more authentic [college] experience.

—Marcelle, Catholic University of America

Many people think alcohol will clear their minds. This is completely untrue. Many times I have gone out with my friends to drown my sorrows in a few beers only to come back to the room crying. Alcohol is a depressant, and adding it to an unstable mind-set is dangerous. The best way to get rid of stress in college, in my opinion, is to go for a hard run or take a nice, quiet nap. These are the best ways to reboot your mind and energy.

—Kelsey, freshman, University of Iowa

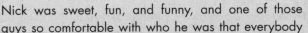

Nick was sweet, fun, and funny, and one of those guys so comfortable with who he was that everybody around him felt they could be themselves, too. Lots of people start drinking when they head off to college, but Nick hit it hard. His friends were worried. He was spending all weekend, every weekend, as wasted as he could get. Academically he barely managed to keep his head above water. He pledged a fraternity that was one of the biggest party houses on campus.

After his first year it was hard to imagine the person Nick used to be. He was still a nice guy, but he didn't have the same level of energy or investment in anything. The next year he wrapped his car around a light post on campus, got arrested for drunk driving, and just barely avoided time in jail.

Don't be satisfied with a social life that leaves you weirded out, babysitting, feeling guilty, or holding somebody's hair while she pukes every Friday night. Keep looking for people to hang with whose interests and tastes match your own. Trust us, they're out there.

Party with a Plan

Whatever you decide, when you're going out, have a plan. It'll be much easier to not drink or limit your drinking to a less dangerous level if you've made a commitment ahead of time not to overdo it. Jillian, a senior at Boston College, received some good advice from an unlikely source. "If I don't feel like drinking very much, am not feeling well, or just don't want to get drunk, my mom told me to simply fill my cup with something nonalcoholic and drink that throughout the night. People are happy as long as everyone has a drink—no one checks to see who is drinking what. It seems like a no-brainer, but I'm really glad she told me. I still do it to this day."

For Jillian the issue wasn't simply whether to drink or not, it was more a matter of authenticity. "The most common mistake freshmen make is pretending to be somebody they are not," she says. "For many people, this takes the shape of drinking and partying in an attempt to look cool. I always found that the coolest people are the people who are independent and sure of themselves."

Online Survival Guide: *Ask our online resident assistants any questions you may have about college life by visiting "Interactive RA" at http://TheFreshmanSurvivalGuide .com and clicking on "Ask."*

SEEK → FIND

What struck me—and I'm working with very high-achieving kids—is to what extent alcohol was self-medication. The kids had poor social skills, didn't know how to interact, and this was the model that was given to them and it was a real social lubricant. I got very tired of students reviewing with each other how drunk they were. Finally we passed a rule in the chaplain's house, where we have our meals and gatherings, that you could never utter a sentence that began with "I was so drunk..." The students needed a space where that wasn't what we talked about. It so much rules the culture, and people need to have space away from that self-defeating conversation.

—Rev. Ian Oliver, Protestant chaplain, Yale University

When it comes to alcohol, I encourage people to be far from it as much as possible. I don't want them to alienate themselves from their fellow Christians and Jews and friends because they drink. I tell them, "Yes, you can socialize with people, but you need to set your own parameters, your own ethics."

—Imam Yahya Hendi, Muslim chaplain, Georgetown University

Consider Waiting

Earlier we recommended living like a monk for the first month, which, of course, is a bit of an exaggeration. But please think seriously about this: If you plan to drink, don't do it right away. According to Joseph A. Califano Jr., chairman of the National Center on Addiction and Substance Abuse at Columbia University, "A child who reaches age twenty-one without smoking, abusing alcohol, or using drugs is virtually certain never to do so."[3]

According to the National Institute of Alcohol Abuse and

Alcoholism, "The first six weeks of freshman year are a vulnerable time for heavy drinking and alcohol-related consequences because of student expectations and social pressures at the start of the academic year."[4] We've mentioned that people go pretty wild the first few weekends on campus. The first month, when you're lonely, vulnerable, stressed out, and perhaps still a little afraid is *not* the best time to be diving into a vat of liquid oblivion. Maybe your emotions are at the other end of the spectrum and you feel as if you've finally been set free, you're exhilarated, thrilled to finally be on your own. *Settle down.* All the same opportunities and people will be available to you a month from now. Keep your cool and wait until you've got some good friends you know you can trust before you start experimenting.

You may want to wait even longer. There's pretty compelling research now that shows the benefits of waiting until it's legal for you to start drinking.

According to the National Institute on Alcohol Abuse and Alcoholism, "Another line of research is examining how becoming intoxicated at a young age is linked to later drinking problems during the college years. The results showed that college students who first became intoxicated prior to age nineteen were significantly more likely to be alcohol dependent and frequent heavy drinkers. These younger drinkers also were more likely to report driving after drinking, riding with a driver who was drinking or drunk, and sustaining injuries after drinking alcohol that required medical attention."[5]

These risks go down each year as people approach twenty-one (although they don't disappear). The brain continues to develop throughout young adulthood and is better able to project consequences, and behavior becomes less impulsive. Drinking can have consequences beyond hangovers and stupid decisions. The National Institute on Alcohol Abuse and Alcoholism (NIAAA) states, "About

25 percent of college students report academic consequences of their drinking including missing class, falling behind, doing poorly on exams or papers, and receiving lower grades overall."[6]

Drinking and Sexual Assault

The NIAAA's Task Force on College Drinking reports that each year:

- More than 97,000 students between the ages of eighteen and twenty-four are victims of alcohol-related sexual assault or date rape.[7]
- 400,000 students between the ages of eighteen and twenty-four had unprotected sex.
- More than 100,000 students between the ages of eighteen and twenty-four report having been too intoxicated to know if they consented to having sex.[8]

The problem is, at first binge drinking seems kind of funny. You lose a shoe, drop your phone, and can't remember a thing the next morning. But when you're a freshman girl, you may as well be walking around with a sign that says, I'M VULNERABLE! It's no joke. Guys prey on freshmen girls thinking they're naïve and eager to please. I can't tell you the number of times I've had to literally run when a creeper just wouldn't take the hint . . . but I've been lucky. I've had friends who were date-raped because they were either too drunk or doped out to fight or understand what was going on. I know someone who reported a rape and the case was thrown out because she wasn't sober, so her story wasn't believable. It's disgusting and it's not fair, but until the law catches up to the twenty-first century, it's better to be safe and boring than to be a statistic.

—Sophomore, Muhlenberg College

At many big schools it is very tempting to drink in the dorms. This, however, will get you kicked out of school! No matter how fun or how many people are doing it, you are risking a lot. If you get kicked out of school this will not make you, your parents, or your future very happy. I know this sounds like an obvious piece of advice, but being an RA I can tell you drinking in the dorms happens way too often. We catch two to three groups per week. You are not immune to this devastating result.

—Sarah, RA, University of Iowa

Drugs

You'll run into drugs on campus. Depending on the people you hang out with, it may happen only a few times, or pretty frequently, in your college career. You've already had years of education on the dangers of drugs, but in college, where you may feel freer to do what you want, it can be a bigger temptation. Whether your school costs $20,000, $30,000, or $50,000 a year, that's a lot to pay to party.

With that in mind, here's a quick snapshot of the reality of drugs on campus among full-time college students, courtesy of the National Institute on Drug Abuse. In 2013:

- 39 percent of college students admitted that they had used illicit drugs.
- 36 percent smoked pot.
- 5.3 percent used ecstasy
- 4.4 percent took Vicodin
- 5.4 percent admitted to taking narcotics other than heroin
- 10.7 percent had misused medication for attention deficit hyperactivity disorder (ADHD), specifically, Adderall.[9]

Colleges tend to be considerably less forgiving about drug use than underage drinking. You may feel as if your dorm room is your private property, but you actually have few rights on campus. Avoid the temptation and the chance of getting busted; don't hang with people who use or deal. It's also boring and frustrating to have to babysit friends who are too high to be trusted to stay safe.

Not everyone uses drugs to escape; some students use them to focus. Speed, Adderall, Ritalin, even caffeine pills may help in the short term, but in the long term they can wear you down and wipe you out with some serious side effects. (More on that in the pages ahead.)

No matter where you go to college, at some point you'll probably find yourself in closer proximity to drugs than you ever thought you'd be. Marijuana is a really popular drug in college. It isn't addictive, but it will make you a lazy bum, and you'll forget you even have classes or homework. Do yourself a favor—realize that drugs are everywhere in college, and be informed about what they can do to you.

—Freshman, University of Massachusetts Lowell

I have a few close friends who just messed around their first semester, consuming alcohol and smoking pot. The college almost did not let them return for a second semester because of their poor academic performance. There are a bunch of people who turn to alcohol or even harder things like cocaine to relieve their stress... You could be hanging out with some new guy or girl and they pull out some cocaine or something. You could be going out with some new friends and before you know it the cops come walking into the place and you find yourself in a room filled with underage drinkers. What will stop the cops from assuming you have been drinking, too?

—Freshman, Nazareth College

SEEK → FIND

The basis for a drug experience is about heightened sensitivity. It is worth exploring the nature and effects of the drugs being used—not for the sake of only avoiding drugs, rather for the sake of knowing what else is available to you in life. Is there anything that can accomplish that same feeling or high? I think there are alternatives that can accomplish "special experiences," where a mind-altering and expansive experience can be achieved. This approach, I believe, is a healthy alternative to the "don't do drugs" type of talk.

—Rabbi Yonah Schiller, executive director of Hillel at Tulane University

One weekend I got a call from two friends who had just taken 'shrooms and asked me to come over and trip-sit for them so they didn't hurt themselves. The drugs were done already, so there wasn't much I could do—unless I wanted to seriously risk my friendship with them by calling the police to report them. So I dropped all of my plans for the day to go babysit adults who couldn't take care of themselves. I spent the day watching them stare at inanimate objects, bored out of my mind, because the drugs made my friends about as communicative as goldfish. I couldn't even turn on the TV because it freaked them out (I started to wish I had called the police). When this ordeal was over, I told my friends that if they ever decided to ruin a weekend again this way they should call someone else and that they should also seriously consider if it was worth putting their friend through hell just so they could stare at the walls and be afraid of real life. I never had to trip-sit again and I think my friends realized that their choice was both dangerous and really inconsiderate to those who were around them.

—A reluctant trip-sitter

"Study Drugs"

In competitive environments like college, where getting higher grades could mean a better job or grad school opportunities down the line, some students are turning to prescription drugs to allow them to study and focus for longer periods. "If you can take a drug that allows you to stay awake through finals week and concentrate on relatively boring topics, you can see how the word would spread," University of Wisconsin–Eau Claire psychology professor William Frankenberger told the *Milwaukee Journal Sentinel* in 2006.[10]

Statistics from Partnership for Drug-Free Kids clarify the issue:

1. Among young adults between the ages of eighteen to twenty-five, one in six (17 percent) has abused a prescription stimulant at least once in their lifetimes.

2. More than four in ten (44 percent) say they abuse Rx stimulants in order to study and improve academic performance, while 31 percent say they abuse in order to stay awake.

3. More than one in five (21 percent) report abusing Rx stimulants in order to improve work performance at their jobs.

4. More than a quarter of students (27 percent) who report abuse of Rx stimulants also hold full-time jobs, in addition to attending school (compared to 12 percent of those who do not abuse Rx stimulants).

5. According to one study, between 2008 and 2012, the total number of privately insured Americans using medication to treat ADHD was more than 4.8 million—a 36 percent rise.[11]

Adderall is an amphetamine that, along with Ritalin (an amphetamine-like drug), is among the medications used effectively to treat the neurobehavioral disorder ADHD. When used without a prescription, however, Adderall has been classified by the federal government—along with cocaine, opium, and morphine—as having a high potential for abuse. Side effects include insomnia, irritability, and loss of appetite. In extreme cases, the drug can cause paranoia, hallucinations, and heart attacks.

Students are increasingly using these "study drugs" as academic performance enhancers in much the same way athletes use steroids. "We see a blend of psychological and physical dependence," said Eric Heiligenstein, clinical director of psychiatry at the University of Wisconsin–Madison's health services. "Students take it, get better results, and feel like they can't go off. They say, 'I feel like I've built my whole GPA on this. How can I stop?'" Our advice: Don't start.

The Risks

Risks of using/abusing drugs or alcohol include binge drinking, alcohol poisoning, rape, assault, fighting, hangovers, missed classes, weight gain, overspending, lowered inhibitions resulting in errors in judgment, drunk driving and other accidents, and an increased risk for suicide, arrest, dropping out, or getting kicked out.

It's an ugly list. Proceed with caution around drinking and drugs at college. Become aware of your school's rules and resources on the subject. The consequences of going too far can derail your education.

Sober Sundays, Wasted Wednesdays, and Everything In Between–The Interactive RA

Alcohol in college—it is prevalent in about 98 percent of any college movie. Epic parties every weekend, tons of beer and alcohol, shots, and hangovers. While movies tend to overexaggerate what college is like, alcohol in college is a real issue that, chances are, you will encounter at some point in your college career, if you haven't already.

When it comes to being safe with alcohol in college, there are some steadfast rules that do not need too much elaboration. Just follow the rules!

- **If your dorms don't allow alcohol in the dorms, don't bring alcohol into the dorms!** It isn't worth getting kicked out of the dorms just to have a case of beer in your room.
- **Don't ever drink and drive!** Also, don't get into a car with a drunk driver ever, under any circumstances. It isn't worth gambling *your life* or anyone else's. Speaking from personal experience, it isn't an enjoyable experience having a friend killed due to a drunk driver.
- **Use "Safe Ride."** Most colleges realize that parties and drinking are going to happen regardless of their rules and prevention. So, many campuses offer a "Safe Ride" program, in which they offer a *free* taxi service to and from the dorms to wherever you are in town. All you have to do is save the number in your phone. Use it!
- **If you are over twenty-one, don't buy alcohol for anyone underage.**

Now while you are completely free to experiment while in college, definitely be smart about your choices when it comes to drinking. First, make sure to party off campus. Parties in the dorms usually are highly distracting to neighbors, probably against your dorm's rules, and can be shut down and land you in some trouble quickly. Always make sure to have a designated driver, or use the Safe Ride program as noted above.

Second, know your limit and maintain control of yourself. This may be hard to discover if you are a first-time drinker, but you will feel a change in your body, way of thinking, and personality. If you feel yourself to begin to act outrageous, and do or say things that you regret, then it is probably a good time to put the solo cup down. It is always best to have friends around who can look after you as well.

If you find yourself struggling to overcome a growing tendency to drink, you may be developing an addiction to alcohol. Matters such as these are serious and need to be addressed quickly, regardless if it is with yourself, your roommate, or a friend. I don't know of any college campus that does not have some sort of place where you can seek help with this type of issue and work on getting yourself back on the right track. If you feel you need it, never hesitate to seek the help you need. Drinking is never worth destroying your college career or your life.

—Josh Martin, iRA
Director of Residence Life, Culinary
Institute of America at Greystone

For information on emergencies, how to recognize a drinking or drug problem or alcohol poisoning, what to do in case of sexual assault, check out chapter 29 on handling emergencies.

5 Final Thoughts

1. Just because you're in college doesn't mean you *have* to party.
2. Just because you choose to go to parties doesn't mean you have to drink or—if you do—get drunk.
3. Just because you choose to get drunk doesn't mean you have to get obliterated.
4. Just because you have before doesn't mean you have to again.
5. You can *always* make a new choice.

Online Survival Guide: For more information and resources about alcohol and drugs on campus, visit "Chapter 24" at http://TheFreshmanSurvivalGuide.com/chapters/.

THE TAKEAWAY

At college you'll be around drinking and drugs. You can make choices to put yourself closer to or further from that scene. Making your own choices, thinking ahead, and handling stress in positive ways will help you keep a healthy attitude and set of behaviors around alcohol and drugs on campus.

CHAPTER 25

To Keep Your Act Together, HALT

Survival Strategy #25: Be aware of the warning signs before you crash and burn. Don't let yourself get too Hungry, Angry, Lonely, or Tired.

The acronym *HALT* comes out of the recovery movement and is used to remind recovering substance abusers of the things that can put them at risk for relapse. Okay, *relapsing* might not be an immediate danger for many college students, but *collapsing* because you've neglected to pay attention to some red flags can be a real risk. In the spring of 2014, the National College Health Assessment surveyed 79,266 respondents. Thirty-two percent of the students reported they "felt so depressed it was difficult to function" in the past twelve months. Eight percent of the students reported that they "seriously considered suicide."[1] Being hungry, angry, lonely, or tired doesn't always spell disaster, but keep an eye on yourself and keep in touch with the people who've always kept an eye on you.

Hungry

Your mom's not here to remind you to eat. Get to the dining hall and take care of yourself. Skipping meals messes with your mood and your appetite. Most of us are used to having a plate set in front of us with a pretty balanced meal—something meaty, something green, something carby. We're also used to having someone remind us when it's time to eat something. When you skip meals you can end up overeating at the next meal or just wolfing down a bag of chips (or three) back in the dorm because you've gotten so hungry. Most important, though, it's hard to get everything done when you haven't fueled up, and going hungry makes it easy to crash emotionally.

A study published in the *Journal of American College Health* found a positive relationship between eating breakfast and first-year college students' grade point averages.[2] If you have a tendency to sleep through breakfast, keep some "traveling food" like granola bars, fruit, or pretzels in your room so you can eat on your way to class (see our guide to cheap snacks below). And whenever you start to feel crabby or headachy, ask yourself, *When did I eat last?* (For more advice on campus eating, read chapter 27.)

Cheap Snacks

DIY Trail Mix

Get big bags of raisins, almonds, and chocolate chips and make ziplock bags of your own to-go trail mix. It's far cheaper than buying premade trail mix, and you can add in your own preferences (like peanut butter chocolate chips, mini pretzels, dried cranberries, or M&M's).

> *Eat when you're hungry. Stop when you're full. And do something physical, even if it's going on walks with a friend. Those three things alone will make you feel better physically and mentally.*
>
> **—Erin, sophomore, Point Park University**

Veggie or Fruit Snacks

Buy inexpensive storage containers and take veggies (baby carrots, celery sticks, cherry tomatoes) and little containers of salad dressing along with you for snacking during the day. Or pick up some apples, bananas, and oranges. Check with your dining hall to see if you can take food outside, and save some bucks.

 Online Survival Guide: *For more dorm-friendly recipes— or to share your own—visit "Chapter 27" at http://The FreshmanSurvivalGuide.com/chapters/.*

Bringing healthy snacks back from the dining hall [if it's allowed in your school] is a good idea. When I knew I had a long night of work coming up, I'd bring back a bowl of fresh vegetables and keep snacking on those. This gave me a much more constant supply of energy than coffee did.

—Mike, Middlebury College

In Every Bag

Keep a granola bar in each of the bags you carry (i.e., backpack, purse, laptop bag). That way, if you're running around and haven't thought ahead about meals, you will always have something with you if you get hungry and don't have time to get something to eat right away. Make sure you remember to replace it every time after you eat one. If granola bars aren't your snack of choice, grocery stores stock an enormous selection of prepackaged snacks that are easy to throw in a backpack at the beginning of the day, just in case.

Angry

Manage your emotions by taking a walk, working out, talking to a friend, and especially avoiding alcohol! Angry + drunk = stupid behavior, sometimes involving campus security. Make sure you keep a read on how you're feeling and respond accordingly. People deal with the new stresses that come along with college life in many different ways. Some are healthy, such as going for a run, journaling, taking a break; others not so much, such as driving themselves to the breaking point, using sex or alcohol as a distraction, or taking stress out on other people.

The American Psychological Association (APA) explains that anger "is accompanied by physiological and biological changes; when you get angry, your heart rate and blood pressure go up, as do the levels of your energy hormones, adrenaline, and noradrenaline."[3] Anger is clearly not just in your head. Letting stress or anger build up, trying to ignore it, or dealing with it in unhealthy ways can take a toll. If you feel as if you're constantly ready to explode, deal with that short fuse in positive ways: exercise, prayer or meditation, an episode of your favorite comedy, some great music, or your favorite video game; or spend time with friends who can listen to and support you.

In the article "Controlling Anger Before It Controls You," the APA explains:

Sometimes, our anger and frustration are caused by very real and inescapable problems in our lives. Not all anger is misplaced, and often it's a healthy, natural response to these difficulties. There is also a cultural belief that every problem has a solution, and it adds to our frustration to find out that this isn't always the case. The best attitude to bring to such a situation, then, is not to focus on finding the solution, but rather on how you handle and face the problem.

Make a plan, and check your progress along the way. Resolve to give it your best, but also not to punish yourself if an answer doesn't come right away. If you can approach it with your best intentions and efforts and make a serious attempt to face it head-on, you will be less likely to lose patience and fall into all-or-nothing thinking, even if the problem does not get solved right away.[4]

Most likely college will bring you face-to-face with some of the most difficult situations you've ever confronted. Knowing how to manage the inevitable frustration and anger that accompanies those situations will help keep you sane.

Online Survival Guide: Ask our online resident assistants any questions you may have about college life by visiting "Interactive RA" at http://TheFreshmanSurvivalGuide .com and clicking on "Ask."

Lonely

Make sure you're meeting new people and developing new friendships (see chapter 2). Whether you had a ton of friends back home or just a few, starting over can be really tough, and it's tougher still if you feel as if you're in it alone. It can help to have people to talk to who are going through the same stuff. Every freshman on your campus is in the same boat, so reach out.

Stay connected to your existing support network, too (see chapter 2): Text your old friends, call your mother! "At least until you have strong connections among your college peers and professors, keep the connection with your family alive," recommends Harvard's Dr. Richard Kadison. "Send them e-mails; pick up the phone when they call. It's a little dose of insurance in case the day comes when you're out there alone and you need to hear a kind, familiar voice."

Three weeks into Sarah's first semester, her dad was worried. Sarah was calling home every night in tears. He wondered, *Is this normal? Is she going to be okay?* She'd played a different sport every season in high school but, afraid she'd be in over her head in a tough first-year program, she'd opted out of college sports. Now she had athlete roommates who were great people but were gone all the time. Sarah found herself alone every evening with her anxiety, worrying whether she could make it academically and socially in this new environment. A friend suggested she get out of her room and find *one* activity to join. That was all it took. Within a matter of a few days, she'd found an intramural team and through some new friends there got connected to a volunteer program, where she tutored kids once a week in a local school.

Be honest with your friends about the stress, and let them help you cope with it. Don't pretend everything is going well when it's not, because it's stupid to put up a front like that. Don't worry about your pride or image, and just be honest with the people around you. Dealing with stress alone is the worst idea ever.

—Senior, Northwestern University

Family, whether the one back in your hometown or the one you make at college, is the most important thing in the world. As much work as you have, go grab a cup of coffee with your friends every night, talk to your friends back home, and above all else, give your parents a ring at least once a week. You'll find you could use a little nagging once in a while, though in college it comes with more encouragement than it used to!

—Gerald, State University of New York at Fredonia

Winter Blues–The Interactive RA

If you're going to school in a place where the temperatures can get pretty cold, it's not unusual to get the winter blues and you may need to shake things up a little to cheer up. Here are a few pointers:

Exercise—Getting to the gym, popping in a yoga video, or going for a run can lighten the mood. Also, you could be working toward your New Year's resolution...Exercising with a friend can also help you battle your blues.

Soak Up Some Vitamin D—Spend some time outside. You lucky people who live in the South can do this without freezing your butts off, but those Northerners like me have to resort to keeping the curtains open, or sitting by a window during class or at a restaurant.

Avoid Binge Drinking—It may seem that since days are shorter and nights longer that you must get your drink on. Remember from high school health that alcohol is a depressant and will lower your energy and cause your mood to worsen.

Relax—Spend time with friends or take a break from school. Deep breathing always helps me. Read a book, watch a movie, or start a new TV series on Netflix or Hulu.

Embrace the Winter—Turn winter into something fun. Build a snowman, go sledding, skiing, ice skating, and more!

—Kailynn Cerny, iRA
West Virginia University

SEEK → FIND

Friendship is the most important thing in life, and spiritual friendship's really important. Four years of a concentrated pool of friends [is something] you won't have, most likely, anywhere else in the rest of your life. In addition to all the other things you feel you need to accomplish, learning how to be a friend and finding friends are indispensable life skills. [You started learning these skills] in high school, but it's very different doing that in college. Still, there's a skill to [making and being friends] that needs to be learned.

—Rev. Scott Young, Protestant campus minister,
University of Southern California

Tired

The statistics all point in the same direction: College students are tired. According to one study, only 11 percent of college students slept well consistently,[5] and in another conducted by the American College Health Association in 2007, only 40 percent of college students felt well rested no more than two days per week.[6] Lack of sleep can make your mood plummet. If you find yourself weepy all the time, impose a strict bedtime on yourself and see if that improves your mood.

All-nighters are a bad idea. *No* students do their best work under pressure. Sleep! Do it at night as often as possible. Daytime sleep screws up your body clock and your ability to attend your very expensive classes. Lack of sleep also impairs judgment. It may not seem like a big deal to pull a few all-nighters, but according to Dr. Richard Kadison, chief of Mental Health Services at Harvard, poor sleep quality can lead to myriad problems that can ruin your college years. "It's a myth that the best students stay up all night studying," he says. "It has been scientifically proven that it's the student who gets a good night's sleep, not the student who studies through the night, who does better academically. Less than six hours of sleep per night can lead to deficits in attention, concentration, memory, and critical thinking, along with increased depression, irritability and anxiety."

A semester with seven to eight hours of sleep every night is much better than a semester with five to six hours of sleep every night. When I wasn't getting enough sleep, I couldn't focus during my classes and found it hard to work on homework once it got dark outside.

—Jesse, Rochester Institute of Technology

The smartest thing I did in my first semester—keep my personal schedule as close to what it was at home as it could be in a college setting. My alarm goes off at 8 A.M. every day, because that's when my mom woke me at home, even though my classes aren't until later. I eat dinner around the same time as I would at home.

—Freshman, Stonehill College

I did two all-nighters a week while working on my thesis senior year, and by November I was seeing things that weren't there and getting myself all worked up about nitpicky things because I could not concentrate. Especially when you first arrive, it's important to remember how necessary sleep is for your body to function. Work hard, play hard, yes, but you cannot juggle all those things college has to offer if you can't concentrate and don't sleep. And while eight hours is ideal, it may be impossible, so at least fit in a nap here and there when you can.

—**Graduate, College of the Holy Cross**

Calm Yourself! A HALT How-To

Self-soothing is a person's ability to calm himself down. It's a skill that most of us have to one degree or another, but we're not always aware that it's what we're doing when we do it. Next time you find yourself really stressed out or distracted by intense emotions, go through this checklist and see which activity strikes you as the most appealing option. That's probably the one that will be most effective in settling you down. Even if you have too much to do, some deliberate destressing can make your work time more efficient.

- Take a nap.
- Take a shower (hot or cold—intense is the key to shifting mood).
- Are you hungry? Take your time to eat a decent, relaxed meal.
- Do some escapist reading, such as fun fiction or your favorite magazine or website.
- Talk to a friend.
- Get outside.
- Watch your favorite movie.
- Play your favorite board or video game or sport.
- Exercise.

8 Easy Ways to Add Movement to Your Day

1. Take the stairs instead of the elevator.
2. Stretch before bed or when you wake up.
3. Walk for at least fifteen minutes during your longest break.
4. Keep a Frisbee, football, or basketball next to your bed so you remember to use it.
5. Take a gym class.
6. Join an intramural or a club sport.
7. Take a dance class or join a dance club.
8. Get to know the athletic center, especially if you're not an athlete.

Give yourself twenty to thirty minutes at one of these activities, then try again to get at your work. Don't let your self-soothing turn into avoidance or addiction.

Get in the habit of giving yourself some quiet time as you transition from one kind of activity to another. Sleep space, personal space, and work space are suddenly all the same space when you live in a dorm. You can create space for yourself using a fifteen-minute cushion between activities like studying and sleeping or watching TV and working on a paper.

Online Survival Guide: For more easy ways to get moving—or to share your own ways to energize—visit "Chapter 25" at http://TheFreshmanSurvivalGuide.com /chapters/.

THE TAKEAWAY

Odds are nobody at college knows what normal is for you. You are your own best judge of whether you're operating at peak performance, taking care of yourself, or not okay. If you've never been an introspective person before, now is a great time to start cultivating that skill. Find a few moments each day to think about how you're feeling, how you're acting, what your energy level is like, and how you are interacting with others. HALT: Don't let yourself get too Hungry, Angry, Lonely, or Tired.

CHAPTER 26

How Not to Be Gross

Survival Strategy #26: Not being gross = staying healthy. Simple hygiene will help you avoid whatever bug is being passed around campus, and being clean is significantly more attractive to potential dates than being gross is.

Look, we realize that it doesn't exactly take a rocket scientist to understand that maintaining decent hygiene is a good practice in general for your health, appearance, and well-being. So think of the advice offered here as practical tips, shortcuts, and instructions you might not have heard before that will help you sustain the basics of good hygiene you've known about since you were young.

Hit the Showers

Remember to shower regularly (even during finals). It's not only a matter of cleanliness; it will help refresh you during long, stressful study hours. But for those moments when you simply run out of time, we offer you...

Tips for Cleaning Up Fast

1. Wash your face and brush your teeth no matter how late you wake up. (If somebody ever offers you a breath mint, *take it*. This could be a bad breath message in code!)
2. Use baby powder to freshen up. If you don't have a chance to shower, baby powder can make your hair look cleaner and absorb some of the oil. It's not a permanent solution but a way to look more put together.
3. Change clothes every day. If you fall asleep in your clothes, it may be easier to just walk out the door in what you're wearing, but don't—it will look messy and someone will notice.
4. Wear deodorant ('nuff said).

 Online Survival Guide: *For a complete, downloadable list of college essentials, visit "Chapter 26" at http://The FreshmanSurvivalGuide.com/chapters/.*

Avoid the Bugs

Nobody wants to be paranoid about germs. More important, nobody wants to *look* as if they're being paranoid about germs. On the other hand, nobody wants to get sick, either, and starving yourself of decent nutrition and sleep while living in close quarters with a bunch of other people can make you more susceptible to catching something.

Lots of nasty germs get passed from hand to hand to mouth in dorms, classrooms, and other well-populated buildings on campus. These bugs can be as simple as the common cold or as serious as meningitis. For every two hundred college students, one will come down with mono this year.[1] Though mononucleosis probably won't kill you, it can easily cost you a semester. Luckily your mother probably taught you everything you need to safely navigate this minefield before she put you on the bus for kindergarten—another favorite hangout of ugly little microorganisms—but here's a review to keep you moving at full speed so you can save your energy for more productive things than being sick.

Don't Go Barefoot

Not even in the shower. All manner of invisible things live on shower and locker room floors, and a run-in with one of them can cause anything from athlete's foot and warts to an infected cut full of blood and pus...We won't go into that. Most of this can be avoided with the purchase of a cheap pair of flip-flops at any dollar store.

Wash Your Hands

Try paying attention for a day to what you touch: doorknobs, car keys, cell phone, TV remote, mouse and keyboard in the computer lab—and then you touch your itchy nose, the drinking straw you're about to put in your mouth, and your eye that just got a speck of dust in it. When do you think was the last time anybody sanitized these surfaces? Nail biters and pencil chewers, take heed, wash up, and do it right—the world-renowned Mayo Clinic suggests at least twenty seconds of scrubbing followed by cleaning under the nails, in between fingers, and so on.[2]

Okay, we're not trying to turn you into compulsive hand

washers; we just want to encourage you to wash up every time you use the bathroom, before every meal, and at times in between when you can. Use hand sanitizer when running water is not available; keep a little bottle in your backpack or pocket. (Keep in mind that the desire to be clean has to be kept in balance. Compulsive or excessive use of hand sanitizer can start to peel the skin on your hands and kill what's supposed to be there.)

Get Some Sleep

We get it—college isn't exactly a time to catch up on your sleep or follow curfews. Most students will at some point pull an all-nighter or something close to it. When possible, try to keep regular hours as best you can, and you'll be able to shortchange yourself a little in a pinch without getting sick...or wasting your tuition money on a class you fail (see chapter 25).

Stay on as regular a sleeping schedule as possible when there's not much work. Then you can stay up late when the semester gets rough (e.g., don't stay up all night watching a TV show because you're bored).

Some people suggest not taking naps, but most college students will anyway. Instead of sleeping in your bed half the afternoon, take a twenty-minute power nap outside or in a chair. This will ensure you feel most refreshed and not fall into bad sleep habits. Is napping on your bed the only real option? Another trick we learned for power napping is not to get into pajamas and get under the covers. Instead, try lying on your bed with a lighter blanket and in your clothes from the day.

Listen to how your body reacts to your college-life schedule. If you find yourself nodding off in a class you normally don't, then you are probably not getting enough sleep.

Online Survival Guide: *Ask our online resident assistants your questions about college life by visiting "Interactive RA" at http://TheFreshmanSurvivalGuide.com and clicking on "Ask."*

Use earplugs and an eye mask! Sleep is so important, and you will wear yourself down if you don't get at least six or seven hours a night. Do what you can to schedule some sleep time and to block out roommate noise.

—Emily, junior, Tulane University

Eat Well

It may be the first time in your life you haven't had your mom there to pour orange juice down your throat every morning, but don't make a habit of breakfasting on coffee or cold pizza. Eat a balanced diet. Just because the cafeteria has a self-serve frozen yogurt machine doesn't mean the vegetable section needs to be neglected. Up your fruits and vegetable intake to crank up health and energy.

- Slice bananas or strawberries over your cereal.
- Load your burger with extra lettuce and tomatoes.
- Make salad a habit: Start at least one meal a day with green, leafy vegetables.
- Choose fruit over cake or cookies for dessert whenever you can.
- Be a food adventurer. Never eaten sprouts before? Don't know what an avocado tastes like? Be brave—you might just discover your new favorite food.

How do you determine if something still qualifies as food? If it's been sitting around in the car, in the back of the fridge, under the bed, and you have *any* hesitation over it, don't eat it! Food poisoning can take you out of the game for days or even weeks.

Drink lots of water. Almost nobody gets the recommended sixty to a hundred ounces of water per day. Bring your water bottle to the dining hall morning and night and fill it up with H_2O to make sure you're getting enough. A good rule from http://www.mayoclinic.com—if you rarely feel thirsty, you're drinking enough water. Staying hydrated helps your body, including the immune system, work right, and it staves off headaches and overeating. Water is especially important if you're consuming any significant amounts of caffeine or alcohol.

Janie had boundless energy in high school, bouncing-off-the-walls, nonstop-talking energy. She also had crazy allergies and was superthin, not eating-disorder thin, but fast-metabolism thin. She worked about twenty hours a week from the time she turned fifteen and was always burning the candle at both ends. Her parents were high achievers, and she was following right in their footsteps. At college she seemed to catch every cold or flu that came through campus but didn't slow down until she got so sick she could no longer function. Over break she looked like a ghost, dark circles under her eyes and no bounce at all. She missed two full weeks of classes but was able to rescue the semester with a few incompletes. From there on out she learned to watch her health more closely and take better care of herself.

Be Weather Wise

Dress appropriately for the weather. In some climates this means winter boots, hats, scarves, gloves, even long johns or extra layers... and often sunscreen. Even though you won't actually catch a cold from going out in the cold or melt in the rain, frostbite, windburn, hypothermia, heatstroke, and sunburn can be serious. And UV rays are dangerous all year round, not just in summertime. Skiers know it—sun reflects off snow and can burn you just as surely in January as in July.

Just Say No

Of *course*, drugs are bad for you; you already know that. This goes for alcohol and cigarettes, too. Is it practical to think you'll get through college—or even freshman year—without a single sample? Maybe not, but setting some limits for yourself is good for a whole bunch of reasons, one of which is that you don't want to get sick. And while it's fine to take cold medicine for a cold, sleep aids for insomnia, and painkillers for cramps or headaches once in a while, habitual use can become addiction before you know what's happening. If you're somebody who tends to pop a pill to fix every minor ache or pain, you'll want to keep an eye on that.

Put on Clean Underwear

When was the last time you hung out with someone who smelled a little rank or had visibly dirty clothes on? Yes, doing laundry on a regular basis is a pain in the neck, but nasty little things live in dirty clothes, specifically *E. coli* in your dirty underwear.

(We're talking fever, vomiting, diarrhea, and sometimes death.) You can definitely get more than one day out of a pair of jeans, but don't be gross. And wash your underwear in hot water to kill the germs (the hotter the water the more germs you kill—just watch out that your bright red boxers aren't in the same load as your white towels or T-shirts).

The "You Smell!" Conversation—The Interactive RA

Do your laundry / Take a shower! I think this point is self-explanatory. Your RA does not want to have the "You smell" conversation with you, and neither do you. It is very awkward for everyone. Trust me everyone will appreciate you smelling good (and no, Febreze does not count as a doing your laundry or showering).

—Kailynn Cerny, iRA
West Virginia University

The Freshman Survival Guide's Crash Course in Laundry

So your mom's been doing your laundry all these years, and now you're off at college and don't know how. You're certainly not alone. But it's easier than it looks, and there are lots of online resources with specific instructions. Here are the basics:

Sort. Separate your laundry into three categories—lights, darks, colors—and wash them in different loads, or else you'll end up with gray T-shirts and pink socks.

Check your pockets. You don't want to wash your cell phone or your wallet for obvious reasons, but a stray lip balm or pen can ruin an entire load of laundry, and a single Kleenex will coat everything in tiny bits of fluff.

Any detergent will do. The more expensive ones do more tricks—stain prevention, color saving—but even the cheapest ones are going to get your clothes clean. Read the container's label to see how much to use, or just look inside the cap—there will be a line that shows you. (See? We said it was easy.) A front-loading machine will have a special dispenser drawer that the detergent goes in. For a top loader let the washer fill a little, add the detergent, then add your clothes. A lot of laundry detergent manufacturers are also making pods now—basically small capsules that contain detergent and can include stain-fighting liquid and other goodies depending on which brand you buy. They're geared toward college students, because they're portioned to include just the right amount for one load of laundry, and you can just toss it in with a load—the capsule encasing dissolves to disperse the detergent once the wash gets going.

Wash. There will be a number of settings on the washer: *Normal* or *regular* will serve the laundry rookies best. Some washers will also give you water temperature choice. You can usually choose *cold*; it's an all-purpose setting that saves energy, cleans fine, and is easier on your clothes. You can choose *hot* for towels, underwear, and gym socks to kill germs and odor.

Don't overload. It's tempting to stuff the washer or dryer as full as possible, but resist. If you overfill, it's likely that you'll have to run your clothes in the dryer for a second cycle—totally annoying and not worth it. Three-quarters full is usually the limit for effective cleaning or drying.

Can it go in the dryer? Almost everything can for guys (but not your wool sweater, your linen shirt, or your silk boxers). Girls, read the labels; women's clothing tends to be trickier and uses a wider variety of special-care fabrics. Anything that might not survive a trip through the dryer should be air-dried. Cotton can take high heat, especially your towels and jeans, but some polyester will actually melt, so a medium setting will be safest for most everything else. As you take stuff out of the washer, give it a shake to reduce wrinkles.

> *Online Survival Guide: For a downloadable, printable PDF of the* Freshman Survival Guide*'s "Crash Course in Laundry," visit "Chapter 26" at http://TheFreshman SurvivalGuide.com/chapters/.*

For Extra Credit

- **Stains.** Pretreat by applying your regular detergent or a stain remover directly to the spot. Check stains when clothes come out of the washer. If the stains are still there, don't put the clothes in the dryer—the heat will set the stains permanently. You can reapply a stain remover and rewash—and hope for the best—or you can check online for stain-removal tips. Having a Tide to Go Instant Stain Remover pen and a bleach pen at school is invaluable, especially when you don't have a spare half hour to treat a stain properly.
- **Clean the lint trap before and after drying.** The lint trap is located either on top or inside the door frame of the dryer. Emptying it will make the dryer operate much more efficiently, saving you time and money.
- **Timing is everything.** Evenings and weekends are prime laundry hours on college campuses, so if you're an early

riser or have a longer break for lunch, you will find less competition for machines.

- **Laundry emergencies.** Lip balm, a marker, a pen, or lipstick in your laundry; new jeans in a load of lighter-colored things; or a lone bright-colored item that snuck in with the whites can be the kiss of death for the whole load. If one of these happens to you, try running the load again in hot water (if the fabrics can stand it) with (a little) extra detergent, and don't put anything in the dryer until you're sure you've got it all out.

I brought several weeks' worth of underwear. You can go a long time without doing laundry if you have clean underwear.

—Graduate, California State University, Monterey Bay

Two Weeks Left in the Semester, You're Low on Cash and Skipping Laundry...

- Air and fabric fresheners are lifesavers in college dorms to make rooms and clothes smell less gross.
- Wash clothes in the sink using dish soap or even shampoo.
- Use drying racks. As an alternative to dryers, a drying rack will save the earth, it's easier on your clothes than machine-drying, and it'll save you cash.

The one thing I was really glad I brought was cleaning supplies. I was definitely not a clean freak at home, but moving into a room that had been lived in only months earlier by complete strangers was enough to get me cleaning. Putting clean clothes into a dirty drawer is just gross. And if you are lucky enough to have your own bathroom, be prepared to do some heavy-duty cleaning of the toilet and shower before using them.

— **Lindsay, senior, New York University**

If You Feel Sick, Go to the Nurse

Don't forget that the campus health center is there to help keep you healthy—use it. A round of antibiotics can keep strep throat from turning into rheumatic fever—and keep you from passing the fun around.

A Word About Stress

Nothing weakens the immune system like being in a constant state of anxiety, and the best stress buster you could ever have is a healthy dose of organization (see chapter 13). What if you've gotten all your ducks in a row and you're still wringing your hands over every little thing? Well, first check out chapter 10 on mental health in case you have an actual anxiety disorder, and then try some time-honored techniques for destressing like those mentioned in chapter 25.

SEEK → FIND

I try to encourage students to have some sort of daily discipline for their own well-being, [such as] to stay away from this "Red Bull syndrome," where you work as hard as you can and live a caffeinated life, and then when you crash, you crash. That kind of cycle for study and for living is very unhealthy. So I always encourage them to get a good night's sleep. I also encourage them to maintain at least twenty to thirty minutes of meditation practice every day. During this time they're not thinking about work or planning but simply trying to spend time in their minds, analyzing their emotions and their priorities and how they are progressing.

—Ven. Tenzin Priyadarshi, Buddhist chaplain, Massachusetts Institute of Technology

Don't Share This—You Might Get That

Don't Share	You Might Get
Towels	Ringworm
Cosmetics	Pink eye, other infections
Lip balm	Cold sores, herpes
Razors	Ringworm, other fungal infections
Hats and hairbrushes	Lice
Drinks	Cold, flu, mono
Shoes (especially without socks)	Athlete's foot, warts
Toothbrushes	Cold, flu, mono, gum infections
Nail clippers	Fungus
Bathing suits (duh!)	Most of the above

In general, I think it is important to find quiet time for yourself, especially if you live in the dorms where it is difficult to find peace and quiet. The worst way to deal with stress is by giving up on your schoolwork and just sleeping or partying all the time. I have seen

both routes taken, and both lead to more stress as schoolwork can continue to build up.

—Kate, Iowa State University

The worst ways to deal with stress are to internalize it or try to ignore it. I can't even count the number of times that I have become sick because I let the stress consume me.

—Freshman, Stonehill College

Online Survival Guide: *For a complete packing list of college essentials, visit "Chapter 26" online at http://The FreshmanSurvivalGuide.com/chapters/.*

THE TAKEAWAY

Shower. Don't go barefoot. Brush your teeth. Get some sleep. Eat healthy. Drink water. Wash your clothes and dress for the weather. In short, take care of yourself.

CHAPTER 27

There's No Vitamin C in Orange Soda, and Doritos Aren't a Food Group

Survival Strategy #27: Paying attention to what and how much you're eating and drinking will pay off in terms of energy, good health, mood, and weight.

You're going away to college now; it's time you learned the hard truth. There is no vitamin C in orange soda, and "crunchy" is not one of the five food groups. In this culture, our relationship with food is a very complex thing. It offers us basic sustenance, but food is also an integral part of so many aspects of life— friendship, family, romance, pleasure, culture, religion. It cheers us up, it calms us down, it connects us, it comforts us. It can also be the source of problems in terms of excessive weight gain, unhealthy/unbalanced diets, and perhaps even eating disorders. You probably make a lot of your own food choices already, but as the weight of responsibility for choices shifts more fully and permanently to you, there are some things you should know.

Eating Healthy in the Dining Hall

Making the switch from someone else worrying about what you're eating to your doing it yourself has been gradual up to this point, but now it takes a sudden leap. You're on your own here. The other major change is that you won't be eating from a well-stocked fridge and pantry. Dining-hall eating is more like eating at a restaurant (not always a five-star) for almost every meal. Talk to anyone who does a lot of traveling about eating out and eating healthy at the same time. It's a big challenge. It can be done, though, especially if you pay attention and follow a few simple rules:

- **Start with one.** You may be tempted to load your plate with three of everything, especially if you're walking into the dining hall superhungry from having skipped the previous meal. Start with a single serving of each item. If you still feel hungry, drink a glass of water while you wait five or ten minutes to decide if you really need seconds. If you have to make a conscious decision to go get more food, it can help keep you from eating more than you should. A serving of meat is the size of a deck of cards;[1] a serving of pasta, rice, yogurt, or milk is about the size of your fist; and a serving of fruit or vegetables is about the size of a baseball.[2]

- **Food group savvy.** You don't have to laminate the food pyramid on an index card and carry it around with you, but do try to choose at least one serving from each of the five food groups—meat, fish, and poultry; dairy; grains and cereals; fruits; and vegetables—at every meal. Find out more at the USDA's website, http://www.choosemyplate.gov.

You can get a customized eating plan and even follow MyPlate on Twitter for daily nutrition tips.

- **Processed is bad.** The closer it looks to the way it did when it grew out of the ground, the better. Whole grains and fresh produce are the healthiest and most desirable; refined sugars, enriched flours, and canned fruits or veggies should be eaten in limited amounts.
- **Variety.** Even at schools with dining halls that are top-rated for quality, sometimes what they offer for dinner hardly ever varies. Attending a school that serves steak tips and salmon is great, but you're not going to want to eat it every night for four months. An easy and fun way to help balance your diet is to eat lots of different foods instead of having the same thing over and over. Green vegetables are great for you, and you can't go wrong with "an apple a day," but it's even better to eat a rainbow of different-colored foods—think blueberries and strawberries on your cereal at breakfast and orange juice to drink, a green salad with purple cabbage at lunch, and butternut squash or even a banana with dinner to cover your yellow requirement.

Online Survival Guide: *Ask our online resident assistants any questions you may have about college life by visiting "Interactive RA" at http://TheFreshmanSurvivalGuide .com and clicking on "Ask."*

Food can be one of the most unpleasantly surprising aspects of college life. Try to get the most flexible meal plan your school offers, such as a meal card that can be used in more than one dining section, so you don't eat the same thing every day. Before you go, find out what dining options are in the town or city your college is located in—some schools give students brochures or books on this. Bring snacks for your dorm, but try to limit the just-add-water entrées. You can't live on sodium!

—Chelsea, freshman, Muhlenberg College

The Freshman Fifteen

If you're worried that by the time you go home for Thanksgiving break your pants won't button anymore, you may be happy to learn that on average a freshman's weight gain is closer to four or five pounds[3] in the first year, not fifteen.[4] And it's not everybody. There are people who *lose* weight when they start college. There are also people who gain even more than the freshman five or fifteen. College is a tremendous lifestyle change. Most of the things that influence changes in body weight—available food choices, amount and types of physical activity, sleep, mood, stress level—are also part of beginning college.

5 Ways to Watch Your Weight

1. Become a Label Reader

It's hard to know whether you're eating healthily if you don't know exactly what it is you're eating. Become familiar with the standard nutrition label, which will tell you how big a serving is—for instance, two cookies, not half a box. It also tells you how much fat (bad), saturated fat (worse), and trans fat (awful) a serving contains; other important stats to look for are protein, carbohydrate, and fiber content—higher protein and lower carbohydrates will usually help you avoid gaining weight, and the more fiber, the better.

2. Stop Mindless Munching

This happens when studying, partying, watching TV, hanging out with friends, stressing out—anytime you eat while you're doing something else that seems more important. All of a sudden you realize that you've polished off a whole bag of Doritos without even tasting them. Start paying attention to what, when, and why you eat.

3. Count Liquid Calories

Ever had a Starbucks Venti Caramel Macchiato? This particular nectar of the coffee gods packs a 300-calorie punch, with 8 grams of fat (5 of them saturated), and 43 grams of carbohydrates. If soda is your vice, you should know that a one-liter bottle of Mountain Dew will supply you with 440 calories and 124 grams of sugar (in case you don't notice, the bottle contains not just one, but *four* 8-ounce servings). *That's like eating 31 teaspoonfuls of sugar.* And this site contains an interesting breakdown of the different types of food and drink you might consume to mull over: http://www.calorieking.com.

4. Eat at Mealtimes

Of course this means to cut down on snacking in between meals and snacking with healthier foods when you do, but it also means don't skip breakfast (or lunch or dinner), and try to keep to a regular schedule whenever possible, even on weekends. Skipping meals may seem like an easy diet strategy, but by letting yourself get too hungry you only risk *over*eating later in the day, when your body tries to make up for the food you deprived it of earlier.

5. Think Ahead

Yes, there are going to be times when you just won't have enough hours in the day. For such occasions as these, keep handy a stash of trail mix, protein bars, fresh or dried fruit, beef jerky, or whatever floats your boat—but first read the label and make sure there's something in it besides sugar or salt. And it's never a bad idea to grab an apple or a banana to go on your way out of the dining hall, as long as your meal plan allows this—check the rules first.

 Online Survival Guide: *For more about healthy eating on campus, visit http://TheFreshmanSurvivalGuide.com /chapters/ and click on "Chapter 27."*

Easy and Edible Dorm Recipes

(Made with ingredients that you probably have in your dorm room or can get easily.)

Thai Ramen

Cook one package of ramen noodles and drain. Heat ⅓ cup peanut butter, ⅓ cup water, two packets of soy sauce, one packet of sugar, and some of the seasoning packet to taste. Stir. Toss with cooked noodles.

Deluxe PB and Banana Sandwich

Spread peanut butter on one slice of bread. Slice a banana onto it. Drizzle with honey. Sprinkle with granola. Top with second slice of bread.

Trail Mix Oatmeal

Mix ½ cup instant oatmeal (Old Wessex brand is really good and comes "bulk" rather than in individual packets) with a handful of trail mix and one cup of water in a two-cup microwave-safe bowl. Cook for about two minutes. Top with yogurt or milk.

Don't trust yourself with these? Try this Busted Halo intern's recipe:

Pappa's Pizza Bagel

This one is for students who are less than talented in the culinary arts. All you need are three simple ingredients. Grab a few bagels and store in a ziplock bag in the freezer if you've got one. Then wait for your dining hall to have pizza one night and ask if you can have some extra pizza sauce—the dining-hall staff usually doesn't mind. Finally, grab some mozzarella cheese from the local convenience store. Spread the sauce on the bagel, top with cheese. Put your pizza bagel in the oven on top of tinfoil (you don't want to annoy the rest of your dorm with the smoke and smell from burned cheese). Leave it in the oven for a few minutes to cook on high, then turn on the broiler to make it crispy.

Online Survival Guide: For more dorm room recipes—or to share some of your own—go to http://TheFreshman SurvivalGuide.com/chapters/ and click on "Chapter 27."

I've found it easiest to eat healthy when I cook for myself. This might not be the case for people who can't cook, but I've found it's a hundred times easier to watch what you eat when you're buying the ingredients that go into your meals. It's easy not to eat ice cream all the time when you just don't have it stocked in the freezer, and fruits and vegetables are fresher at the grocery store and hard to find in a good variety in the dining hall. Even if cooking for yourself isn't an option, if you can get to a grocery store or produce/farmers' market a few times a month, having that fresh stuff stocked in a minifridge can make a huge difference in your diet.

—Jenna, Boston College

Going into college, I didn't know how to cook at all. I didn't take a meal plan because that was more money that I didn't need to spend. The first few weeks were terrible because I was just eating sandwiches and nothing else. Bread, spinach, deli meat, and cheese. When my dad visited he brought me my sister's rice cooker. This was probably where my college experience got so much better (in terms of food and sustenance). I used it as a Crock-Pot to make all sorts of things. Three semesters in, I'm still cooking, I'm still using my rice cooker as a cooking pot, and I'm happy that I learned how to cook now instead of after college.

—Austin, University of Advancing Technology, Arizona

What Are You Hungry For?

This is college. It's okay to pig out with your friends now and then. Food is an integral part of your social life. On the other hand, you don't want it to get out of control. If you find yourself putting on weight and wondering how it got there—or if you find yourself with a Twinkie in your mouth and wondering how *it* got there—it may be time to reexamine your eating habits.

When you reach for a snack, stop and think about what you're hungry for. Are you feeding your body, or are you feeding your boredom, anxiety, loneliness, or depression? (Because *they* don't actually want Twinkies, they only *think* they want Twinkies.)

During freshman year, in an effort to eat healthier, Anna went vegetarian. Her mother wasn't very worried—a number of her friends were committed, balanced vegetarians, and they ate really well and consciously. For the first few months, things went fine. The challenge of getting the right nutrients was interesting and kept Anna engaged in the pursuit. But she was a dancer, so making sure she was eating right was important. And with all the changes that came with freshman year, her mom was a little concerned that the learning curve of going vegetarian responsibly might be a little steep.

As Anna's schedule got busier, she found she didn't have as much time to spend thinking ahead about what she needed to eat. After a while she started feeling tired all the time and finding herself defaulting more and more to quick, packaged foods. She decided to start adding some meat back into her diet, but she does still try to eat consciously, healthily, and meat free as much as possible.

Again, bringing healthy snacks back from the dining hall (if allowed) or getting some at a grocery store is a good idea. Keeping a bowl of fresh fruits or vegetables nearby to snack on will give you a healthier, more consistent source of energy than coffee or sugar.

Try keeping a food journal for a week or two, in which you write down everything—and this means *every*thing—you eat and drink. This will not only help you keep track of where your calories are coming from, it will also help motivate you to avoid eating something that isn't worth writing down.

Spoon University

Spoon University is an everyday food resource for college students to intelligently discuss and share tips about eating in college. According to its website, Spoon U (SpoonUniversity.com) is "on a mission to make food make sense...For many of us, this is the first time we're navigating our campuses or our kitchens on our own, and Spoon University is here to simplify and celebrate that." On the site you can find incredibly simple recipes and great restaurants around campus that you haven't discovered yet.

A Salad Never Hurt Anybody–The Interactive RA

Going off to college brings with it an obvious amount of new-found freedom including the sudden ability to eat whatever it is you want and buy whatever it is you want, which means that suddenly all of that junk food that you were most likely forced to eat in moderation back at home becomes readily available 24/7. Everyone's body is different, so adjusting to the college lifestyle will take a toll on everyone's body differently, too. Fortunately, there are easy ways to make slight adjustments to your eating habits that make for overall healthier results.

- Eat three meals a day! It may be hard to eat breakfast when you are rushing out of your dorm to get to your 8 A.M. class, but grabbing a granola bar, a piece of fruit, or even dry cereal helps you from overeating during later meals and also provides brain food during those early mornings before lunchtime.

- Snacking can help to keep your appetite in check! This one comes with an asterisk—by snacking I don't mean an entire bag of Doritos between lunch and dinner. Snacking moderately on something light and healthy actually helps keep you going during the day and lowers your appetite with those bigger meals. Personally, I have a bag of trail mix for such a purpose. A handful here and there between my meals does wonders. Other snack ideas may be yogurt, precut fruit, or string cheese.

- Balance your food groups! We aren't saying to never indulge in those three slices of pizza on a Friday night when kicking back with your buddies. Just don't eat it every day. And when eating at the dining halls, try your best to get a good balance of dairy, grains, fruit, vegetables, and protein. Don't go for the cheeseburger and fries every single meal. A salad never hurt anybody.

- Some colleges provide special kitchenette areas in the common areas of their dorms, or have apartment-style housing with a full kitchen available for cooking. A quick Google search will find you easy college recipes that will not break the bank. A common website frequented by myself and one I share with my residents at the beginning of the school year is http://www.supercook.com. It allows you to enter in the ingredients you have, and it pops out a meal you can make using those ingredients.

Josh Martin, iRA
Director of Residence Life, Culinary
Institute of America at Greystone

Eating Disorders and Body Image Issues

According to the National Eating Disorders Association, as many as 10 million females and 1 million males struggle with an eating disorder such as anorexia or bulimia. In terms of college-age students:

- 40 percent of female college students have eating disorders.
- 15 percent of women seventeen to twenty-four have eating disorders.[5]
- The rate of eating disorders among college men ranges from 4 to 10 percent.
- Large-scale surveys have concluded that male body-image concerns have dramatically increased over the past three decades, from 15 to 43 percent of men being dissatisfied with their bodies; these rates are comparable to those found in women.[6]

Millions more have binge-eating disorders, and 40 percent of newly identified cases of anorexia are in girls fifteen to nineteen years old. If you have already been diagnosed with an eating disorder, you should check out what help is available on campus before you head off to school. The stresses of college will most likely impact your ability to manage your health. Eating disorders—anorexia, bulimia, and/or binge-eating disorder (compulsive overeating)—are a complex and serious health problem.

Male Body Image

The traditional understanding of eating disorders and body image issues generally focused on women but the pressure for an idealized vision of physical perfection has also taken its toll on men as well... but in different ways. A recent study from the *Journal of the American Medical Association* (*JAMA*) found that "high concerns with muscularity are relatively common among adolescent boys and young men. Males with these concerns who use potentially unhealthy products to improve their physique are at increased risk of adverse outcomes."[7]

The major difference they're finding between men and women in terms of weight concerns is that while girls generally want to be thinner, boys are as likely to feel pressure to *gain* weight as to *lose* it. "There are some males who do want to be thinner and are focused on thinness," said Dr. Alison Field, the lead author of the study, "but many more are focused on wanting bigger or at least more toned and defined muscles. That's a very different physique."

"The media has become more of an equal opportunity discriminator," says Dr. Raymond Lemberg, a clinical psychologist and an expert on male eating disorders. "Men's bodies are not good enough anymore either."[8] The idealized and unattainable body proportions characterized by the "Barbie" doll has its male equivalent. One study from the late 1990s examined G.I. Joe action figures and found that in 1964, the action figure had what would equal a thirty-two-inch waist and twelve-inch biceps. By 1991, Joe had a six-pack and had lost three inches off his waist, but bulked his upper arms up to sixteen-and-a-half-inch biceps—nearly impossible-to-attain dimensions.[9]

The desire to attain male physical perfection is having adverse effects on behavior as well. A 2012 study of adolescents revealed that "more than a third reported downing protein powders or shakes in an effort to boost their muscularity; in addition, almost 6 percent admitted to using steroids, and 10.5 percent acknowledged using some other muscle-enhancing substance."[10]

The consequences of this behavior can be severe, according to Dr. Rebecka Peebles, codirector of the Eating Disorder Assessment and Treatment Program at the Children's Hospital of Philadelphia. She cites concerns about the "natural" powders or shakes that teenagers can purchase anywhere. The truth is, she says that "natural" in terms of these products simply means unregulated: "They actually can include all kinds of things in them... [Some] are actually anabolic androgens and just packaged as a natural supplement."[11]

The *JAMA* study found that males who had high concerns about muscularity and used potentially unhealthy products to achieve their desired physique were "more likely than their peers to start binge-drinking frequently... In addition, males with high concerns about muscularity and thinness... and those with high concerns about muscularity who used products to improve muscle size or strength... were much more likely than their peers to start using drugs."[12] Suffice it to say, like the eating disorders discussed above, this is a serious issue. If you find yourself becoming preoccupied with body image, excessive working out, using supplements and whatnot, you need to seek out professional help immediately.

SEEK → FIND

I teach a vegetarian cooking class, and 80 to 85 percent of the students we get aren't from a Hindu background. Students I come across who are becoming vegetarians are doing it for three reasons: health, environment, and compassion... Their understanding of what's happening in terms of violence to the animals and how the meat industry is having a really terrible impact on the environment is growing. As these facts are becom-

ing better known to young bright minds, students don't want to have anything to do with it. A lot of them are looking to become vegetarians, but they're having problems because their families and schools aren't facilitating it... They're already going through so many stresses being away from home, new roommates... If they can't get proper nourishment, that's an additional burden in their lives and it's a big one.

—Gadadhara Pandit Dasa, Hindu chaplain,
Columbia University

6 Easy Ways to Eat Healthier

1. Drink more water. It'll keep your appetite under control and help your whole system function better. Approximately sixty-four ounces per day is recommended. Buy a water bottle that has ounces measured on the side to keep track.

2. Up your protein intake and lower your carbs. More meat, nuts, cheese, eggs, dairy; less bread, pasta, and crackers.

3. Cut back on soda and sweets. Keep an eye out for any farmers' markets near campus where there will be lots of great opportunities for good eating.

4. Eat simply. More raw and whole foods, fewer processed foods, meals with fewer ingredients.

5. Strive for five or more servings of fruits or vegetables daily—juice counts.

6. Slow down. You're busy, but mindfulness about eating, tasting your food, being attentive to what you're eating helps you eat less and benefit more. Relax and chew, don't chomp and gulp.

Our relationship to food can get very complicated at times. It can be used for everything from nutrition and comfort to relieving stress and damaging self-image issues. As with any relationship, trying to maintain a healthy sense of balance and awareness is key. Try to eat healthily, regularly (three meals a day), and for the right reasons.

CHAPTER 28

Is This Really Where I Belong?

Transferring

Survival Strategy #28: Adjusting to a new situation takes time. *So* much has changed since you left high school, but being patient with yourself and your new surroundings can really pay off. If you're not happy where you are, transferring *might* be your best move. Just be sure you've given yourself and your school enough time to be sure.

At some point during freshman year nearly every student asks the question "Is this where I belong?" For about one-third of them, according to the National Association for College Admission Counseling, the answer to that question is "No."[1] For a significant number of students, their initial college choice isn't their eventual choice.

But just because a lot of students make the decision to transfer, that doesn't mean it's a choice that anyone should make lightly. There are so many reasons why people choose to transfer. Some students find themselves at a college that just isn't the right fit. They thought they would enjoy a big campus, but they found it overwhelming. Or maybe they fell in love with a small private college on their campus visit, but now that they're living there it seems restrictive and boring. Some students start a program that they have been interested in for years and realize it's not that interesting to them anymore. There are lots of other reasons people transfer: Their program is too rigorous or not rigorous enough, homesickness, or family circumstances. Sometimes it's because a student is simply uncomfortable in a new environment or still sorting out what he or she would like to pursue. A conversation with an advisor or just a little more time can usually solve—or at least settle down—those worries. Although these situations are not always an easy fix, switching schools, transferring to a new college when you've just gotten used to one, is a big decision.

What's the Problem?

If you are unhappy where you are, one of the best things you can do is take some time to get specific. Think, talk through, and even write down what you're unhappy about. There are things that every college student struggles with no matter what college they ended up at. (Look at the chapter titles in this book, and you'll notice you're not the only one who has problems.) Once you've made your list, take some time to consider whether your problems are with college in general or this college in particular. General college problems—roommates, friendships, homesickness, time management, learning how to study, research, or write papers—are the kind of problems that will resurface wherever you go. If those are the primary source of your discontent, it's usually best to stay put and tackle those things head-on without adding to them by trying to start over someplace new. It may mean you'll be less than perfectly comfortable for a little while longer. But often, time to adjust is the biggest factor. When everything is still new it's hard to know what the real problem is.

Problems specific to your college—it's too big or too small, there's too little diversity, or the program you chose isn't what you were hoping for—are still worth trying to solve without a move if you can. Transferring, especially midsemester, can end up losing you money, time, and credits, and rather than solving problems, it sometimes just creates new ones. Again, as you're adjusting to this new environment it can be easy to mistake *I'm just not used to this* for *I really don't like this.*

Another important step to take if you do decide to transfer is to do some research with the school or schools you're thinking of transferring to. Talk to their transfer staff and make sure you'll get maximum credit. Ask specific questions, especially about the things you're dissatisfied with currently. Transferring for the right reasons can make a big difference in your long-term success in college as well as your short-term happiness. Talk to other people who have transferred and collect some wisdom there. Often it's the things that don't turn out the way we'd planned that teach us the most about ourselves and about what's important. A more philosophical way of putting it—experience is what you get when you don't get what you want.

We asked some transfer students to share their stories.

Erin was the classic "so good at everything" student. She had to make a choice and dive in so she could find out what was right for her. She ended up finding out what *wasn't* right for her. Patti started out at small women's college. She made some great friends right off the bat but found the small college environment a little *too* small.

Erin's Story

I was told college is the time to learn about yourself: who you really are, what you actually want to do, how loud you can play

Journey without the RAs hunting you down. You don't even notice, but your actions fall into patterns that you begin to recognize, and you really get a grasp on what your strengths are.

Leaving high school, I didn't know my strengths at all. I had no idea what to major in or what college to look into, because I didn't specialize in one thing. I was that kid who did everything—I had no real calling. Everyone said to follow my heart, but the things I loved to do were dance and write, and what do you do with a degree in English or dance?

I ended up going to a local state school undeclared and thought I would figure it out eventually, but when Cornell offered me a guaranteed transfer as an environmental engineering major, I accepted. I did it because I knew I would never pick unless I threw myself into something and decided if I liked it or not. The plan was to go to my school for a year taking specific classes and then transfer to Cornell my sophomore year. The classes I had to take made me a biophysics major at my school, something so defined and difficult that I would either love it or fail miserably.

By October I knew I wouldn't be going on to Cornell. I had found a home at my school and didn't want to leave that behind. But in November I finally accepted that I was under a ton of stress and that it was more difficult to handle than I wanted to admit. In December, I realized I wasn't just stressed out, I was unhappy. At the end of the semester, I compiled a list of things I learned about myself in the first few months of college.

First of all, I should *not* be a biophysics major. As luck would have it, I hate biology. Some people love it, but I think biology is the most boring subject I've ever taken. Yes, I made it through that semester. Yes, I can make myself learn biology and even biophysics. In fact, I'm pretty good with math and physics. Still, as much as I appreciate the physical universe, I don't want to be a biophysicist and I don't want to be a doctor. As a matter of fact, I am that person we all laugh at in bio lab who questions animal testing.

Second, I should *not* be an engineer. One of my roommates calls me Whole Brain because I do well in math and science, but my artistic side is just as strong. I guess she's right, because I can't stand only doing the technical stuff. I'll be the first to stand up and announce that I love physics, but when I went to see my old dance studio's holiday show, I realized that by cutting all the artistic things out of my life I had left a part of myself behind. I'll never get that out of calculus and physics. Someone else might, but I won't. Engineering is a wonderful profession that takes a lot of intelligence, but it is not the kind of intelligence I want to commit my life to.

Third on my list is this: This was not the school for me. I knew this when I visited my senior year, but I questioned myself, and when I couldn't decide what to study I went to the only place I had applied undeclared. Don't get me wrong—it is a beautiful campus, I made friends who mean the world to me, I've had opportunities I never expected—but I couldn't do what I want to do there.

I have two passions: dancing and writing. Now I'm pursuing them. I didn't return second semester and started instead at Point Park University in Pittsburgh as a dance major with a concentration in jazz. I'm now declaring a double major in print journalism. It's a far cry from biophysics, I'm well aware. It also all happened very quickly.

I returned home for Christmas break and got a chance to really think about being unhappy at school. I knew the stress wasn't the true problem, because the feeling of stress was very different than the feeling of being sad when I thought about my days as a dancer, or the detached feeling I got when I walked past students in the arts building.

I tried to find what I was looking for where I was—I joined swing dance club, I went to campus club performances, I was a novice rower on the crew team—but I needed more. I realized that I had done just what I expected: thrown myself into a crazy major and hated it. It was time to try something else.

My first semester at the new school was hard—I wouldn't recommend transferring halfway through your first year. People had already settled into their groups of friends, and the most difficult part was finding a way in. I missed my old friends. I missed our Thursday night *Grey's Anatomy* tradition and the roommate who was my best friend. At Point Park, I didn't watch *Grey's*, and my new roommate went home most nights. Soon enough I found a best friend, though, and I fell into another group of friends who spent their Thursday nights glued to a different set of TV shows.

I still miss my old school sometimes. It still feels like home to me when I visit or talk about it. I know, however, that I did the right thing in leaving. I learned more about myself in those few months than I ever would have if I'd stayed. The experience alone is enough to make me say I'm glad I transferred.

Patti's Story

There are many reasons why I decided to transfer, some more influential than others, but they were all important. I started my freshman year at Cedar Crest College, a small school in Allentown, Pennsylvania. It was not my first-choice school, but a series of unfortunate events led me there. Think Murphy's Law times ten. I ended up having only one choice left of the five schools where I was accepted, that I could actually still go to. I tried to think positively about everything. It was an all-women's college, and I was skeptical about that right off the bat. I had always found it easier to be friends with guys than girls, but since I had no other choice, I decided to step up to the challenge. What I found was that it was really cool, almost like being at summer camp all year round. You didn't always have to primp or worry about looking your best, because it was just you and your girlfriends going to class. There was a lot of female empowerment going on, and I really loved that feeling while I was there.

I really enjoyed my time at Cedar Crest, but I knew there was something missing. I had wanted to do Navy ROTC, and the opportunity for that just wasn't available in Allentown. I also missed home, not necessarily my family, but my friends and just having something to do. Allentown is in the middle of nowhere, and I was bored. Then there was the boy factor. It wasn't necessarily the lack of them at school, but there was one in particular that lived in Rochester and I wanted to be with him.

So I looked at my options and applied to schools in the area. I've always been a bio major, that didn't change when I switched schools. I chose Rochester Institute of Technology because I liked the feel of the College of Science. And I loved it. RIT was the place I was meant to be, but I like to think that I was also meant to go to CCC for a year, and meet some really awesome people who I will now be friends with for the rest of my life.

Both Erin and Patti took the time to think about why their first college wasn't a good fit. They made a good-faith effort to solve the problems they were experiencing, but ultimately the choice to transfer led to good things. Keep in mind that if your first college isn't right for you, there is probably another one that is.

I started out at a small private school for freshman year. I liked the school well enough but felt I wasn't being challenged at all. I credit my Catholic school background for that. I was shocked to be in a freshman philosophy class with students who had never written a term paper. I applied to a bunch of schools (including some Ivies) for sophomore year transfer. I ended up at a safety school—a big university. I stayed there for one semester. I hated everything about it: classes with five hundred students, a campus with the feel of a small city, the dorm (I was a commuter at my first school). So over Christmas break, I visited the U of R and loved it. I lucked out and hooked up with a transfer counselor who liked me, and she expedited my application, and I started there in the spring. I commuted there and loved it until I graduated. I even did the Take Five program and stayed an extra year. It was the perfect fit sizewise and academically. I occasionally still hear grumbles from my dad because I had a full scholarship at my first school, but even though it took me three moves, I know I ended up in the right place. For me, that's the most important thing.

—Jill, University of Rochester

As a freshman I went to a very small, very conservative college in the middle of nowhere. My first semester there was really awesome; I made a lot of friends and I got to play soccer. Once soccer season ended I noticed a drastic change. I didn't fit in with everyone else because I didn't have such high conservative views, and in the second semester I noticed a lot of my "friends" were trying to change me and the way I think. That's when I knew I needed to leave that school. Their transfer process was also very ridiculous, I had to have meetings with a school counselor and my resident director, [and they] both tried to convince me to stay because they felt I still needed to be helped by them. And that's when I really knew I needed to run and never look back. And in the end, I transferred to the best school ever. (I'm a little biased, I know.) And I don't think I could have been happier with my decision.

—Bailey, Saint John Fisher College

It's such a strange feeling, thinking that you're where you're meant to be and then figuring out that you were wrong all along. My gut always told me that I wasn't 100 percent happy with where I was attending, but it took me three semesters to admit it. I was a student at Point Park University in Pittsburgh with a great group of friends, in a major I loved. I had an amazing freshman year filled with homework and partying and fun. But when I returned for sophomore year after a long summer home in Delaware, it clicked that I wasn't happy. To be successful, you need to be happy, especially regarding the university that you're paying thousands of dollars *to attend. I was a broadcast production major, but my true calling is elementary education. I want to help children. I wasn't going to stay at an expensive arts university if I was unhappy just to become a teacher. Transferring schools was my best and cheapest option to achieve my dreams. I'm really excited to be a student at Wilmington University because it's where I'm meant to be. I'll be closer to family and friends, I'll have access to my car, I can work more. This decision to transfer has been an emotional roller coaster, but I think I'm on the right path now and I couldn't be happier. Oh yeah, and my biggest tip for anyone who is thinking about transferring:* Do not *base your decision upon your friends. Leaving them will be hard, but don't risk your future and your happiness just to be in close proximity to your BFFs.*

—Madeline, Wilmington University

I lived on campus with three other suitemates; luckily we all had our own rooms. One suitemate—the Party Addict—would stay up til 3 A.M. each night, have friends over and be banging on the walls. When he was partying too loud and couldn't hear the front door banging, I would have to get up and let people inside. He did this almost every night. He covered the smoke and fire detector with plastic so he could smoke inside of his room. Great. He'd steal food and wouldn't clean up after himself. Roommates weren't the only problem. I really didn't like the two-year-school atmosphere. I had no real friends, no groups to join. Then one of my friends who I had bowled with in high school asked me to come down to Pikeville to see the campus and meet the bowling coach. When I stepped foot on the campus I knew for a fact that this was where I belonged. I met the coach and the team and fell in love. Pikeville had the major I was interested in, and the coach offered me a half ride to go here. I couldn't say no. He said that I'd be rooming with other bowlers and if I had any problems to let him or any professor or staff know, and it would get taken care of. At this moment I couldn't be happier. My advice if you're thinking of transferring is to make the effort and do campus visits. See what you like and don't. I hated big cities where the campus is spread out over an entire city, and I really like the small campuses where everyone knows each other.

It's going to be a struggle to get away at first. I was always a homebody, never wanted to leave home, and would rather play videogames than go on a field trip. But don't be afraid to make a jump and try to get out there. I went from never wanting to leave my city to now wanting to travel places. When we travel for tournaments, it's a blast to see a whole new side of the U.S. I would never have thought to have gone to Vegas, or to go see my aunt and uncle in Georgia. Don't be afraid to take a risk!

—Matt, University of Pikeville

Seek → Find

You are midway through your first semester of college, and things do not seem to be going the way you originally envisioned. You and your roommate are not BFFs; your classes do not engage you; and the food, well, it is certainly not your mom's home-cooked lasagna. You begin to question your choice in schools. After the honeymoon phase of orientation is over, the college routine often becomes ordinary. More often than not, transferring will not change these experiences. Before you start updating your Common Application, trust in what originally brought you to the college you chose. Begin to explore new friends groups and clubs; speak to an academic advisor about other majors that might better suit your gifts and talents; and look for opportunities that get you off campus to volunteer and engage you in your new surroundings.

—Jamie R. Fazio, chaplain, Nazareth College

If You Do Decide to Transfer

Starting over can be a challenge, but you have some experience under your belt now. It actually can be a little easier because you know a little more about what to expect. Usually transfer students will be in an orientation group together so you'll get to meet other students in the same situation as you.

I think the hardest part of transferring for students is the fear of no longer having a social life. When you transfer, you go into a new school with no friends, and it seems that everyone is already settled into their friend groups. If there is one thing I couldn't stress enough, it's to make friends with freshmen! Honestly they are in the same social boat as you, they don't have any friends, and they are looking to make some. In addition, your newfound friendships also give you the chance, as the older student, to help the freshmen out. Come middle of the semester when they think their life is ending because school is tough, in my experience they really appreciate someone telling them that it's a normal situation, and you're the person they can ask advice about living on your own for the first time.

—Andrew, junior, State University of New York at Geneseo

THE TAKEAWAY

If you're thinking of transferring, take a hard look at your reasons and be sure you've given yourself time to adjust to college life. If you're sure this isn't the place for you after talking it over with friends, family, and advisors, know that getting into the right program at the right college for you can make college a great experience.

CHAPTER 29

In Case of Emergency

 Survival Strategy #29: Alcohol poisoning, drunk driving, eating disorders, sexual assault, getting arrested, suicidal feelings—college life has a dark side as well. The information here will help you see the warning signs of potential emergencies and help you deal with them when they actually occur.

Okay, so you've finally arrived at the proverbial Danger Dumping Grounds of this book. You may have noticed along the way that we've discussed crises that come up in college and then referred you to this chapter for help. The fact is, fortunately, emergencies like the ones we're going to talk about don't occur every day. Hopefully you'll never have to deal with them at all, but in case you do, we've tried to include all the basic information you'll need. We've included resources showing you whom to contact for some of the most common college emergencies. In any emergency, try to keep a cool head and get help.

Alcohol Poisoning

As you've gathered from previous chapters, the college culture encourages a lot of drinking. Sometimes if you join a sport or other organization, part of the "induction" ceremony is consuming mass quantities of alcohol. Even when that isn't the case, it's easy to drink too much with partying and drinking games. Because of this, it's also terrifyingly easy to get alcohol poisoning.

Alcohol poisoning occurs when too much alcohol is absorbed into your body's system. The body can process 1 to 1.5 ounces of alcohol an hour, which is the amount in a single standard drink. But most partiers don't stop at one standard drink an hour. Because alcohol is a depressant, it slows down your central nervous system and dulls the nerves that regulate your breathing, heartbeat, and gag reflex (which is what makes you vomit when your body doesn't want to absorb more alcohol). If left untreated, alcohol poisoning can lead to permanent brain damage or even death.

Signs of Alcohol Poisoning

A person doesn't need to show all these signs to have alcohol poisoning. Use your best judgment—it's better to be safe than sorry.

- Mental confusion, stupor, coma, or person cannot be wakened
- Vomiting
- Slow or irregular breathing
- Hypothermia or low body temperature
- Bluish skin color or paleness, caused by dehydration
- Seizures

If You Think Someone Has Alcohol Poisoning...

Always get help—no matter what. Many times people don't want to call medical services or 911 because they're afraid of what will happen to *them*. They're afraid the party will get broken up, they'll be humiliated, or they will get in trouble for underage drinking. The truth? None of that matters. According to the Center for Disease Control, the annual average deaths between 2010 and 2012 due to alcohol poisoning deaths was 2,221. On average, six people (predominantly male men, and varying greatly by state) die from alcohol poisoning each day in the United States.[1] Just get help. RA Bryan Heinline says, "If you're worried about someone and you're in the dorm, go immediately to your RA. You may not know what someone with alcohol poisoning looks like, but I do. Even if you're drunk yourself, don't hesitate to seek help from your RA."

Online Survival Guide: Ask our online resident assistants your questions by visiting "Interactive RA" at http://The FreshmanSurvivalGuide.com and clicking on "Ask."

3 Steps to Take to Deal with Alcohol Poisoning

Remember that not all symptoms have to be present for a person to have alcohol poisoning.

1. Try to wake the person up. Don't bring the person home or put him in a bed, where no one will watch him. Don't assume he will just sleep it off.
2. Call 911 or your campus emergency medical services.
3. Never leave someone who has passed out from excessive alcohol intake by himself. A person might vomit unconsciously and choke or accidentally inhale the vomit, which will cause serious damage or death.

Online Survival Guide: *How prepared are you in case of an emergency? Visit http://TheFreshmanSurvivalGuide .com/chapters/ and click on "Chapter 29" to find out.*

Friends Don't Let Friends...

Friends are one of the most important elements in the effort to keep car keys and drunk people from getting together. If you have a chance to stop someone from getting behind the wheel when he or she is under the influence, *take it!* Consider this scenario:

It's the end of a pretty wild night and one of your friends, the one who was *supposed* to be the designated driver, is headed for his car talking loudly, weaving as he walks, and clearly not fully in control. He wasn't supposed to be drinking at all! Now you can either let him go or try to stop him. It might not seem like that big a deal—really, how dangerous is it? People drive drunk all the time, you may think. In 2012, 29.1 million people admitted to driving under the influence of alcohol, and the rate of drunk driving is highest for people aged twenty-one to twenty-five (23.4 percent).[2]

In 2013, 10,076 people were killed in alcohol-impaired driving crashes, accounting for nearly one-third (31 percent) of all traffic-related deaths in the United States.[3]

Actually, this situation is as much of an emergency as any of the others listed in this chapter. At all levels of blood alcohol concentration (BAC), the risk of being involved in a crash is greater for young people than for older people. Among drivers with BAC levels of 0.08 percent or higher involved in fatal crashes in 2013, one out of every three were between 21 and

24 years of age (33 percent). The next two largest groups were ages 25 to 34 (29 percent) and 35 to 44 (24 percent).[4] Your slightly drunk friend is impaired enough that he doesn't realize how impaired he is. And even though everybody should know by now, people who've been drinking aren't exactly famous for their good judgment. Here are a few strategies for keeping this scenario from turning into an accident scene:

- Just ask for the keys. Don't tell him you think he's too drunk to drive and don't argue. Just ask. (Next time, get 'em before he starts drinking.)
- Lie. Say, "I need to get something out of the trunk," "I want to see if your key is bigger than mine," or "[Insert your own witty key joke here]."
- If he gets belligerent, call security. Better to have him busted for being too loud than arrested for drunk driving.
- If you can't get the keys and you can't stop him, don't be afraid to call the cops. That way you can visit him in jail instead of identifying his body at the morgue.

Many campuses and municipalities have ride programs to get students home safely and prevent drunk driving. Know what's available to you, and program the number into your cell so you won't be tempted to ride with someone who's under the influence. The designated drivers should be designated before anyone starts drinking and shouldn't be drinking at all. We've been indoctrinated to the point of its becoming a joke, but talk to anyone who's lost a friend or family member to drunk driving and it will remind you just how serious a situation it is. Don't let your friends drive drunk, and *don't* get into a vehicle with a driver who's been drinking.

Eating Disorders

In this new high-pressure environment, some people respond by controlling the one thing they feel they can: what they eat. A nationwide survey found that four out of ten Americans have either suffered or know someone who has suffered from an eating disorder, and 40 percent of new cases of anorexia are in girls fifteen to nineteen years old.[5] You probably already know if this is a danger for you. The people who would normally help you keep an eye on your eating problems are also the people who would help you deal with the stress that causes them—and they're not with you at college. But you can hook up with some help at the counseling center—a number of colleges now have eating disorder support groups that meet right on campus— find yourself a supportive friend (or two) you can share your struggles with, and stay accountable to friends or family from back home who can encourage and support you. Watching your weight can become a dangerous obsession that will distract you from your goals just as surely as any other addiction!

If you've never had problems with dieting, binge eating, or weight obsession but you find yourself distracted by calorie counting or controlling your weight, or you are avoiding eating—it's important to recognize you may be in trouble and to find a way to get help.

Symptoms and Behaviors of Eating Disorders

Anorexia nervosa is a condition in which a person is obsessed with food and being thin, sometimes to the point of deadly starvation. The attempts to limit calorie intake are sometimes paired with excessive exercise.

Symptoms
1. Excessively thin appearance
2. Dry skin and dehydration
3. Fatigue, dizziness, or fainting
4. Frequently being cold
5. Brittle nails and hair that thins or falls out
6. For girls, menstrual irregularities or loss of menstruation
7. Low blood pressure, bone loss, and abnormal blood loss
8. Constipation

Warning Behaviors
1. Refusal to eat and skipping meals
2. Making excuses for not eating and denial of hunger
3. Excessive exercise
4. Weighing food and eating only a few certain "safe" foods (like those low in fat or calories)
5. Frequently complaining about being fat or checking mirror for perceived flaws
6. Checking weight repeatedly
7. Having a flat mood, lack of emotion, or difficulty concentrating

Bulimia nervosa is a condition in which a person has a pattern of binging and purging, where she typically eats a large amount of food in a short amount of time and then tries to get rid of the calories by forcing herself to vomit or overexercise. In between, she may eat very little or skip meals altogether.

Symptoms
1. Self-induced vomiting
2. Dry skin and dehydration

3. Damaged teeth and gums
4. Sores in the throat and mouth, as well as possibly on the knuckles or hands
5. Swollen salivary glands in the cheeks
6. Abnormal bowel functioning
7. For girls, menstrual irregularities or loss of menstruation
8. Fatigue

Warning Behaviors

1. Frequently going to the bathroom after eating or during meals
2. Constant dieting
3. Excessive exercise
4. Use of laxatives
5. Unhealthy focus on body shape and weight
6. Depression or anxiety

There are many other subtypes of eating disorders, but these two are the most prominent.

If You or Someone You Know Has an Eating Disorder...

Many times people with eating disorders refuse to think they have a problem. But if your desire to control your weight becomes the most important thing in your life—interfering with your schoolwork, extracurricular activities, and social life—then you should get help. Schedule an appointment with a doctor or therapist to talk about your weight, eating habits, and body image.[6] Even if you don't think you have a problem, it is always a good idea to get a professional opinion from a doctor or therapist before you dismiss friends' or family's concerns.

If your roommate or a friend is showing signs of having an eating disorder, *don't* get caught up in daily arguments about how much she is eating or exercising. *Do* talk to your RA or someone in health services or counseling. As we've mentioned, many campuses have staff that specialize in eating disorders. You can also call the National Eating Disorders Association's Information and Referral Helpline at 1-800-931-2237. They also have a Click-to-Chat option on their website that offers another way to speak with a live, trained Helpline volunteer. This offers a potentially less nerve-wracking added layer of anonymity for someone who is nervous to take the first step to get help. (Go to http://www.nationaleatingdisorders.org and click on "Find Help & Support" on the top navigation bar.) If untreated, an eating disorder could create permanent damage in your body, and it's more important for you to be healthy and happy than "perfect."

Online Survival Guide: Ask our online resident assistants any questions you may have about college life by visiting "Interactive RA" at http://TheFreshmanSurvivalGuide .com and clicking on "Ask."

Rape and Sexual Assault

According to a 2014 report from the White House Task Force to Protect Students From Sexual Assault, one in five women fall victim to sexual assault in college.[7] The 1in6 organization also cites research conducted by the U.S. Centers for Disease Control that indicates that one in six men have had abusive sexual experiences before age eighteen.[8] And this is probably a low estimate. It is extremely important to stay alert and aware when you get to college. With new friends and new social situations, sometimes it's easy to forget to stay safe. College-aged women are four times more likely to be sexually assaulted. Use RAINN's tips for reducing your risk.

1. **The college environment creates a false sense of security.** As an incoming freshman, you feel like everyone you meet is a new friend and your dorm is your new home. While it is a lot of fun, remember that these people are also strangers. Don't assume people you've just met will look out for your best interests.

2. **Get to know your surroundings.** Learn a well-lit route back to your dorm or place of residence. If you are new to the campus, familiarize yourself with the campus map and know where the emergency phones are.

3. **Never loan your room key to anyone, and always lock your door.**

4. **Be careful when leaving your address, contact information, and location online.** When you use the check-in feature on Facebook, it notifies people that you are away from home...and also notifies them of your exact location. Updating your status or leaving online "I'm away" messages about your whereabouts and activities can make details of your location accessible to everyone. Avoid putting your dorm room, campus address, or phone number on your personal profile where everyone can see it.

5. **Try not to go out alone at night.** Walk with roommates or someone you trust. If you'll be walking home alone, ask a trusted friend to accompany you. Avoid the ATM and jogging at night. Don't use music headphones so you can be more aware of your surroundings.

6. **Keep the phone numbers of both your campus escort service as well as the campus police with you at all times.**

7. **Avoid being alone or isolated with someone you don't know well.** Let a trusted friend know where you are and who you are with when you go out.

8. **Form a buddy system.** Arrive with your friends, check in with each other throughout the night, and leave together. Don't go off alone. Make a secret signal with your friends for when they should intervene if you're in an uncomfortable situation.

9. **Practice safe drinking.** Don't accept drinks from people you don't know or trust, and never leave your drink unattended. If you've left your drink alone, just get a new one. Always watch your drink being prepared.

10. **Trust your instincts.** If you feel unsafe in any situation, go with your gut. If you see something suspicious, contact your resident assistant or campus police immediately.

Was It Rape?

There are many misconceptions about rape, and sexual assault and legal definitions of rape vary from state to state. Rape can be committed by a stranger or by someone you know well. There's no such thing as "asking for it" when it comes to rape. Just because one person made mistakes or poor choices does not give another person the right to commit a violent crime against them.

 Online Survival Guide: To find out more about myths and misconceptions about rape and sexual assault, go to http:// TheFreshmanSurvivalGuide.com/chapters/ and click on "Chapter 29."

If You or Someone You Know Is Sexually Assaulted...

First know that it is not your fault. Now you should do what is best for you in terms of getting help and support. Consider reporting the attack to the police by calling 911. Preserve evidence of the attack by refraining from bathing, brushing your teeth, or washing your clothes. Write down all the details you can remember.

SEEK → FIND

I think that the pressure not to report [sexual assault] is so huge that many women walk around, sometimes maybe years, not being able to share this traumatic experience. So they stay and face that person who assaulted them. In the few times that someone does approach me per year, they're wondering whether they need to get health services or meet with a spiritual advisor, with someone who is neutral. Some people don't want to talk with someone who is religious because that's very scary—they feel that the blame is on themselves, that they've broken some kind of rule—particularly more traditional Jewish women, certainly Muslim women...If you get to that point, we need to ask the women what they feel is the appropriate next step. Sometimes it's transferring; sometimes it's having the young man leave the campus because she didn't do anything wrong—why should she be punished?...The bottom line is we need to empower women.

—Rabbi Serena Fujita, Jewish chaplain, Bucknell University

We asked Megan Foster of RAINN what a student should do if she is raped, what issues may arise for her in the aftermath, and what resources she might find on (or near) campus to help. She told us the student should put her clothing in a paper bag to preserve evidence and immediately seek help. She needs medical attention for any injuries, to test for STIs and pregnancy, and to have the option of a rape kit. A student can take a friend along or an advocate from the campus or local rape crisis center. The advocate can help with resources and reporting to the police if the student wants advice and help.

Leah called a trusted friend on a Saturday. She sounded strange, shaken. She recounted haltingly her account of the night before—the show, the party, how much she'd had to drink, and the jerky guy who'd followed her around all night and then to her car. There were parts she didn't remember clearly, but the jerky guy was bragging later that they'd had sex. Leah remembered trying to get him out of her car, trying to get him to leave her alone. And then she told her friend she knew she'd been stupid. "Maybe so," the friend replied, "but it doesn't make it okay and it doesn't make it your fault. He committed a crime." Her friend took her to the hospital, where they talked about whether she wanted to press charges and where she could find support on campus. At the hospital she got medical help, information, and support, and back on campus she had some great friends and an on-campus counselor who helped her through the aftermath.

Individuals react to rape and sexual assault in a wide variety of ways. There is no singular normal experience, but extreme mood swings, depression, anger, and self-blame are all very common reactions. Many campuses have some sort of victim services advocate or sexual assault team, and there is usually a rape crisis center in the area. These resources can provide immediate support or referrals for more long-term services.

If you have any questions or need support immediately, or long after the experience, the National Sexual Assault Hotline (1-800-656-HOPE) and the Online Hotline (https://ohl.rainn.org /online/) can provide you with free confidential counseling services 24/7. For more information on sexual assault, visit RAINN's website at http://www.rainn.org. The Joyful Heart Foundation was founded by actress Mariska Hargitay (*Law & Order: Special Victims Unit*) to heal, educate, and empower survivors of sexual assault, domestic violence, and child abuse, and to shed light into the darkness that surrounds these issues. Visit their website, http://www.joyfulheartfoundation.org, for more information.

NOTE: A rape kit is designed specifically for collecting evidence of sexual assault, including semen and blood. Even if you do not want to press charges now, going to the hospital and having a rape kit done preserves evidence in case you decide later—even months or years later—that you *do* want to press charges.

Online Survival Guide: Ask any questions you might have by visiting "Interactive RA" at http://TheFreshmanSurvival Guide.com and clicking on "Ask."

Getting Caught by the Police

Some of the "fun" things college students do aren't only stupid or dangerous, they're also illegal. It's important to be smart about what you do, when you do it, and where you are.

Ways You Might Get in Trouble

Schools, cities, and states have different laws and regulations. Know the laws that apply to your school, city, and state, and *follow them* to the best of your ability. Statistics show that it's unlikely that as a college freshman you will stay completely away from drinking and parties. However, there's a difference between having fun at a party and getting so drunk that you disturb the public peace, or walking around with drugs in your backpack, or streaking right in front of campus security.

Here are some examples of actions that will get you in trouble, depending on where you go to school and what laws are in place:

1. Having an open container of alcohol outdoors when you're underage
2. Serving alcohol to underage drinkers
3. Buying alcohol when you're underage
4. Drinking and driving
5. Possessing, using, manufacturing, or selling illegal drugs
6. Illegally downloading music on your campus Internet network
7. Drawing graffiti or otherwise defacing and damaging public or school property
8. Possessing and/or using dangerous objects like firearms, ammunition, hunting knives, swords, and explosives like fireworks
9. Stealing
10. Arson
11. Physical assault
12. Sexual harassment or sexual assault[9]

Punishments

If you get caught doing something illegal, you will be punished. For example, in Washington, D.C., if you are caught trying to buy alcohol or going into a bar while underage, you may be fined up to $1,000 and have your driver's license suspended for a year. Having an open container of alcohol in a public area results in a fine of up to $500 and/or a prison term of up to sixty days.

Possession of a controlled substance can get you a fine of up to $1,000 and/or 180 days in prison.[10]

What to Do If You're Caught

If you're caught by the police doing something illegal, do what you're told. The police are there to enforce the law, and disobeying them will just make things worse for you. While some of these reactions in the following list may seem bizarre, if you're scared or intoxicated you may not think about staying calm and doing what the police say to do.

1. Stay calm and in control. Don't panic.

2. If they ask, give them your name.

3. Be polite and respectful. Resist the temptation to yell at the police, even if you have been wrongly stopped. Being drunk isn't an excuse to be belligerent, and it will just make the police more likely to be harsh with you.

4. Don't run. It's unlikely that one person could outrun several police or police cars, but sometimes people who haven't even done anything wrong get scared and bolt. This will make the police suspect that you *have* done something wrong, and you'll risk being arrested.[11]

5. Don't resist arrest, even if you believe the arrest is not fair or justified. Police may "pat down" your clothing if they suspect you might be carrying a weapon. You should not physically resist, but you are within your rights to not consent to any additional search.[12]

6. If you're stopped in a car, again, do what the police tell you to do. Stay in your car, turn on your interior light so the officer can see how many people are inside, keep your passengers still and quiet, keep both hands on the steering wheel, and don't make any sudden movements.[13]

Suicidal Thoughts: Yours or Someone Else's

Constantly feeling as if nothing will ever get any better, fantasizing about dying, saying things like "I want to go to sleep and just not wake up," and/or making a plan to end your life are all signs that you (or your friend) are in imminent danger. Human beings have a very strong survival instinct. When circumstance or brain chemistry is somehow overcoming that primal urge, it's time to get help and get it fast, today, *now*. An RA, campus medical personnel, or campus security are all appropriate avenues for help here—so is 911. You should be clear with anyone you call that you are having feelings that you want to die and that you need to go to the hospital. Don't downplay your feelings. Be honest and as clear as you are able.

The Jed Foundation—which was founded by Phil and Donna Satow, whose son Jed committed suicide while attending the University of Arizona in 1998—created the "It's on My Mind" campaign to raise awareness of the warning signs of mental health problems and suicide among college students. You can find out more about the program on their website: http://www.jedfoundation.org.

Another organization that is dedicated to people who struggle with depression and other harmful issues is To Write Love on Her Arms. TWLOHA actually has student organizations on campus that work diligently to promote mental health awareness and reduce the stigma around depression and anxiety. Find out more: https://twloha.com.

Should you hear or see anyone exhibiting any one or more of the following signs, get help *immediately* by contacting a mental health professional, calling your college's emergency number, or calling 1-800-273-8255, the National Suicide Prevention Lifeline, for a referral:

- Someone threatening to hurt or kill him- or herself, or saying or wanting to hurt or kill him- or herself
- Someone looking for ways to kill him- or herself by seeking access to firearms, pills, or other means
- Someone talking or writing about death, dying, or suicide, when these actions are out of the ordinary for the person
- Someone who shows physical signs of self-injury

If you cannot reach the contacts we've listed during a crisis, take the individual to an emergency room or mental health walk-in clinic. Do not leave the person alone until professional help is with him or her. Remove any firearms, alcohol, drugs, or sharp objects that could be used in a suicide attempt.[14]

Online Survival Guide: For more information on any of these emergencies—and resources for dealing with them— visit "Chapter 29" (go to the "Chapters" drop-down menu) or "Interactive RA" online at http://TheFreshman SurvivalGuide.com.

THE TAKEAWAY

No college experience will be completely trouble free. If you need help, ask. If people are being stupid and someone's going to get hurt or killed, take action. It can be a drag to be the responsible one, but it beats feeling responsible for someone getting hurt or killed.

CHAPTER 30

Overwhelmed Yet? Don't Despair

 Survival Strategy #30: You'll be okay. If you're feeling a little overwhelmed at this point, you have a right to. Actually, if you weren't at least a *little* concerned, we'd worry about you. You're facing some of the biggest changes of your life, leaving behind people who have been the most important in your life so far, and taking on one of the most difficult challenges in your life. A healthy respect for all that just shows that you've got your head screwed on straight.

At the same time you shouldn't be losing too much sleep over starting college. Lots of people succeed at it, and you don't have to do it alone. Though you are leaving important things behind, what's ahead of you—the new friendships, mentors, experiences, successes, and learning—might be better than you could even imagine. Will you have days that are total disasters? Sure. Will you make mistakes? You bet, probably some pretty spectacular ones. But overall this should be a great ride.

Here's a brief recap of some of the tips that will help you survive and thrive at college.

Don't Go It Alone

Of course, your academics are primary, but forming the relationships that will sustain you through college is one of the most important responsibilities you have. Time invested in finding the right friends and mentors—the ones who are like the person you hope to become—will pay off in the short term by way of companionship, support, and good times. These valuable new people will help you in the long term by pushing you to achieve, encouraging you to keep going when you've run out of steam, and being there for you when the really tough things come along.

Still, keep in touch with friends and family from home and let them know how you're doing. Because these are the people who know what "normal" is for you, they're also the ones who will know if you've headed into a danger zone. (See chapters 2, 5, 19, and 22.)

Go to Class!

The single clearest indicator of success in college is whether or not you're missing class. It's the big one. If you haven't finished your paper, go to class. If you're tired, go to class. No matter what happens, if you can get upright and get your feet underneath you, go to class. It matters.

As much as possible, get to know your professors. Some of them will be among the most interesting people you'll meet in your life. Do your reading, schedule study time—every day—and use the resources your college provides: academic advisement, professors' office hours, tutoring, writing labs, math labs, study groups, and library resources and staff. The help available to you on campus is usually top-notch and will make an enormous difference in your capacity to complete your work and score well. (See chapters 12–16 and 22.)

Stay Healthy

Sleep, food, and exercise in the right amounts, enough but not too much, are often forgotten elements in the college equation. Sleep as normally as possible—for a college student—and know that when you have to skimp on sleep you'll also be reducing your emotional resilience and your ability to focus, as well as increasing your tendency to procrastinate. If you start to struggle academically, one of the first things you'll want to think about is how much sleep you're getting and whether you can get more.

The quality of the food you're eating will impact how you're feeling physically and emotionally. Choose wisely. Avoid excessive amounts of sugar, salt, and processed foods. Whenever you can, eat whole grains, fresh fruits, and vegetables, and drink lots of water. Soda, alcohol, and comfort eating—eating to feel better rather than because you're hungry—will all pack on the pounds. Make sure you're getting enough protein.

Keep moving. Even a short walk after meals can help, but a regular exercise routine or participation in a sport will help protect you from the freshman fifteen, keep you healthier overall, and give you a physical outlet to reduce stress and improve your mood. (See chapters 10, 24, and 25.)

 Online Survival Guide: *Follow up with the freshmen featured in our Survival Stories throughout the book and see if/how they survived by visiting "Chapter 30" at http:// TheFreshmanSurvivalGuide.com/chapters/.*

Find the Balance...

...between kicking yourself in the butt and giving yourself a break, between work and play, between asceticism and excess, between fear and recklessness. So much of freshman year is about finding that place between the extremes where you can survive—in academics, in relationships, and in risk taking. A little stress can keep you motivated; a lot can shut you down.

Find organizations that connect you with the activities and people you enjoy, but don't get so involved in extracurriculars that they start pulling you away from schoolwork. Watch your commitment level. If you're a busyness junkie, be prepared to let some things go if you start feeling like you've got too much going on. Take risks, meet new people, try new things—just maintain a pace that helps you keep in mind what you want and who you are. (See chapters 6, 14, 18, and 25.)

> *Relax. In the long run, what honestly matters is your happiness, and your major won't make you happy. You might love what you're studying, but you can't expect loving your major to make you happy. Surround yourself with people who are fun, interesting, smart, and happy themselves. Building those relationships is what will make you love this part of your life.*
>
> **—Erin, sophomore, Point Park University**

Identity

You're the same person you were before; you're just in a new place. Bring your sparkling personality, your excellent judgment, and your keen intelligence to bear on this new situation. Don't be misled or pushed around by people or things going on around you. Stick up for yourself. If you want to head in some new directions, go for it. Just do it on purpose with your eyes wide open, not because it's the path of least resistance or because someone else is pressing you to.

Be aware of the choices you're making and that these choices influence the person you are becoming. Drinking, drugs, sex, and dating, how much and what you choose to study, and how you spend your free time—all these things matter.

Don't sweat the small stuff, but remember that it's not all small stuff. Don't let anyone use you, and don't be a person who undervalues other people, either. Keep one eye on the past, who you were, and the things and people important to you; and one on the future, the person you want to become, and be sure that what you're doing now will lead you there. (See chapters 8, 9, 11, 13, and 24.)

Watch Yourself

Remember that even though campus can feel pretty safe, a little bubble of like-minded people, there are dangers there. From property crime to date rape, alcohol poisoning to emotional abuse, bad stuff can happen. Take steps to reduce your risk. Paranoia isn't necessary, but travel through your freshman year with a healthy dose of skepticism. People should earn your trust—don't just give it to them. Be a little protective of your personal information and your personal history. Most people are honest, but the ones who aren't are often highly skilled at scamming others. It's worth watching your back. (See chapters 2, 6, 8, 23, and 29.)

Get Back Up

You will get knocked down. More than once. You'll find your limits. You'll experience failure, disappointment, betrayal. Learning to let go of hurt and anger, at least to the point of not letting it keep you from what you want, is an important life skill.

Sometimes when you fall, it'll be your own fault. Another vital skill for getting through is learning to forgive yourself. You will make mistakes. They may be small errors or they may be devastating disasters. Give yourself permission not to be perfect. College is tough: It's meant to push us, test us, show us what we can accomplish, and help us understand ourselves more deeply. None of that is easy, and there will be days that you have no desire to keep at it.

SEEK → FIND

 There is no right way to get through school. Whenever one engages in any form of learning experience, one is bound to make mistakes. When we make an error of judgment, the best thing is to reflect on it and work on a way of correcting it. There is no point dwelling in the guilt of error; guilt is a waste of time at its best and a threat to one's well-being at its worst. What is important is to recognize all this as a valuable learning process.

—Ven. Tenzin Priyadarshi, Buddhist chaplain,
Massachusetts Institute of Technology

Although college life may feel overwhelming at first, you are not the only one feeling that way. Know that after a few weeks you will know where your chemistry class is and your new friend's dorm is located, and that there are some great faculty and staff that seem to care. And most of all, know that thousands of us have shared the same experience and we all survived our first semester of college life. It is one of those amazing transitions that when you come out the other side, you will be transformed into a college student.

—Rabbi Serena Fujita, Jewish chaplain, Bucknell University

The transition from adolescence to young adulthood can be fraught with terrifying excitement and exhilarating struggle. The college/ university experience is a time to maximize discovery of who you are and discern your potential role in the world. There is no better time to practice the arts of humor, diligence, directness, and celebration. Spiritual habits and religious rituals often can augment your campus life with insight and perspective not available in the dorm and in the classroom. Finding God at this juncture in your journey might be one of life's great pleasures.

—Rev. Scott Young, Protestant campus minister,
University of Southern California

Know how to handle a potential disaster, and know going in that there will be bad days. Count on the people who care about you when times get tough. (See chapters 22, 25, and 29.)

Online Survival Guide: *Remember, help is always nearby. Visit us online or go to "Interactive RA" at http://The FreshmanSurvivalGuide.com and click on "Ask."*

THE TAKEAWAY

Being in college means you're being challenged to work harder, think more, and grow up. This story has the potential to be a drama, a comedy, a tragedy, maybe even a romance, and it will surely have elements of each. Whatever it becomes, it's sure to be a pretty incredible experience. But most important, it's *your* story. So when you run into trouble, remember you have help, support, and instruction from highly qualified people who are invested in your success. You'll be okay.

Acknowledgments

Long before we ever thought about putting it into book form, *The Freshman Survival Guide* was a web-based resource for incoming college freshmen. As such it was a dynamic, collaborative forum for college students, professors, administrators, orientation staffs, RAs, campus ministers, and other professionals to share their experiences, insights, and advice on how to handle college life. The reaction to the guide when it debuted on the Busted Halo website (http://BustedHalo.com) was phenomenal, and our online version was forwarded and passed out to tens of thousands of freshmen across the country.

Though it is far more comprehensive than anything we were able to do on the web, the book you are holding in your hands is a result of that initial interactive experience and sense of collaboration online. Once the foundation was laid, however, it took a small army to help us turn it into a book that was practical, relevant, and—most important—helpful to college students.

Without the hundreds of students and recent graduates from all around the United States who filled out our surveys and answered our questions both in the classroom and online, this book wouldn't exist. Their input formed the backbone of *The Freshman Survival Guide* and kept us firmly grounded in the reality of college life today.

Busted Halo development director Brittany Janis offered numerous thoughtful comments and clever ideas throughout and improved our section on Greek life immeasurably. Project manager Jarrad Venegas, along with research intern Mike Pappa, rounded out our reading team and offered critical insights and critiques (and recipes) as we got down to the wire. Monica Bradbury-Lareau provided edits, input, humor, and encouragement above and beyond the call of sisterhood. Nora's interns, Claire Mongeau and Erin Kouwe, brought their hard work and innate smarts to bear on countless issues that needed resolving. Kate Hunt's experience and enthusiasm for the project—born out of the three years she actually used the online *Freshman Survival Guide* as an RA—helped us clarify how we could integrate the *FSG*'s online dimension. The incredible staff and contributing editors at Busted Halo, especially Mike Hayes, Phil Fox Rose, Mirlande Jean-Louis, Joe Williams, Tara Devine, and Elias Demopolous, offered crucial feedback and support all the way through. Dr. Christine Whelan provided guidance on our survey design and wise counsel in general. Fr. Dave Dwyer, CSP, and his crew from *The Busted Halo Show* on Sirius XM Satellite Radio—Robyn Gould, Brett Siddell, and Brian Zagen—have been unfailingly supportive, and they regularly go above and beyond to help synchronize and coordinate the multiheaded beast that Busted Halo can become.

Joelle Delbourgo's experience and wisdom about the publishing industry from both an agent's and an editor's perspective was invaluable. Her calm guidance and perceptive comments were instrumental in turning our idea for a book into a reality.

Kate Hartson, our editor at Center Street, came on board at a crucial moment in the book's original publication and has continued to champion it. She was key in making sure this second edition became a reality. Michelle Rapkin instantly understood what we long believed was unique and valuable about the *FSG* when it was still exclusively online. Holly Halverson and Leah Johnston Tracosas, along with Adlai Yeomans and Veronica Sepe, helped make the transition from the web to the printed page as productive—and painless—as possible. Andrea Glickson, director of marketing for Center Street, has been a great ally and has gone above and beyond the call of duty on many occasions. Carol Meadows at Center Street was an early supporter and helped make sure that countless colleges could purchase copies for incoming first-year students and have them arrive on time. Alexa Smail has been an invaluable editorial voice on this second edition, helping us clarify our thoughts and ideas throughout. Her patience and good nature in dealing with so many of our questions has made the process of creating a second edition as painless as possible.

Joe Durepos at Loyola Press was an early and enthusiastic advocate (thanks for the introduction).

Jenna Wang took time out of her busy schedule at Boston College to do some critical research for the second edition. Natalie Vielkind has become an enormous asset in terms of running our social media.

Of course our Interactive RAs—both past and present—figure prominently in the second edition. Danielle Shipp, Michelle Lowry, Megan Stamer, Josh Martin, Kailynn Cerny, and Sam Harbison have contributed enormously on a volunteer basis. Their willingness to offer their time to this project despite their own busy schedules has been incredible. We can't thank you enough.

Dr. Richard Kadison's book *College of the Overwhelmed* and his input for both online and print editions of the *FSG* helped give us some clinical insight into vital mental health issues on campus. Courtney Knowles at the Jed Foundation was also enormously helpful in our understanding some very sobering facts about college life. Michelle Goodwin's generous input on roommates and campus safety improved those sections enormously.

Dan Olsterdorf at ResidentAssistant.com and everyone at Campus Advantage helped to bring our "Interactive RA" feature out of the realm of mere possibility. Bryan Heinline, Michelle Lach, Anne and Katie Vogtle, Dr. Noelle Hannon, Zarah Ektefai, Kimberley Mauldin, Dr. Tom O'Brien, David Nantais, Lee Chase, Patti Czarnecki, Cecilia Christopher, Sr. Rita Marie Schroeder, Michaela McDonald, Jeff Guhin, Becky Guhin, Dr. Tim Pychyl, Dr. Stephen Prothero, Megan Foster of RAINN, Dr. Albert Matheny, Dr. David McMillen, Kate Knebels, and Robert McDonald shared their extensive experience and expert advice. Meredith Teasdale stepped in at the last minute and added new graphics that really helped the book's design.

Michael Galligan-Steirle; Charlie Currie, SJ; and Fr. Marty Moran offered their enthusiasm for the project and key input along the way. Bill Byron, SJ, gave us the Study Budget, which is one of the most practical bits of advice we've ever come across. We're thankful he shared it with us.

Special thanks to Chrysta Bolinger, Mary Matunis, and all the wonderful campus ministers of CCMA who helped promote the guide with their own students. To Vernon LaSala and the chaplains of NACUC; to Dr. Bob McCarty, Michael Theisen, and Matthew Robaszkiewicz at NFCYM; to the ACCU and AJCU staffs; to our God on Campus panelists, who helped us realize how important the spiritual lives of students are.

Our extensive interviews with people like Jeff Rubin at Hillel; Ven. Tenzin Priyadarshi; Rick Malloy, SJ; Ivan Tou, CSP; Rabbi Yonah Schiller; Dr. Amir Hussain; Imam Yahya Hendi; Jack Collins, CSP; Ven. Bonnie Hazel Shoultz; Larry Rice, CSP; Rev. Ian Oliver; Rev. Eric Andrews, CSP; Scott Young; Gadadhara Pandit Dasa; Charlie Donahue, CSP; Rabbi Serena Fujita; and Imam Abdullah T. Antepli helped reinforce our gut feeling that *The Freshman Survival Guide* was for spiritual seekers and students of all faith traditions.

Doug Mandelaro's media savvy and shameless plugs have been very helpful. Thanks also to many others in the Diocese of Rochester and St. Paul's and Patrick's Parishes for their ongoing help and support, particularly George Slack, Rev. Robin Olsen, Jamie Fazio, Lynne Boucher, Sue Versluys, and Shannon Loughlin. Thanks to Tyler Wheelock and his students at Saint John Fisher College, the first-generation class, for their input on first-generation students and commuter students: Mitch Lalik, Sam Capadano, Brent Lindsay, Cassie Ripley, Scott Swigart, and Allison Koczur.

Finally, thank you to the Paulists, who sponsor Busted Halo, the website where *The Freshman Survival Guide* was developed long before it became a book.

Notes

CHAPTER 2. Be Generous with Your Friendship but Stingy with Your Trust
1. "This Year's Freshmen at 4-Year Colleges: A Statistical Profile," *Chronicle of Higher Education*, accessed July 29, 2009. http:// cpe.ky.gov/NR/rdonlyres/F7CD1719-2285-49D3-BAF0 -E4B426D58CFB/0/Thisyearsfreshmanat4yearcollegesstatistical profile.pdf.

CHAPTER 3. Living with a Weirdo and Other Roommate Issues
1. "The First Year Is a Big Deal," Higher Education Research Institute, University of California, Los Angeles. http://www.heri.ucla.edu /infographics/2012-YFCY-Infographic.pdf.
2. "How to Get a College Roommate You Can Live With," Michigan News, University of Michigan, accessed June 5, 2009. http://ns.umich.edu/htdocs/releases/story.php?id=6695.

CHAPTER 5. I Miss My Old Life!
1. "The First Year Is a Big Deal," Higher Education Research Institute, University of California, Los Angeles. http://www.heri.ucla.edu /infographics/2012-YFCY-Infographic.pdf.

CHAPTER 6. Dealing with Differences

1. Gary J. Gates and Frank Newport, "Special Report: 3.4% of U.S. Adults Identify as LGBT," Gallup. http://www.gallup.com /poll/158066/special-report-adults-identify-lgbt.aspx.

CHAPTER 7. Embracing the Awkward(ness of Dating)

1. Heather Fishel, "7 Surprising College Dating Statistics," Campus Explorer. http://www.campusexplorer.com/college-advice-tips /E6F6928C/7-Surprising-College-Dating-Statistics/.

2. Sharon Jayson, "Less Commitment and More 'Hookups,' but Also More Virgins," *USA Today*, March 31, 2011. http://usatoday30 .usatoday.com/printedition/news/20110331/1avirgins31_cv.art.htm.

CHAPTER 8. Sex and the University

1. http://www.acha-ncha.org/docs/ACHA-NCHA-II_ReferenceGroup _ExecutiveSUmmary_Spring2013.pdf#page=11&zoom=auto,-99,38.

2. Stephanie Pappas, "College Sex: 'Hookups' Are More Talk Than Action," Live Science. http://www.livescience.com/16055-college -sex-hookups.html.

3. Maia Szalavitz, "The Truth About College Hookups," *Time*, August 13, 2013. http://healthland.time .com/2013/08/13/the-truth-about-college-hookups/.

4. "Northwestern Offers Sex 101 for Freshmen, Public," *ABC 7 Eyewitness News*, September 28, 2015. http://abc7chicago.com /health/northwestern-offers-sex-101-for-freshmen-public/1006283/.

5. Sandy Keenan, "Affirmative Consent: Are Students Really Asking?" *New York Times*, July 28, 2015. http://www.nytimes.com/2015/08/02 /education/edlife/affirmative-consent-are-students-really-asking .html?_r=0.

CHAPTER 10. Real Stats and Strategies on Mental Health

1. "The State of Mental Health on College Campuses: A Growing Crisis," American Psychological Association. http://www.apa.org/about/gr /education/news/2011/college-campuses.aspx.

2. American College Health Association, *National College Health Assessment: Reference Group Report*, Spring 2000.

3. "Depression," ULifeline. http://www.ulifeline.org/topics/128-depression.

CHAPTER 11. Being a Seeker

1. Blaise Pascal, *Pensées*, rev. ed., trans. A. J. Krailsheimer (New York: Penguin Books, 1995), p. 45, no. 148.

2. Susan Jacoby, "Blind Faith," *Washington Post*, March 4, 2007, accessed April 24, 2009. http://www.washingtonpost.com/wp-dyn /content/article/2007/03/01/AR2007030102073.html.

3. "The U.S. Religious Landscape Survey Reveals a Fluid and Diverse Pattern of Faith," Pew Research Center, February 25, 2008, accessed March 18, 2009. http://web.archive.org/web/20090203060101/http:// pewresearch.org/pubs/743/united-states-religion.

4. "Chapter 4: The Shifting Religious Identity of Demographic Groups," Pew Research Center, Religion and Public Life, May 12, 2015. http://www.pewforum.org/2015/05/12 /chapter-4-the-shifting-religious-identity-of-demographic-groups/.

5. " 'Nones' on the Rise," Pew Research Center, Religion and Public Life, October 9, 2012. http://www.pewforum.org/2012/10/09 /nones-on-the-rise/.

6. The Center for Spiritual Development in Childhood and Adolescence, *With Their Own Voices: A Global Exploration of How Today's Young People Experience and Think About Spiritual Development*, November 5, 2008.

7. Ibid.

8. "What Works: Meditation," BustedHalo.com, accessed December 26, 2009. http://www.bustedhalo.com/features/what-works-2-meditation.

CHAPTER 12. Go to Class!

1. "College Dropout Statistics," College Atlas. http://www.collegeatlas. org/college-dropout.html.

2. Eduardo Porter, "Dropping Out of College, and Paying the Price," *New York Times*, June 25, 2013. http://www.nytimes.com/2013/06/26 /business/economy/dropping-out-of-college-and-paying-the-price. html?pagewanted=all&_r=0.

3. Troy Onink, "College Costs Could Total as Much as $334,000 in Four Years," *Forbes*, January 31, 2015. http://www.forbes.com/sites /troyonink/2015/01/31/college-could-cost-as-much-as-334000-total -in-four-years/.

CHAPTER 14. Thrill Seekers, Avoiders, and Other Procrastinators

1. Kathleen D. Vols et al., "Making Choices Impairs Subsequent Self-Control: A Limited-Resource Account of Decision Making, Self-Regulation, and Active Initiative," *Journal of Personality and Social Psychology*, 94:5 (2008): 883–898, accessed November 1, 2009. http://www.apa.org/pubs/journals/releases/psp945883.pdf.

2. "Are You a Procrastinator?" Procrastination Research Group, accessed November 5, 2009. http://http-server.carleton.ca/~tpychyl/prg/self _help/self_help_links.html.

CHAPTER 15. The Care and Feeding of the College Professor

1. Author interview with Dr. Thomas O'Brien, DePaul University, June 29, 2009.

2. P. A. Mueller and D. M. Oppenheimer, "The Pen Is Mightier Than the Keyboard: Advantages of Longhand Over Laptop Note Taking," *Psychological Science* 25:6 (2014): 1159–1168.

3. Joseph B. Cuseo, Viki S. Fecas, and Aaron Thompson, *Thriving in College AND Beyond: Research-Based Strategies for Academic Success and Personal Development* (Kendall Hunt Publishing, 2007).

CHAPTER 17. Online Is Forever

1. "Wikipedia Survives Research Test," BBC News, December 15, 2005, accessed June 19, 2009. http://news.bbc.co.uk/2/hi /technology/4530930.stm.

2. Larry Gordon, "Wikipedia Pops Up in Bibliographies, and Even College Curricula," *Los Angeles Times*, June 14, 2014. http://www .latimes.com/local/education/la-me-wikipedia-20140615-story.html.

3. "Sex and Tech," National Campaign to Prevent Teen and Unplanned Pregnancy, accessed July 14, 2009. http://web.archive.org /web/20081215025523/http://www.thenationalcampaign.org/sextech /pdf/sextech_summary.pdf.

4. Kathy Martinez-Prather and Donna M. Vandiver, "Sexting Among Teenagers in the United States: A Retrospective Analysis of Identifying Motivating Factors, Potential Targets, and the Role of

a Capable Guardian," *International Journal of Cyber Criminology*, 8:1 (2014): 21–35. http://www.cybercrimejournal.com/prather Vandiverijcc2014vol8issue1.pdf.

5. Eric J. Moody, "Internet Use and Its Relationship to Loneliness," *CyberPsychology and Behavior* 4:3 (2001): 393–401.

6. Catherine Steiner-Adair, "Are You Addicted to the Internet?" CNN, July 17, 2015. http://www.cnn.com/2015/07/17/opinions/steiner-adair -internet-addiction. "Many Young People Addicted to Net, Survey Suggests," BBC News, October 15, 2014. http://www.bbc .com/news/technology-29627896.

7. Moody, "Internet Use and Its Relationship to Loneliness."

8. Kimberly Young, "Signs of Internet Addiction," Center for Internet Addiction Recovery, accessed June 21, 2009. http://www .netaddiction.com.

CHAPTER 19. "Growing Up" Your Religion

1. Susan Jacoby, "Blind Faith," *Washington Post*, March 4, 2007, accessed April 24, 2009. http://www.washingtonpost.com/wp-dyn /content/article/2007/03/01/AR2007030102073.html.

2. "U.S. Religious Knowledge Survey," Pew Research Center, Religion and Public Life, September 28, 2010. http://www.pewforum .org/2010/09/28/u-s-religious-knowledge-survey/.

3. Stephen Prothero, *Religious Literacy: What Every American Needs to Know—and Doesn't* (New York: HarperCollins, 2007), p. 41.

4. Cathy Lynn Grossman, "Americans Get an 'F' in Religion," *USA Today*, March 14, 2007, accessed April 24, 2009. http://www.usatoday .com/news/religion/2007-03-07-teaching-religion-cover_N.htm.

5. "The Spiritual Life of College Students," University of California, Los Angeles, Graduate School of Education and Information Studies, Higher Education Research Institute, accessed April 13, 2009. http:// spirituality.ucla.edu/docs/reports/Spiritual_Life_College_Students _Full_Report.pdf.

6. "Strong Majority of College and University Faculty Identify Themselves as Spiritual," University of California, Los Angeles, Graduate School of Education and Information Studies, Higher

Education Research Institute, press release, February 28, 2006. http://
spirituality.ucla.edu/docs/news/faculty_report_release.pdf.

7. Neil Gross and Solon Simmons, "How Religious Are America's
College and University Professors?" Social Science Research
Council, February 6, 2007. http://religion.ssrc.org/reforum/Gross
_Simmons.pdf.

8. "Are Students Losing Their Religion on Campus?" ABC
News, accessed April 12, 2009. http://abcnews.go.com/GMA
/Story?id=1375842&page=2.

CHAPTER 20. When You're the First: First-Generation Students

1. Linda Banks-Santilli, "Guilt Is One of the Biggest Struggles
First-Generation College Students Face," *Washington Post*,
June 3, 2015. https://www.washingtonpost.com/posteverything
/wp/2015/06/03/guilt-is-one-of-the-biggest-struggles-first-generation
-college-students-face/.

2. Liz Riggs, "First-Generation College-Goers: Unprepared and
Behind," *Atlantic*, December 31, 2014. http://www.theatlantic
.com/education/archive/2014/12/the-added-pressure-faced-by-first
-generation-students/384139/.

CHAPTER 21. Come Early, Stay Late: How to Do College as a
Commuter

1. Susannah Snider, "Weighing the Pros, Cons to Living at Home
in College," *U.S. News and World Report*, August 5, 2015. http://
www.usnews.com/education/best-colleges/paying-for-college
/articles/2015/08/05/weigh-the-benefits-drawbacks-to-living-at-home
-during-college.

2. George D. Kuh, Robert M. Gonyea, and Megan Palmer, "The
Disengaged Commuter Student: Fact or Fiction?" Indiana University
Center for Postsecondary Research and Planning, accessed June 19,
2009. http://nsse.iub.edu/pdf/commuter.pdf.

3. Scott Bland, "Obama Aims to Lift College Graduation Rates, but His
Tools Are Few," *Christian Science Monitor*, August 9, 2010. http://
www.csmonitor.com/USA/Education/2010/0809/Obama-aims-to-lift
-college-graduation-rates-but-his-tools-are-few.

4. "College Costs: FAQs," Big Future by The College Board. https://bigfuture.collegeboard.org/pay-for-college/college-costs/college-costs-faqs.

CHAPTER 22. Help Is All Around

1. Richard Kadison and Theresa Foy DiGeronimo, *College of the Overwhelmed* (San Francisco: Jossey-Bass, 2004), p. 158.
2. Andrew L. Turner and Thomas R. Berry, "Counseling Center Contributions to Student Retention and Graduation: A Longitudinal Assessment," *Journal of College Student Development*, 41:6 (2000): 627–636.
3. Kadison and DiGeronimo, *College of the Overwhelmed*, p. 156.

CHAPTER 23. Am I Safe?

1. "School and Campus Crime," National Center for Victims of Crime. http://victimsofcrime.org/docs/default-source/ncvrw2015/2015ncvrw_stats_school.pdf?sfvrsn=2.
2. Kathy Psencik, "Universities Bait Bike Thieves, with Mixed Results," *USA Today*, May 22, 2013. http://www.usatoday.com/story/news/nation/2013/05/22/colleges-bait-bike-thieves/2351903/.
3. Steve Weisman, "Why College Students Are at High Risk of Identity Theft," FT Press, October 3, 2013. http://www.ftpress.com/articles/article.aspx?p=2141481.
4. *Consumer Sentinel Network Data Book for January–December 2013*, Federal Trade Commission, February 2014. https://www.ftc.gov/system/files/documents/reports/consumer-sentinel-network-data-book-january-december-2013/sentinel-cy2013.pdf/.
5. Weisman, *50 Ways to Protect Your Identity in a Digital Age: New Financial Threats You Need to Know and How to Avoid Them* (Pearson Education), p. 18.
6. Weisman, "Why College Students Are at High Risk of Identity Theft."
7. "Report: Current Term Enrollment Report—Fall 2014," National Student Clearinghouse Research Center, December 10, 2014. http://nscresearchcenter.org/currenttermenrollmentestimate-fall2014/.
8. "College Drinking" fact sheet, U.S. Department of Health and Human Services, National Institute on Alcohol Abuse and Alcoholism. http://

pubs.niaaa.nih.gov/publications/CollegeFactSheet/CollegeFactSheet
.pdf.

9. "College Students Beware," National Bike Registry, accessed May 20, 2009. http://www.nationalbikeregistry.com/college.html.

CHAPTER 24. Too Much of a Dangerous Thing

1. "College Drinking," U.S. Department of Health and Human Services, National Institute on Alcohol Abuse and Alcoholism. http://www
.niaaa.nih.gov/alcohol-health/special-populations-co-occurring
-disorders/college-drinking.

2. Ibid.

3. National Institute on Addiction and Substance Abuse, accessed April 20, 2009. http://www.casacolumbia.org/newsroom
/op-eds/hands-parenting.

4. "College Drinking" fact sheet, U.S. Department of Health and Human Services, National Institute on Alcohol Abuse and Alcoholism. http://
pubs.niaaa.nih.gov/publications/CollegeFactSheet/CollegeFactSheet.pdf.

5. "What Colleges Need to Know Now," U.S. Department of Health and Human Services, National Institute on Alcohol Abuse and Alcoholism, November 2007, accessed April 21, 2009. http://www
.collegedrinkingprevention.gov/1College_Bulletin-508_361C4E.pdf.

6. "A Snapshot of Annual High-Risk College Drinking Consequences," U.S. Department of Health and Human Services, National Institute on Alcohol Abuse and Alcoholism, accessed April 20, 2009. http://www
.collegedrinkingprevention.gov/StatsSummaries/snapshot.aspx.

7. "College Drinking" fact sheet.

8. "A Snapshot of Annual High-Risk College Drinking Consequences."

9. "Monitoring the Future: National Survey Results on Drug Use, 1975–2013," Institute for Social Research, The University of Michigan. http://monitoringthefuture.org//pubs/monographs/mtf-vol2_2013.pdf.

10. Megan Twohey, "Pills Become an Addictive Study Aid," *Milwaukee Journal Sentinel*, March 26, 2006, accessed April 29, 2009. http://
web.archive.org/web/20060329151320/www3.jsonline.com/story
/index.aspx?id=410902.

11. "Report: Turning Attention to ADHD," Express Scripts. http://lab.express
-scripts.com/insights/industry-updates/report-turning-attention-to-adhd.

CHAPTER 25. To Keep Your Act Together, HALT

1. American College Health Association, *American College Health Association–National College Health Assessment II: Reference Group Executive Summary Spring 2014* (Hanover, MD: American College Health Association, 2014). http://www.acha-ncha.org/docs/ACHA -NCHA-II_ReferenceGroup_ExecutiveSummary_Spring2014.pdf.
2. "Diets of College Students," Internet FAQ Archives, Nutrition and Well-Being A to Z, accessed May 6, 2009. http://www.faqs.org /nutrition/Ca-De/College-Students-Diets-of.html.
3. "Controlling Anger Before It Controls You," American Psychological Association, accessed May 6, 2009. http://www.apa.org/topics /controlanger.html#strategies.
4. Ibid.
5. W. C. Buboltz, et al. "Sleep Habits and Patterns of College Students." *Journal of American College Health*, 50 (2001): 131–135.
6. American College Health Association, *National College Health Assessment*, Fall 2007 Report.

CHAPTER 26. How Not to Be Gross

1. "Mono: The Makeout Disease," video, Healthguru, accessed May 14, 2009. http://college.healthguru.com/content/video/watch/100486 /Mono_The_Makeout_Disease.
2. "Hand Washing: Do's and Don'ts," Mayo Clinic, accessed May 16, 2009. http://www.mayoclinic.com/health/hand-washing/HQ00407.

CHAPTER 27. There's No Vitamin C in Orange Soda, and Doritos Aren't a Food Group

1. "Portion Size and Weight Loss," WebMD, accessed July 21, 2014. http://www.webmd.com/diet/control-portion-size.
2. Ibid.
3. "Freshman 15: Is It Myth or Reality?" Cornell University, Gannett Health Services, accessed May 25, 2009. http://www.gannett.cornell .edu/topics/nutrition/info/freshman15.cfm.
4. Mitch Ritter, "The Freshman 15—It's Really the Freshman 5," University of Guelph, January 12, 2006, accessed May 25, 2009. http://web.archive.org/web/20101203131417/http://www.uoguelph.ca /research/apps/news/pub/article.cfm?id=87.

5. "Eating Disorders Among College Students," Walden Center for Education and Research. http://www.waldencenter.org/popular-searches/eating-disorders-among-college-students/.

6. "National Eating Disorders Awareness Week," Cornell University, Gannett Health Services. https://www.gannett.cornell.edu/topics/nutrition/NEDA.cfm.

7. Alison E. Field et al., "Prospective Associations of Concerns About Physique and the Development of Obesity, Binge Drinking, and Drug Use Among Adolescent Boys and Young Adult Men," *JAMA Pediatrics*, 168:1 (2014): 34–39. http://archpedi.jamanetwork.com/article.aspx?articleid=1766495.

8. Jamie Santa Cruz, "Body-Image Pressure Increasingly Affects Boys," *Atlantic*, March 10, 2014. http://www.theatlantic.com/health/archive/2014/03/body-image-pressure-increasingly-affects-boys/283897/.

9. Melissa Dahl, "Six-Pack Stress: Men Worry More About Their Appearance Than Their Jobs," *Today*, February 28, 2014. http://www.today.com/health/six-pack-stress-men-worry-more-about-their-appearance-their-2D12117283.

10. Cruz, "Body-Image Pressure Increasingly Affects Boys."

11. Ibid.

12. Field et al., "Prospective Associations of Concerns About Physique."

Chapter 28. Is This Really Where I Belong?

1. Kelci Lynn Lucier, "5 Reasons for College Students Not to Transfer," *U.S. News and World Report*, September 15, 2011, accessed October 31, 2015. http://www.usnews.com/education/best-colleges/articles/2011/09/15/5-reasons-for-college-students-not-to-transfer.

Chapter 29. In Case of Emergency

1. Centers for Disease Control and Prevention, "Vital Signs: Alcohol Poisoning Deaths—United States, 2010–2012," *Morbidity and Mortality Weekly Report*, 63:53 (2015): 1238–1242. http://www.cdc.gov/mmwr/preview/mmwrhtml/mm6353a2.htm.

2. "Drunk Driving Statistics," Mothers Against Drunk Driving. http://www.madd.org/drunk-driving/about/drunk-driving-statistics.html.

3. "Impaired Driving: Get the Facts" fact sheet, Centers for Disease Control and Prevention. http://www.cdc.gov/motorvehiclesafety /impaired_driving/impaired-drv_factsheet.html.

4. Ibid.

5. "Statistics: Eating Disorders and Their Precursors," National Eating Disorders Association, accessed August 10, 2009. http://www .northwestern.edu/counseling/clinical-services/eating-concerns /statistics/index.html.

6. "Eating Disorders," Mayo Clinic, accessed August 10, 2009. http:// www.mayoclinic.org/diseases-conditions/eating-disorders/basics /symptoms/con-20033575.

7. "Not Alone: The First Report of the White House Task Force to Protect Students from Sexual Assault," White House, April 2014. https://www.whitehouse.gov/sites/default/files/docs/report_0.pdf.

8. "The 1 in 6 Statistic," 1in6. https://1in6.org/the-1-in-6-statistic/.

9. For example, see "Code of Student Conduct," Georgetown University, Office of Student Conduct, accessed August 8, 2009. https:// studentconduct.georgetown.edu/code-of-student-conduct.

10. "Policies on Alcohol and Other Drugs," Georgetown University, accessed August 8, 2009. https://studentaffairs.georgetown.edu /policies/alcohol-and-other-drugs/.

11. Brian Dinday, "Ten Things Not to Do If Arrested," Free Advice, accessed August 8, 2009. http://www.freeadvice.com/resources /articles/arrest_donts_dinday.htm.

12. American Civil Liberties Union, "Know Your Rights: What to Do If You're Stopped by the Police," July 30, 2004, accessed August 8, 2009. https://www.aclu.org/know-your-rights /what-do-if-youre-stopped-police-immigration-agents-or-fbi.

13. "Police Stops: What to Do If You Are Pulled Over," Nolo. http:// www.nolo.com/legal-encyclopedia/police-stops-when-pulled-over -30186.html.

14. "Symptoms and Danger Signs," Suicide Awareness Voices of Education. http://www.save.org/index.cfm?fuseaction=home. viewpage&page_id=705f4071-99a7-f3f5-e2a64a5a8beaadd8.

About the Authors

NORA BRADBURY-HAEHL is a writer for teens and twenty-somethings and is a twenty-year veteran of youth ministry. Two decades of launching young people into college life have given her a unique perspective into the challenges they face, their fears and concerns, and the real risk involved in beginning college.

PHOTO CREDIT:
STEVE LOSH

BILL McGARVEY was the editor-in-chief of the award-winning Busted Halo website (http://BustedHalo.com) for over six years. He has written and commented extensively on the topics of pop culture and faith for BBC, NPR, the *New York Times*,

PHOTO CREDIT:
JARRAD VENEGAS

the *Washington Post*, *America*, the *Tablet* (in London), *Time Out New York*, Sirius-XM Radio, *Commonweal*, and *Book* magazine.